# 365 Days of a Journey Through Loss and Pain

Lorraine Brosious

ISBN: 1495922308

ISBN-13: 9781495922305

# DEDICATION

This book could not have been written but for my own losses with which God has entrusted me. My husband's sudden death in 1984 drove me to God in a way that no other happening could. HE became my Comforter, my Strength, my Guide as I took care of my four children and began to make my own way through life. Then once again on September 11th, 2001 when I had to watch my own daughter as she lost her husband and began the task of bringing up three children alone, I was thrown into a mourning that only God could get me through. One prayer that never left me was, "Lord, don't let me waste this time, as painful as it is. Let me see YOU".

Those losses, as well as others, remain for my family and me, but we have One Who sustains us in them, Who is redeeming them for His purposes.

This book is dedicated to two great men who loved the Lord and their families and whose deaths taught me so much that I can't help but share with others, my husband, Paul Brosious, and my son-in-law, Todd Beamer. I miss both of them beyond what words can express, and I look so forward to seeing them in eternity.

# ACKNOWLEDGEMENTS

Several people deserve my gratitude and praise for their help in bringing this book to fruition.

Karen Urbanowicz not only spent a year reading and making corrections on every page, but she encouraged me to continue to bring it to completion at a time when I may have otherwise not proceeded.

Pastor Corby Angle, a master in technology, also at a critical point, took over the project and made it become an actual book, still a mystery and miracle to me.

My granddaughter, Morgan Beamer, now 12, also was instrumental in helping me stay on task, asking me if I were still working on my book, if I had a cover, when would it be finished, simply assuming that it would happen.   I could not disappoint her.

God gave me the idea, the words, and the fortitude to keep going.   I thank Him for that and for the people He allowed in my life to be part of His work.

# PURPOSE

Pain and suffering are constants in life, and are seen, like a thread, in Scripture on nearly every page from Genesis to Revelation. Pain has a purpose, and that purpose is to point us to our great need for God, Who desires to redeem it and use it in our lives and in the lives of others so that we can know Him in the deep way He planned and desires.

Loss is inevitable. The day we are born we begin to experience losses - some small and easily negotiated, some so immense that they require a lifetime to negotiate. Losses occur because we live in a fallen world, we contribute to our own losses by irresponsible living, others cause losses in our lives by their sin, Satan attacks us, and at times God may send losses for a specific purpose, always meant for our good. Whatever the cause, God intends to redeem them and use them to show us more of Himself, to equip us to edify others, and to make us into the people He intends for us to be. I know this because His Word teaches me this and my own experience has confirmed it.

I have experienced the same losses we all face: leaving home, rejection by someone we value, children leaving home, aging, loss of health on occasion, death of parents and others we hold dear, even something so simple and routine as change of seasons, to name a few. Then there were those losses that can send one's world spinning out of control: the sudden death of my husband when I was 39 years old and the myriad of losses that entailed, particularly the loss of a father to my four children, and then the loss, seventeen years later, of my daughter's husband in the terrorist attack on September 11th, and again, the loss of a father for her three children.

Some of us experience losses that are difficult to name, such as loss of trust of people at an early age or never having enough resources to feel secure. Those kinds of losses can greatly affect every area of life.

In His Word, God address the problem of pain and loss repeatedly. Only He can make sense of it. It is for this reason I write this daily devotional by using every book of the Bible from Genesis to Revelation to see what God wants us to see as we experience difficulty in our lives. He wants us to see HIM so He can redeem our pain for Himself and use it for His good. My prayer is that He will use this book for His honor and glory.

Exodus 7:5                                                    January 01

## Redeeming Last Year's Losses

In everything that comes into our lives, this is God's plan: That we will see Him. As you think of the pain and losses that came into your life in the past year, do you see them in relationship to Him? No matter their source, do you readily submit to the fact that He allowed them, and no matter how difficult they are, that He longs to use them in your life, or are you stuck in any of the typical stages of loss: denial, anger, bargaining, or depression? These are natural, human reactions to loss, but they are meant to be worked through so we can get to the place of acceptance, to the place where we can see Him as we never have before. Hebrews 13:5b tells us that He will never leave us or forsake us, meaning He desires to walk with us through our pain. Think of a time when you were in a difficult phase of life and someone came along side and walked with you. Wasn't there a strong bond that formed between you and that person? God desires to be that One Who helps you carry that pain so a stronger relationship can be forged. Let Him. Don't shut out the One who cares for you like no other, the One who knows you and desires to be known by you. He longs to mourn along with you and then move you to a place where He can redeem your pain for good. He never intends that our sorrows be wasted.

A new year lies ahead. It is certain that many of us will encounter new wounds. We will make decisions to trust Him to walk with us through them, or not to trust Him in them. He is longingly waiting to redeem them for our good and His glory.

In the days that lie ahead in the New Year, we will go through God's Word, seeing the pain that the people there encountered, how they responded and what God did. Make this journey your own.

Think of the pain you have encountered in this past year.

Are there any losses that you have not given over to the Lord to let Him use for His glory and your good?

Are you willing to begin the journey of doing that?

Genesis 2:18-25                                    January 02

## Needs and Desires

In this section of Scripture God creates a helpmeet for Adam so he will not be alone, so he will have a companion like himself, meant to come along side to complement him, to fit him. She was to be exactly right for him.

So, why does this relationship, created so lovingly and so perfectly by God, so often not measure up to our expectations, or His? Of course, we know that our sin is the answer. As it says in James 4:1, we fight because we want what we want and we don't get it. We ruin relationships.

I see the heart of this as being a confusion about needs and desires. Only God meets the basic needs that we have, for love, significance, and belonging. The problem is that many do not let Him do that, and then turn to a spouse or other person to demand that they meet their needs. They cannot. They are incapable. Often, knowing they cannot meet the needs of the other, the spouse retreats, resulting in anger and a feeling of rejection. Then the battle is on.

So, if God is the only One Who can meet the heart of our needs, then what can we expect from a spouse? He or she can meet our desires. We desire his love, his protection, and his companionship, particularly as women, but we don't NEED those things from him. God has already met them so we are free to approach a spouse with no demands, just desires, albeit legitimate desires, important desires.

Think of it as bread and butter. We can eat a piece of bread without butter or jam. It will sustain us, but when we put butter or jam on it, then we have a complete and satisfying food. There is the idea of completion again, as Eve was for Adam. Genesis 2 shows us that God met Adam's needs, even before Eve was created. There is no record of Adam's complaining that God was not enough, but when Eve came into his life, she put "the butter on the bread", completed him by meeting his desires.

How much better relationships would work if we got our needs met first by God and then looked to another for our desires.

Are you hurting relationships by expecting others to meet what only God can?

Genesis 2:8-15                                     January 03

## Blaming Our Circumstances

As we begin our journey through God's Word, one of the first things we see is that Adam and Eve failed, even though God had provided them with everything they needed to succeed. God gave them a garden with trees and fruit and a river that flowed, watering the garden. God even gave Adam a satisfying vocation, caring for the environment He had given him. Everything surrounding Adam was perfect, but he fell, choosing sin. He could not blame his parents, his peers, poverty, or lack of work. Later he made a weak attempt to blame Eve and even God, but that did not work because it wasn't true. It was Adam himself who chose his route and created his own pain.

Certainly I have seen many people whose circumstances were contributing factors to their difficulties and adversities, but they themselves also made choices that led them to their destination. Bad environments are tough to overcome, but many people do it. I have seen clients whose childhood stories bring tears to my eyes and pain to my heart, yet in many cases they found the Lord in those environments and came to the place of making a solid impact on those around them. However, others also with painful stories in their backgrounds, blame their environments for the difficulties they are in today, and never move forward. While impacting us, our background situations do not need to define who we become. God knows about every detail of our stories and will use those circumstances for His honor and glory, if we allow Him to do it. His desire is for every pain in our lives to be redeemed for good by Him.

Do you take responsibility for your situations, or do you play the blame game?

Genesis 3:16-24                                      January 04

## Man's First Loss

It doesn't take many chapters in the Bible before we see man suffering his first loss, and it was as big as it gets. In Genesis 3 Adam and Eve, who thus far had known a life free of pain, chose to disobey God's direct command, and as a result, we see them losing relationship with Him, trust with each other, internal peace, their home, and eventually, life itself. Catastrophic. Yet, even in this, God immediately had a plan in place for their good and His glory: "I will send my own Son to redeem you" (Gen. 3:15). In this case, Adam and Eve caused their own pain, yet God stood ready to redeem it. He showed them Who He is: A God of love, mercy, and grace. Maybe you have brought on some of your pain, just as Adam and Eve did. His grace is much greater than your sin could ever be. Confessing and repenting of your sin is agreeing with God that you are responsible and then turning from it. After you have received His forgiveness, His desire is that you walk free, not burdened down any longer. There, however, may be natural consequences that follow you, as there were in the lives of Adam and Eve (They had to live under the curse, they had to leave the garden, they still died), but you can allow Him to use these consequence in your life to refine you so that you will be becoming the person God always intended for you to be. Dealing with consequence enables us to trust Him more, to know Him better. That's why we are here: To know Him and to be known by Him. Difficulties in our lives are opportunities to move us toward that.

Ask God if there are any difficulties in your life that are a direct result of your sin.

If He shows you that is the case, sit with Him while you confess, repent, and receive His forgiveness.

See the opportunity to know Him better as you sit with Him, talk to Him, and listen to Him about this.

Genesis 4:1                                        January 05

## Adam and Eve's Subsequent Loss

Adam and Eve gave up a life devoid of pain to enter a life of distrust, broken relationships and insecurity. Yet we read that because of God's promise of future redemption, they were able to have their relationship with Him restored, to a degree. When Cain was born, Eve said, "I have acquired a man from the Lord", acknowledging her dependence on Him. After Cain killed Abel and their third son, Seth, was born, Adam said in Gen. 4:25, "For God has appointed another seed for me instead of Abel". Because God offered hope to them in the great devastations of their lives, they had the opportunity to see what the character of God was like. He did not abandon them. In fact, quite the contrary occurred. He provided for them, He blessed them with children, and He made Himself known to them. That is always His plan in our pain- to make Himself known.

After all that Adam and Eve had lost due to their own sin and the sin of their son, Cain, they could have given up on themselves and God, but they apparently saw that God was the One in control and still had a plan for them. Genesis 4:26 tells us that after Seth had a son, Enosh, that men began to call on the name of the Lord. Good things, God's things, followed their pain, not because Adam and Eve were deserving but because it is in God's character to be merciful and loving to us.

Look at some of the hope God has been offering you in some of your recent losses.

Ask Him to reveal to you more of His character as you deal with your difficulties.

Ask Him to show you if there are any areas where you are doubting His intent that good will prevail.

Genesis 5                                                    January 06

## "And they Died"

Genesis 5 could be considered a very sad chapter. Many of the verses end with, "And he died". As it says in Romans 5:12, death entered the world through one man and then passed to all people, just as it will to us one day.

Verse 24 is an exception to, "And he died". Enoch did not die. Scripture says "He walked with God, and he was not, for God took him". Enoch's experience provides hope from the physical consequences of the sin that began with Adam and Eve. Perhaps God recorded this for us as a reminder that even though we sorrow when our loved ones die, and we also sorrow considering what our own end in this world will be, we will be with the God with Whom we were privileged to walk while on this earth. Right here at the beginning of His Word, God showed us that when we are in relationship to Him, we will enter into His Presence after death. We will experience everlasting life with our Lord and Savior.

While I have sorrowed, more than I can express, at many funerals of loved ones , I cannot, for their sakes, wish them back to a world of suffering and pain. They are in the very Presence of Jesus. When I cry, I cry for myself being separated from them, but I do not cry for them. How can we cry for those who are right now seeing the face of Jesus? That truth comforts and sustains like no other as we go through the mourning process for those we have loved.

Meditate on Genesis 5:24 and Hebrews 11:5 with God. Let Him comfort you with this truth.

Genesis 7:4 and 9:20 and 22                                    January 07

## Noah's Reaction to Loss

In the seventh chapter of Genesis, we see God revealing to Noah that, with the exception of him and his family, God will destroy all living things on the earth. Can you imagine receiving that message? Verse 5 says, "And Noah did according unto all that the Lord commanded Him." The life he had known was about to end. We read of no hesitance or protest from Noah. He believed God would be with him as He said He would, and Noah simply obeyed. This is an example of an impending loss. It is similar to God moving us to a new phase of life, giving us time to consider what we must leave behind. It is good to grieve that, but not to the point where we hang on to what we have and refuse to let go. As with Noah, God desires for us to embrace the new thing He has for us and trust Him to show us more of Himself. As we see more of Him, we will know that what He is doing is ultimately for our good.

In Genesis 8:21 we read "that the Lord smelled a soothing aroma". That was Noah's sacrifice he was offering on the altar to God. While it is true that Noah and his family were spared, the life, the people, the things they had always known were gone. We don't usually consider that when we look at the account of Noah and the ark. They were beginning anew with very little in the way of possessions, but they had God. They would be beginning with a deeper knowledge of His holiness and His care for them. One thing they saw very clearly about God: He would not tolerate sin forever. There was a new bond between God and them. God indeed had a plan, but it could only come about if there were major losses in Noah's life. A plant must die in order for its seed to be spread to offer new life the next year. Jesus had to die so that we might have life. We have to suffer losses so that God can give us the something new which He has for us, always with His glory and our good in mind. Our response needs to be acceptance, sacrifice and praise, as it was with Noah.

What is your typical response when loss is looming ahead for you?

Sit now with God and praise Him in the midst of impending loss, knowing He has a better plan for you

Genesis 11:7                                        January 08

## Losing Friendships

Broken relationships cause a great deal of the suffering I see in my counseling ministry. In the account of the Tower of Babel, not only were the people scattered, but their language was confounded, and they could no longer understand one another. It is difficult to understand the loneliness that would result from a situation like that. Pain comes when communication fails and even more so when relationships become broken.

When I consider the reasons why people walk into my counseling office, I see that most have to do with the distress coming from relationships that are not working well: relationships between husbands and wives, parents and children, brothers and sisters, between friends, between neighbors, and often between the person and God Himself. Most of us know the pain of a troubled relationship. James 4 poses a great question: Why do we fight with one another? Verse 2 gives the answer: We don't get what we want, so we fight. Isn't that true? In the pain that results from our fighting, we must get into God's Presence and check on our own motives and behaviors. Am I causing or contributing to this rift.? Most of the time the answer will be yes. In the case of the Tower of Babel, the answer is a definite yes. The peoples' pride and desire to be independent of God orchestrated all that followed. When we see our contribution to the problem, God's Word is quite clear: Go to the person with whom you are having difficulty and try to resolve it (Matthew 23 & 24). Often, if you are honest about your fault and your motives are correct, fellowship can be reestablished. It is always our responsibility to take the initiative when there is broken fellowship, whether God shows us our fault or not. When we are obedient to God in this, He really does work miracles. More important than getting the relationship back where we desire it to be, is keeping our relationship with God in tact by our obedience to Him.

If after doing what God asks of us and the relationship remains broken, pain will most definitely ensue. What then? That is the opportunity for you to give it over to your Lord in prayer, allowing Him to comfort you and give you further direction. He will.

Talk to the Lord about a troubling relationship in your life.

Ask Him what He wants you to do in it.

Genesis 11:8 January 09

## Losing Geographical Position

Once again we see men having to be disciplined by God due to their sin. In this case they, in their pride, wanted to reach heaven and make a name for themselves. God's response? He confounded their language so they could not understand one another and scattered them abroad upon the face of the earth, Scripture tells us.

None of us have experienced anything like this, but many of us have experienced being moved away from all we know and love. We have felt the pain of the separation. A child going to school for the first time feels the loss of his mother, a college student stresses over leaving her friends and family, young couples leave their home town behind to pursue a career, retirees often have to leave the home where their children grew up. These are all good things, but they come by way of having to give something up. It is necessary to acknowledge and mourn them so we are then free to embrace the next phase of life God has for us. Do you put these kinds of losses into proper perspective? For whatever reason, God has taken you from places and people you have always known. Even though it is painful, do you trust Him to go with you, to make a new place and a new fellowship for you? Do you submit, perhaps after a season of mild protest, to His plan, recognizing that He is God and you are not. That is what got the people in Genesis 11 in trouble. They forgot that truth. He sees the whole picture, and He will place you exactly where you ought to be, if you are seeking Him. Perhaps there are people there for you to minister to or to minister to you. Perhaps there is more opportunity for growth there for you. Perhaps you can honor God more there. It doesn't matter the reason. Our responsibility is to submit to Him, Who always has our best in mind. He will be there with us as we move to the next season of our lives.

As you think of a time when God moved you from a familiar place and people, what was your response?

As you sit in His presence today, talk to Him about how you would respond if He were to ask you to leave people and things behind to take a new assignment from Him.

Genesis 16:1                                    January 10

## Sarai Bore No Children

As a counselor I find some cases more heart-wrenching than others. An example of this is when a couple desires children and is unable to conceive. This was the case in Genesis 16 of Abram and Sarai. Sarai looked on her infertility as the Lord "restraining" her [Gen 16:2]. So we see that her view of God was not entirely accurate. On the basis of her wrong view, she worked out her own plan for having a child, and that plan has ramifications even to this day. Sarai didn't seem to be sure that God had her best interest in mind so was not able to submit to His plan for her. Her wrong view of God brought on more pain in many lives. Despite her sin, we know that God, in His grace, blessed her with a child.

Sometimes that happens with people who have infidelity issues. Sometimes it doesn't, and the longing remains, understandably so. The longing is not the problem- the belief that I must have what I want, and I will not submit to what God has for me is where the problem lies. That attitude still leaves us with empty arms and more importantly, without the comfort of the Great Comforter- He Who can redeem even that loss if we allow Him to. Since we only have narrow vision, we miss the whole picture that He sees. The pain that comes from not getting what we long for can be redeemed by Him, used in our lives and in the lives of others. Matthew 5:12 assures us that we shall be comforted in our mourning.

Is there something you think you must have that is destroying your fellowship with God?

Give it to God and let Him redeem it as you sit with Him today. Let Him comfort you in your pain.

Genesis 22:2                                        January 11

## Facing Potential Losses

Abraham was one hundred years old when God fulfilled His promise to give him a son, Isaac. Imagine the joy that filled the hearts of Abraham and Sarah as they looked on their son as he was growing up, not only because he filled their own home but because he was fulfilling the promise that God was forming a great nation from him. Then we read in Genesis 22:2 that God asks Abraham to sacrifice this beloved son, the one who had been promised for so long, the heir to what God was going to do. In the next verse we read of Abraham's response. He rose up early in the morning and went with his son and the wood for the burnt offering to the place where God had told him. When they arrived, Isaac asked where the lamb for the offering was. Abraham's answer is found in Genesis 22:8, "My son, God will provide for himself a lamb for a burnt offering." As a father, his mind must have been filled with myriad thoughts, fears, confusions, but one thing he knew, God could be trusted in this potential loss.

Some of us have had the experience of looking ahead to losses that might come: waiting for a questionable medical report for ourselves or a loved one, sitting by the bedside of one who has been critically injured, wondering if they will survive, contemplating whether our job will be the next to be eliminated, along with our income in the next wave of layoffs…. There are many opportunities to look ahead and imagine losses that may occur. Can we say with Abraham, "God will provide for Himself a lamb". He will meet the need. Actually He already did that in meeting our greatest need, the need to have our sins covered. He sent Jesus, Who paid the price for our sin, something we could not do. He also stands ready to provide for our every need we have right now.

Do you know God at the level Abraham did, being able to say, "God will provide"?

Are there potential losses you are anticipating that need to be turned over to Him?

Genesis 27:34 &35                                      January 12

## Estrangement

As we continue in Genesis we see that much loved son, Isaac, marrying Rebekah and having twin sons, Esau and Jacob. We read that Isaac loved Esau while Rebekah loved Jacob. Esau, being a man devoted to his own fleshly needs, in a moment of hunger sold his birthright to Jacob in exchange for food. After giving up his birthright, he then took a wife from the unbelieving Hittites, bringing "a grief of mind" unto Isaac and Rebekah [Gen. 26:35]. Subsequently, Rebekah and Jacob scheme and succeed in stealing Isaac's blessing to Esau as well. Verses 34 and 35 record Esau's pain: "He cried with a great and exceedingly bitter cry, and said unto his father, 'Bless me, even me also, O my father'". Grief seems to envelope this family. It continues with Jacob fearing for his life because of Esau's anger, and fleeing to his Uncle Laban's home in Haran, never to see his dear mother again. Esau's sin caused him the loss of his birthright while Jacob's sin caused him the loss of his brother's fellowship and subsequently, the loss of his family and home. Rebekah's scheming took her son away from her.

Much of our grief comes because we live in a sinful, fallen world, some comes because of the sin of others, some comes from Satan, and there is that grief that God Himself allows us to suffer but always with the plan of redeeming it in our lives for our good and His glory. In this instance, however, the members of Jacob's family brought pain on themselves through their many sins.

Genesis 33:4 tells us that many years later when Jacob returned home, Esau ran to meet him, embraced him, and fell on his neck and kissed him, and they both wept. In verse 20 Esau erects an altar to the Lord. Restoration of relationships came but only after years of the pain of separation.

If there is hurt in your life from estrangement, ask God to show you if you have played a part in it.

Sit with the Lord now and talk to Him about your part in it and listen to Him concerning what He wants you to do.

Genesis 37:28                                          January 13

## Loss of Home and Family

Joseph, the favored of the twelve sons of Jacob, was sold by his brothers and taken to Egypt. In a few short minutes he was torn away from his home and all his loved ones. This was compounded by the betrayal of those he trusted and loved. It is difficult to imagine the horror going on in the mind of a young boy in this circumstance. We read that he was sold to Potiphar, an officer of Pharaoh's. In Genesis 39:2 we read that the Lord was with Joseph, and He blessed him greatly as he served his master. Even Potiphar saw that the Lord was with him, so he put Joseph in charge of his entire household.

Joseph, despite his confusion and despair of leaving all he knew, made a choice to not only do what he needed to do, but to excel in it. He apparently clung to the Lord and was obedient to Him, putting himself in a place to be greatly used by Him. He proved himself to be a young man of great honor.

It is not what happens to us that determines what will transpire in our lives, but rather it is how we think about what happens to us. Scripture tells us that "as a man thinks, so is he." If we maintain a correct view of God and a correct view of who we are in Him, we can be victorious in any situation, no matter how painful it may be. We get through the situation knowing He is never going to leave us or forsake us, though everyone else may have. We also know that He stands ready to turn our sorrow into something that is beyond what we can imagine.

If you are in turmoil from loss, how are you viewing God?

Is this what you THINK about God or is it the truth as seen in Scripture? Talk to Him about it and let Him correct any wrong thinking you may have.

Genesis 37:34                                          January 14

## Loss of a Child

Jacob's response to the presumed loss of his beloved son, Joseph, was: "He tore his clothes and put sackcloth on his waist and mourned for his son many days." Verse 35 tells us he refused to be comforted, wept, and declared he would die in his mourning. Totally understandable. Years later we see Jacob continuing to mourn for Joseph as he refuses to allow his youngest son, Benjamin, to leave him for fear of losing him also, saying the loss of him would cause him to die in his sorrow.

Mourning for the loss of a loved one, particularly a child, is perhaps the darkest, loneliest experience we know. There is little anyone can say to bring comfort. The pain and sense of loss go on for the remainder of life, but again, it is an opportunity, an opportunity that no one wants, but nevertheless, an opportunity to Know God at a different level than ever before. Little did Jacob know what God was doing with his son in Egypt. He only had the view directly in front of him while God saw all the way to Egypt and into eternity. God was redeeming Jacob's pain by preparing Joseph to save his people. Little did Jacob know that God was allowing Joseph to be a picture of Jesus, Who would be the future Redeemer of all people. His pain, albeit beyond description, had a purpose beyond anything Jacob could imagine. When we are suffering, we can trust God to use it for good, in our lives as well as in the lives of others, even though at the moment of loss, we can only see our pain. We have to trust Him with the bigger picture than we are able to see. We have to trust Him to be our comfort while we can't see that bigger picture.

Is there a loss that is going to be with you for the remainder of your life?

Trust God to use your pain in ways that you can't even imagine. Tell Him you want to do that.

Allow Him to surround you with His comfort.

Genesis 39:17-20 and 40:23                               January 15

## Dealing With Betrayal

If there is anyone who knows how it feels to be betrayed by those around him, it is Joseph. First his brothers, out of their own jealousy, sell him, then his master's wife, out of her own lust, lies about him when he won't be seduced by her relentless temptations. Her false accusations result in his being jailed, where he correctly interprets dreams for the king's butler and baker, one of whom, out of his own self- centeredness, forgets about him as soon as he is released from prison. In all of this we do not read that Joseph did anything wrong. What we do read in Genesis 39:21 is "But the Lord was with Joseph". While Joseph, being human, must have suffered much pain and anguish, he prevailed because one thing he knew, as he says in Genesis 41:32 when he is speaking to Pharaoh, "...the thing is established by God, and God will shortly bring it to pass". Then when Pharaoh looks for one to manage the famine situation in his land, "one in whom the Spirit of God is", he looks no further than Joseph. Joseph didn't look at other's behavior or on circumstances to determine how he would act, but he kept his eyes on his God. Later the names he gives his children is revealing of his heart and mind: Manasseh, meaning "God has made me forget all my toil, and my Father's house", and Ephraim, meaning "for God has caused me to be fruitful in the land of my affliction". He indeed suffered greatly, but God rewarded Joseph for keeping his eyes on Him in times of deepest betrayal by other people. It's never about our circumstances- it's about our attitude about them.

In circumstances of suffering due to other's betrayal of trust, do we let them decide how we are going to think and behave or do we keep centered on God, knowing He knows and stands ready to redeem them for good?

Let God show you Himself as you sit in His Presence today.

Genesis 45:2, 5-8, 14 &15                                     January 16

## Pain's Opportunity

In this area of dealing with hurts, one could perhaps write an entire book on Joseph.  When the time comes for him to reveal himself to his brothers, Genesis 45:2 says, "he wept aloud" so that all in the house heard him.  The suffering he had endured all those years came pouring out.  Beginning in verse 5 he tells his brothers not to be angry or grieved because it was God Who went before him to save their very lives and the lives of others.  It was indeed an opportunity for Joseph.  In his great pain, he took that opportunity and submitted it to God so that, as he says, "I am able to be a father to Pharaoh, lord of his house and ruler throughout all the land of Egypt" [verse 8].  God took the most devastating things in Joseph's life and turned them into unbelievable, unimaginable good because Joseph never took his eyes off of Him, Who is the only One able to do that.  Verse 14 tells us that Joseph fell upon his brother, Benjamin's, neck and wept while Benjamin also wept upon his neck.  In verse 15 we read that he kissed all of his brothers and wept upon them and then they talked together.

Because we are able to keep our eyes on God and know that He has a plan to bring good out of bad does not mean that we don't hurt, sometimes beyond words.  We hurt but not without hope.  We hurt but not alone.  Mourning is part of the process of loss.  We need to weep as Joseph did.  God gave us the emotions to do that but always with the truth that God will use it in our lives and the lives of others.  Oh yes, and He has promised to be with us in it.

Do you agree that God intends for us to express our pain?

Express it to Him now with the knowledge that He has a plan to redeem it.

Genesis 50:1 & 20                                    January 17

## God Prevails

We know of one more loss with which Joseph has to contend. The death of his father occurs in Genesis 49:33. We see Joseph falling on his father's face, weeping upon him, and kissing him. Forty days of mourning then took place. We read that even the Egyptians mourned for him. Many of them, as well as all of Jacob's family, went to the land of Canaan to bury him when the forty days of mourning were over. Genesis 50:10 says they mourned with a great and very strong lamentation for 7 more days. Does this leave any doubt in us that it is okay to mourn, not just okay, but expected and necessary? Sometimes Christians are the worst when it comes to offering glib responses to those who are in the throes of pain. It is as if we don't want to acknowledge that God allows us to suffer also. If we believe that, then we also deprive ourselves of seeing what God will do with it. We limit Him. We are also cheating ourselves out of the sweet fellowship that comes when we sit with God and let Him touch our wounds. We cheat ourselves out of the fellowship we have with others when they sit with us, albeit without answers, and cry along with us.

If we deny our losses, we will never be able to say as Joseph did when speaking to his brothers, "You meant evil against me, but God meant it for good". [Gen 50:20]. This is one of my most treasured Scriptures. We need to see and feel the pain of it if we are also to see and rejoice in the good.

Are there losses you have minimized or denied in your life, or in the life of someone else?

Will you allow God and others to mourn them with you and then see how God will redeem them for good?

Genesis 50:20                                       January 18

## God Wants to Redeem Our Sorrows

The book of Genesis, as we have seen, is about loss and redemption: loss of fellowship with God and with others, loss of home, loss of a child, loss of all material things, loss of everything familiar, infertility, potential, impending loss, loss of trust in others due to betrayal....... Some of these are repeated several times in the lives of the people in Genesis. They are also repeated in our lives. As I look over my list of clients I am counseling, even for the last month, I see all of these things going on in lives. I see abandonment by loved ones, unloving husbands, disrespectful wives, divorce, empty nest issues, disobedient and rebellious children, the loss of freedom that ensues when caring for elderly parents, children with health problems or profound disability, chronic, progressive health problems, family of origin issues, addiction, job loss, children dealing with split family situations, sensing no direction from God in making a major decision..... This is our world. Again, these are some of the sorrows that the clients I have seen in the last month are dealing with. I have not even named all of them.

I do not find this at all daunting or discouraging. On the contrary, when I have a client walk through my door in great pain, I sympathize with them, but I know it is an opportunity for God to do His work in their lives. He is waiting to offer Himself and His comfort. I so look forward to their coming to the place of Job where he says, "I used to hear you but now I see You." It is God Who stands ready to redeem their hurts. It is not my answers or the answers the world offers. They need to come face to face with their Redeemer Who not only redeems them from their sinful state but longs to redeem all the hurts they are enduring right now. Just this week, as I write this, I have seen God take a devastating situation in a couple's life and miraculously bring them to a place with Him and each other where they had never been before. What a privilege to see that.

Which of these areas of sorrow can you identify with?

Allow your Redeemer to walk with you and show you Himself in whatever sorrow you are experiencing today.

Exodus 1                                              January 19

## Disappointment with God

God used Moses to free His people from their bondage in Egypt. Not only did God rescue them, but He caused the Egyptians to give them jewels of silver, gold, and clothing as they left. He Himself went before them in a pillar of a cloud by day and in a pillar of fire by night. All was well until the Israelites realized Pharaoh and his army had second thoughts and were pursuing them. They, being in great fear, cried out to the Lord, "It had been better for us to serve the Egyptians than that we should die in the wilderness [Exodus 14:12]. They didn't know God well enough to trust Him. They were disappointed that God hadn't done things the way they thought He should. Beth Moore refers to those times as "God not behaving". When that happens, we balk, we become discouraged, we whine, we dishonor God. It is we who misbehave. Our sinful arrogance says we know better than God about how things should be done.

Fortunately, our God is a God of grace and mercy. He parted the Red Sea so His people could pass through on dry land. They didn't even have to get their feet wet! Oh yes, He also destroyed their enemies in that same sea. He did indeed have everything under control. After this experience, they get a much better view of their God and come to praise Him in Exodus 15:11, saying, "Who is like thee, O Lord, among the gods. Who is like Thee, glorious in holiness, fearful in praises, doing wonders?" He did what He did so they would know.

Talk to God as you sit with Him today about your disappointments, when He didn't do what you expected.

Ask Him to show you more of Himself. Ask Him to show you yourself.

Exodus 1:14                                                           January 20

## Death of a Child

As we move to Exodus we see different kinds of sufferings. Joseph and all his generation have died. God's people, the Israelites, have greatly multiplied and become mighty, filling the land, making the Egyptian king quite anxious. His answer was to make their lives bitter with hard bondage. He also instructed the midwives to kill any sons who were born to the Hebrew women. Because the midwives feared God, they did not obey that command, and God's people continued to grow in number and in strength. Pharaoh, since he was unsuccessful in controlling the midwives, commanded his people to cast into the Nile River any son born to the Hebrews. It is impossible to imagine the weeping and wailing that followed such a circumstance. I do not personally know anyone whose young child was murdered, but I do know quite a few people who have suffered the loss of a child from other means. I have often thought that must be the greatest of pain to endure. It is one of those losses where the mourning, while somewhat abated over time, never fully subsides. With every holiday, every birthday, every graduation, every milestone in life there is the wonder of what might have been. Does God understand that pain? Remember, it was He Who watched His Own Son die so that we might live. He freely gave Him up so that we, who have no ability to atone for our own sin, might be forgiven by His shed blood. The death of His Son made the way for me to be acceptable to him and to spend eternity with Him. He is the only One Who could possibly understand and have the ability to comfort one whose child has been lost. We are tempted to think that because He is God that His suffering was minimized. I think the opposite was true. He had to watch His Son leave Him and in His Holiness take on all of our sin. He had to watch Him suffer alone, knowing He could stop it. Yes, He knows beyond our ability to comprehend the pain of seeing a child suffer and die.

Whether you are suffering from the loss of a child or something less severe, He stands ready to hear your weeping and protests. Let Him.

Exodus 2                                                    January 21

## Being Set Aside for a Time

Moses was born into a Hebrew family during the time when baby boys were ordered by pharaoh to be killed. His Mother, in her desperation to protect him, made him an ark of bulrushes and pitch, put him in it and set his sister to watch him from afar as he was on the water. He, as Exodus 2 tells us, was seen by Pharaoh's daughter, who having compassion on him, took him as her own. His own Mother was called on to serve as a nurse for him. She had done everything she knew to do for him, and God rewarded her.

The story continues. Moses grows up in Pharaoh's house, but being in a position to see his people being mistreated, takes action by killing an Egyptian oppressor. Moses, then fearing for his life, must flee to Midian where he marries and has a son to whom he gives the name Gershom, meaning, "I have been an alien in a foreign land". He remains there many years, seemingly set aside by God. We have already seen how Noah waited 120 years before the predicted rains came, how Abraham waited 25 years for the promised son, and how Joseph waited 14 years in prison before moving to what God had next for him. Now we see Moses waiting. But what we don't see during these times is what God is doing in their lives. He is deepening their understanding of Him, He is maturing them while they wait, He is preparing them for a mighty work. Moses gave up the palace and all that entailed in an attempt to protect His people, forcing him to leave behind all he knew. There must have also been the confusion and pain of being set aside by God. Little could he have known what God was preparing for him.

I have known people who were seemingly put on a shelf for a time. I have even experienced it myself at times. It is painful. God, however, never stops working. He stands ready to walk with us in our pain and discouragement and always has a plan for us. I Thessalonians 5:24 says, "He Who calls you is faithful, Who also will do it". We just need to trust in Who He is as we wait, and to make it as our main goal to know Him more intimately.

Consider a time when you felt put on a shelf or set aside. Were you able to see at a later time what God was doing? Can you trust in Who He is in these times?

Exodus 3:4                                              January 22

## Out of Our Comfort Zone

"I can't do what you are asking me to do"! How could being called by God to do a special task for Him be considered painful? If we doubt ourselves and Him it most certainly will. If we are to obey, it causes us to allow Him to take over more of our lives. There is that natural bent we have for independence. We have to give up things about ourselves that have always been part of us. We have to let go and let Him. We have to embrace a new way of being and doing since we know we can't do the task on our own. We like what is familiar and comfortable, even though it may be unproductive.

Moses, in his exile from Egypt, had established a family and was content [Exodus 2:21] to dwell with them and his father-in-law in Midian. One day God showed Himself to Moses in a flame of fire out of the midst of a bush. God introduced Himself [3:6] as the God of Moses' father. Verse 6 tells us that Moses hid his face. He saw God as he never had before. While it is an awesome thing to see God in a deeper way, it also requires something of us. It certainly required something of Moses. His placid days of keeping Jethro's flocks were about to end. His new life would entail going to Pharaoh and bringing God's people out of Egypt [verse 10]. Yes, he was to be way out of his comfort zone.

I can so identify with Moses' response in verse 11: "Who am I that I should go unto Pharoah and bring forth the children of Israel out of Egypt?" Then Moses' next question was: "Who should I say sent me? Moses knew that he himself didn't have the ability to do what God was asking, and he had some doubts about Who God was as well. There lies the antidote to our fears about leaving our known way of living and moving on to what God has for us: Seeing Him as He is and seeing ourselves in Him. He is God, and if He calls us to do something even way out of our comfort zone, with Him we will be victorious.

As you spend time with Him today, ask Him if He is calling you to something new, something you find to be beyond yourself.

Consider Who He is. Consider who you are in Him.

Exodus 3:7 & 3:9                                      January 23

## God Knows Our Every Sorrow

In the account of Moses being called by God to deliver His people out of slavery, we are given the opportunity to see so much about God. He says in Exodus 3:3 that He has seen the affliction of His people and has heard their cry. He sees, He hears. "I know their sorrows, He says." Verse 9 says that the cry of the people has come to Him.

We can get so centered on our grief that we forget that God knows every detail of what is happening. He even knew before it happened. He sees. He hears. He cares.

He is waiting for us to come to Him and receive the comfort He is longing to shower on us. I think of Jesus lamenting over Jerusalem in Matthew 23:37: "How often would I have gathered thy children together, even as a hen gathers her chickens under her wings, and you would not". Never let it be said of us that we would not be gathered under His wings. Never let it be said that we would not receive the comfort with which He is waiting to encompass us. Whatever sorrows you are facing today- a health issue, loneliness, an unsaved mate, a wayward child, an unmet dream, financial loss, job uncertainty.....whatever it is, know that He knows. He knew before you were even conceived. He says the very hairs of your head are numbered by Him. If Jesus is your Savior, He says He will never leave you nor forsake you. He will walk with you through whatever sorrow you are facing today.

Name your sorrows to God.

Name the truths about God pertaining to your sorrows.

Exodus 4 January 24

## Inadequacy for the Task at Hand

As we continue with the account of Moses being called by God to lead His people out of slavery in Egypt, we see him centering on his inadequacies. His first objection was that the people would not believe that God sent him, and his second was that he was not eloquent. How many times I have used that one! It can be a daunting thing to go out and perform things that we know are beyond our own abilities. It will also be the very thing that will cause us to succeed in what God has given us to do. Knowing we don't have the ability in ourselves will make us look to Him, the One Who made Moses' mouth....and ours. [Exodus 4:11, 15]. It is a painful thing to look at ourselves and know that we are incapable. After all, the first sin and the one so basic to our nature, is pride, the desire to be independent and not need God. We continually battle this strong tendency. When we see our inadequacies, then we humble ourselves before the Lord and let Him give us what we need to carry out His work.

From the beginning of my counseling ministry, I have had a sign on my desk that reads, "This is not my work. It is His." I often tell Him that if He is not there in that room to do the work, I am not going in. Who am I? I am not at all adequate to hear the issues my clients present. He is. He is so much more than adequate. Moses obeyed, even in his self doubt, and we must also, knowing that He has made our mouths or whatever else it is that we need to perform what He has called us to do. He will never call us to something that He does not equip us to handle.

What are you using as an objection to doing what God has called you to do?

Talk to Him once again about how you see yourself and about how you see Him.

Exodus 16-17:7                                          January 25

## Disappointment in the Good

The Israelites find themselves without food and water. That can indeed be a loss of significant proportion. Exodus 16 tells us that the whole congregation complained against Moses and Aaron. God sends them manna and later has Moses strike the rock in Horeb so water could also be provided for them. The people had a need but it wasn't the real need. God chose these people. He loved them. He desired good for them, just as a loving parent desires good for his children. The problem was that His children were oblivious to what good was. Of course, their bodies needed sustenance, but more so, they needed an intimate encounter with their God. God allowed them to suffer forty years so they could get the most important thing that would not just be good, but would be the ultimate best: knowing Him. It was not an accident that there was no food or water for them, but it was ordained by God so they would have the opportunity to see Him, really see Him. That is what brings real joy and pleasure to us. The forty years in the wilderness could be looked on as a tragedy, wasted time, but God looked on that long journey as necessary miles in bringing His children to an understanding of Who He is. He had so much more in mind for them than food and water. Their desires and expectations were way too low. He longed to give them the best.

We are also hungry and thirsty- for Him. But often we don't recognize that and go off looking for other things to satisfy. They never do. They never will. Pain is a good teacher to show us that.

Do you see yourself seeking the good and not the best?

Talk to God about the best for you.

Exodus 18:13-27                                          January 26

## The Pain of Bearing Burdens Alone

Moses's father-in-law, Jethro, witnessed the great burden Moses carried in judging and teaching the people from morning to night. Jethro's assessment of this is given in Exodus 18:17: "The thing that you do is not good." That was quite direct. It was not good because it was too heavy for Moses and would eventually wear him down. Jethro offers this counsel in verse 21: "Provide out of all the people able men who fear God, men who know the truth, and place them over the people to be rulers and judges." They were to bear the burden with Moses. Then, he says, Moses would be able to endure and the people would be cared for. A similar idea is presented in the New Testament in choosing deacons to carry the load.

We get physically worn down when we carry too much alone. That is never God's intent. We are to be in community with other believers, to carry burdens together. When we follow God's plan and don't revert to our own independent bent, we preserve ourselves physically, mentally, emotionally, and spiritually to carry on to the end. We avoid the loneliness of solitary struggles, which is a recipe for pain and discouragement. God stands ready to present Himself to us, but He also intends for us to be in deep fellowship with others. That is the second reason He made us. We, at this point, are quite familiar with the first.

Is there an area of your life where you are choosing to go it alone?

Can you recognize that this may be causing unnecessary pain?

Exodus 19:9-20:23                                            January 27

## The Pain of Seeing Ourselves Next to God's Holiness

As God prepares to give the law to Moses, He tells Moses to sanctify the people and to have them wash their clothes [Exodus 19:10]. He continues by telling Moses to set bounds around Mt. Sinai to keep the people from touching it. When God came to the mount, there were thunderings and lightnings and a thick cloud upon it. The voice of the trumpet sounded so loudly that the people trembled. Verse 18 says "The Lord descended upon it in fire and the smoke ascended as the smoke of a furnace and the whole mountain quaked greatly." This is the picture presented when God was ready to give His Holy Law. When the people saw all of this, Exodus 20:18 says, "They moved and stood afar off." Wouldn't you? They then asked that Moses tell them what God said. They thought they would die if they heard God directly. Maybe they would have. At any rate, God had indeed gotten their attention. As God then begins to present His law to them and His plans for His dwelling place, the Tabernacle, the contrast between Who He is and who they were is staggering. It cannot be comprehended. It would seem that after this experience, the people would never again fail to trust Him or be bold enough to make complaints against Him and His servants, but, of course, that would not be. After seeing Him as He is and the contrasting insignificance of themselves, they would again and again attempt to put themselves in His place, just as we so often do.

It is a painful thing to see my sinful nature in full bloom and then to meditate on His attributes. The antidote to that pain is to consider that, even though the immense span between us is unattainable for us, He chose to reach down, way down, to us through His Son, Jesus. The pain of our separation I no longer need to carry. He took care of it for me.

Meditate with Him on how He chose to take care of the immense chasm between you and Himself.

Praise and thank Him.

Exodus 32                                                    January 28

## Disappointment in People

Moses has a mountaintop experience with God, literally, on Mt. Sinai where God gave him laws for Israel, including the Ten Commandments. The people grew impatient and concerned with Moses' absence, so they persuaded Aaron to make a god for them, a golden calf. They were also involving themselves in other activity that was contrary to God's expectations of them. God tells Moses in Exodus 32:10 that he will consume them and make of Moses a great nation. We know that Moses also burned with anger toward these "stiff-necked" people because when he returns and sees the golden calf and the revelry, we read that he broke the tablet on which God had written the Ten Commands. To say Moses was disappointed in the people doesn't begin to express what he must have been feeling. He was also bitterly disappointed in his brother's leading of the people while he was gone. Moses had poured so much of himself into these people and now it all seemed in vain.

Now here is what we see about Moses' handling of this enormous set-back in the work he had been given to do. At the end of this chapter we read that Moses fully acknowledged the sin of the people, reiterating what they had done, but then puts himself between them and God as their intercessor, much like Jesus does for us. Moses asks that if God will not forgive their sin, that he, himself, be blotted out of the book which God has written. This was a real test for Moses. What are you going to do when everyone around you, the very people to whom you have given yourself, fails so miserably? When the work you have poured yourself into seems for naught? Moses passed his test when he willingly sacrifices himself for the good of the people. In his great sorrow over what had occurred , He didn't consider himself but instead stayed centered on what God had called him to do.

Think, as you sit with the Lord, on what major disappointments you have endured concerning other people. Think on how you responded.

Ask God to help you stay centered on Him, no matter what others around you are doing. Ask Him also what you can learn from this disappointing experience in Moses' life.

Exodus 33                                                      January 29

## Fearing Separation from God

Moses had grown so dependent on God and had been with Him and seen Him in so many ways that when God informed him in Exodus 33:3 that because of the rebellious nature of the people, He would not go up to the Promised Land in the midst of them, Moses protests. He needs God's presence and can't contemplate functioning without it. He asks God, in his momentary panic, to show him the way that he might know Him (verse 13). He asks God to not move them from where they are if God will not go with them. God's answer to Moses' beseeching of Him is in 33:17: "I will do what you have asked. I know you by name." How wonderful. Moses then asks to see God's glory- He wants and needs more of Him. Another test passed by Moses. God puts Moses in a cleft of a rock and covers him with His hand as He passes by. Moses gets to see God's back- because he asked.

Sometimes we sense God's presence in a way we cannot describe. Other times, He may seem far from us. When this happens, especially when we are in the midst of adversity, it can send us directly to spiritual doubt and cause us to turn to other things. Not for Moses. He reminded God of what they had together. He sought so much more of Him. That is what God desires for us. Remember, God created us first and foremost to be in fellowship with Him. We know how much He loved Moses' response because He showed him more of Himself than He ever had before. If we seek Him, we will find Him.

I often tell God before I enter our counseling room, "If you don't go in there with me, I'm not going." I can't. I have nothing to offer. He does.

Have you come to the place where you know you need God for every single step you take?

Spend time with Him right now and tell Him how much you need Him.

Exodus 34                                                                January 30

## Results of Being With God in Adversity

Moses and the children of Israel had been through a season of adversity, due, of course, to the sin of the people. After showing Himself to Moses, Moses went down from Mount Sinai with the two tablets of testimony which God had so graciously given to him once again, and Moses' face was shining, so much that the people were at first afraid to draw near him. He had to put a veil on his face in order for them to be near him. It was obvious in his appearance that he had been with God.

In the adversity that we go through, is it obvious to others that we have been with Him? We can be real about our feelings, and we must be, but if we have sought Him as Moses did, others will see beneath our pain, a steadfastness, a joy, however muted it may be at times, that can only come by being in His Presence. Beneath our tears our faces can shine-because of Him! When we look on His face we see His love, His grace, His mercy, His compassion, His forgiveness, His long-suffering, His goodness, His righteousness, His holiness…. We see His acceptance of us wherever we are. We see His great love and His desire to work out His perfect plan for us- if we let Him.

Sit in His Presence today until He shows Himself to you- and feel your face begin to shine.

Leviticus 11:44-45, 19:2, 20:                                    January 31

## Separation from the World

The book of Leviticus presents laws regarding offerings, consecration of the Priests, the feasts the Israelites were to observe, holiness, personal relationships... God wanted His people to be separate, different from the other nations around them, and He gave them what they needed to do that. His desire for them was that they would be holy as He is holy. This is repeated at least five times in the book. He expected His people to be separate because they belonged to Him.

He expects that of us as Christians today, but how we fight that. It calls for us to give up wanting to be like everyone else, a desire to fit in, if we are to be pleasing to Him. In the New Testament, II Corinthians 6:17 tells us "to come out from among them and be separate". While it is a privilege beyond our understanding to be His child and to be called out to a holy way of living, it requires us to give up things we might enjoy. We have to sacrifice our penchant for wanting to be like everyone else in order to be who God has called us to be- His child. The family He has called us to has different standards and manner of living than the world. Young people often have to do battle in this area. They so desire to fit in and often suffer when they can't, but it is a sweet suffering because it is pleasing to God. It is also a temporary suffering, not even to be compared to the joy that awaits us, and the joy that presently comes from being in deep fellowship with Him. In Leviticus God talks about the blessings that come from obeying His statutes and commands (bountiful harvests, peace, victory over enemies, fruitfulness, God's covenant with them, God's Presence with them), as well as the consequences of not allowing ourselves to be set apart.   Being His child and not following His commands sets us up for real suffering, needless suffering. In obeying Him we find satisfaction and joy.

Do you battle Him over having to be different from those around you?

Reframe that and consider with Him what a privilege it is to be His child and be called by Him to be separate.

Numbers 6:1-21                                    February 01

## Called for a Specific Purpose

As we continue through the Word of God looking for losses and how they were experienced by God's people, we come to the book of Numbers.  In chapter 6 we read of a man who makes a vow to separate himself unto the Lord and be a Nazirite.  How could that possibly be considered a loss?  As we read through the chapter we see that he needed to commit to abstaining from wine or strong drink, to leave his hair uncut and to avoid contact with a dead body.  He needed to come apart from the practices of the day and be different.  Verse 8 says, "All the days of his separation he shall be holy to the Lord." He gave up his rights in order to live at a higher standard, so he could be used in a special way by God.  He had to be willing to sacrifice what was lawful in order to live a life of discipline for God's higher purposes.  It was a sort of loss for him, but the gains stood to be such that the losses could scarcely be categorized as such.

How true that is in our lives.  God calls us to "Come out from among them and be separate"[II Corinthians 6:17].  We think of that as a sacrifice we need to make when we can't live like others do, but perhaps a better word to apply would be privilege.   We have been called by the Creator of the universe, our Savior, to come apart to Him, to be holy as He is holy.  What kind of sacrifice could I possibly make for Him Who gave up so much for me?  It is impossible to think in terms of sacrifice when I realize how God suffered in giving up His Son that I might live.

Do you sometimes balk at not being able to live like others in the world?

As you sit with Him today, rejoice that He has called you to Himself- to be His child, to be different.

Numbers 11                                                    February 02

## Sharing our Burdens with God

Numbers 11 gives us a review of the Israelites' complaints and how God's anger was aroused as a result, such that He caused some of them to be consumed by fire. The fire was only quenched when the people cried out and Moses beseeched the Lord. The people continued in their cravings for the food they had once enjoyed in Egypt, and they wept as they were given manna every day. Numbers 11 says, "Then Moses heard the people weeping throughout their families, everyone at the door of his tent; and the anger of the Lord was greatly aroused; Moses also was displeased." This incident was already recorded in Exodus 18, but here we are given more insight into Moses' feelings as he says to God, "Why have you afflicted your servant? And why have I not found favor in your sight, that you have laid the burden of all these people on me? Did I conceive these people? Did I beget them, that You should say to me, 'carry them in your bosom, as a guardian carries a nursing child, to the land which you swore to your fathers'? Where am I to get meat to give to these people? For they weep all over me, saying, 'Give us meat, that we may eat.' I am not able to bear all these people alone because the burden is too heavy for me. If you treat me like this, please kill me here and now- if I have found favor in your sight- and do not let me see my wretchedness!" (Verses 11-15].

How gracious of God to allow us into these deep feelings of His meek servant. How gracious of Him to then provide Moses with 70 men to help carry the burden. He responded so wonderfully to Moses' pain, giving the 70 men the same Spirit that was upon Moses, to bear the burden with him so he would not have to bear it alone.[verse 16&17]. God hears our pain, and it is His delight to respond.

Allow God to hear your burdens.

Allow Him to respond, knowing it is His delight to do so.

Numbers 12                                          February 03

## Sin Brings Separation from God and Others

Numbers 12 recounts the incident of Miriam and Aaron speaking out against Moses because he had married an Ethiopian woman. It appears that they may have had an issue also relating to the special relationship God had with Moses. Whatever their complaint, verse 3 says that God heard it, and verses 6-8 record His response: "Why were you not afraid to speak against My servant Moses?" He said this after reminding them that He speaks to His servants in the way He chooses. He is God, and they are not. Verse 9 says God was angry with them, and He left them. Miriam then suddenly becomes leprous, and Moses cries out to God to heal her. After seven days of being shut out of the camp, she is healed of the leprosy and again received in the camp. During those seven days, the entire camp could not move forward. God obviously does not see this offense as a trivial one and responds accordingly, but it is also an opportunity for Him to show His grace.

Miriam's sin brought separation from God ["He departed", verse 9] and separation from others ["Miriam was shut out of the camp seven days", verse 14]. These were major losses for her, as was the humiliation of holding up the entire congregation from journeying forward. Our sin brings all kinds of loss and sorrow into our lives, as well as into the lives of others. Thankfully, God's grace stands ready to redeem us if confession and repentance are present, as they were when Aaron recognized their "foolish" sin [verse 11}, and interceded for his sister as did Moses.

Are there "foolish " sins in your life for which you need to confess and repent so God can offer His grace?

Do you see how sin can be an obstacle between you and God?   Or between you and others?

Numbers 13 &14                                    February 04

## Loss from Listening to the Wrong People

It is recorded in Numbers 13 that the Lord told Moses to send out men to spy out the land of Canaan, which was to be His people's inheritance. These spies were to appraise the land and the people and bring back some fruit from the land. The report brought back by all the men, with the exception of Caleb and Joshua, was that the land did indeed flow with milk and honey, but it was inhabited by very strong people and was highly fortified. Caleb wanted to go at once and take possession of their land, knowing God's people, with Him , were able [verse10]. However, the other spies countered Caleb's proposal by stepping up their assessment of the situation: "The people in the land are stronger", "The land devours its inhabitants", "The men there are giants", "We were like grasshoppers in comparison".... The reaction of the Israelites to this report is found in Numbers 14:1: "All the congregation lifted up their voices and cried, and the people wept that night". Then they followed their usual pattern and complained against Moses, saying they would rather have died in Egypt or in the wilderness. They even suggested selecting a leader and returning to Egypt.

At this point God was ready to disinherit them and begin a new nation with Moses [verse 12] but once again, Moses places himself between God and the rebellious people, asking for pardon for them as He recounted God's attributes: longsuffering, abundant in mercy, forgiving, yet just. God's justice required a payment for their continued sin: this generation, except for Caleb and Joshua, would wander in the wilderness for forty years and never enter the promised land. The men who brought the evil report died of the plague before the Lord. The people mourned greatly because of their sin and the consequence that followed. They listened to the wrong people, rather than keeping their eyes and ears on God and His chosen servants. Tremendous loss and pain resulted.

Who are you listening to?

Can you think of a time when pain resulted in your life because you didn't stay centered on God and His people?

Numbers 13:30, 14:6-9,30,38                    February 05

## Avoiding Pain by Staying Centered on God

While all the spies and their generation of the children of Israel suffered grave losses due to looking at circumstances rather than looking to the One Who had released them from bondage and sustained them thus far, Joshua and Caleb were able to assess their situation from God's perspective because they stayed centered on Him. Numbers 14:8 says, "If the Lord delight in us, then He will bring us into this land and give it to us…" It is reminiscent of "If the Lord is for us, who can be against us?" They knew that nothing was going to get by God without His approval. Their reward for believing that everything was under the Father's control? Only they among all their generation would be allowed to enter the land that God had promised them.

It is not what occurs in our lives which determines what the outcome will be, but it is our attitude and response to it. Two people can suffer similar heartache. One can allow it to make him bitter and unusable to God. The other, even while in sorrow, can offer it to God to be used for His glory and their good. We always have a choice as to how we will respond to that which passes through our lives. If we choose to stay centered on the Lord and know that He not only knows what is going on but has either given it to us as our portion, or has, at the very least, allowed it, we will rise above the circumstances and be victorious in them.

Will you work with Him to accept with thankfulness the portion He has offered you, knowing He only has your good and His glory in mind.

Know that this is a process, seeing Him as He is and yourself as you are.

Numbers 16                                                    February 06

## Loss Results from Rebellion Against God's Servants

In chapter 16 of Numbers we read of 14,700 Israelites dying of the plague, another 250 men consumed by fire, and three entire families and their goods swallowed up by the earth.   The cause of these devastating losses? Man's own sin.  Korah, a Levite, along with 250 other leaders, gathered themselves against Moses and Aaron, complaining about their exalted leadership positions.  Korah, himself as a Levite, had been set apart to serve the congregation in worship of the Lord, but he wanted the position that God had assigned to Moses and Aaron.  Even after Korah, his family, and his 250 followers died, the congregation continued to complain against Moses and Aaron, saying they had killed the people of the Lord. Their behavior resulted in God's sending of the plague.

Every day I see people suffering because of their own sin.  Often they are dissatisfied with what God has given them, desiring instead what God has given to others, and so they have no peace.  When they take matters into their own hands to get what they want, disaster results, as it did in Numbers 16.  When we come to the understanding that God has a plan for each one of us, that he gifts us and desires to use us in specific ways to edify His Church, we will be more than satisfied with where He has us and how He has chosen to use us.  Instead of loss we will experience fullness and joy as we submit to Him.

Are you aware of suffering unnecessary pain because you are dissatisfied with where God has placed others and you?

What do you want to say to God about this?

Numbers 20                                            February 07

## Ungodly Reactions Bring Sorrow

We see a familiar pattern in Numbers 20: the people gathering themselves against Moses and Aaron again because they had no water.  Once again they utter how they should have died earlier.  The pattern continues with Moses and Aaron falling on their faces before God and His glory appearing to them.  After God tells Moses to speak to the rock at Meribah so that water will come flow from it, the pattern changes.  Moses, angry at the rebels, as he calls them, reacts in anger and strikes the rock two times, disobeying God's direct command to speak to it.   Water came out, the people and animals drank, but there had to be a payment for Moses' sin because as God says in verse 12, "You did not believe Me to hallow Me in the eyes of the children of Israel…" Moses' behavior showed disrespect for God before the people.  The payment was that neither Moses nor Aaron, the two who had dealt with the rebellious and complaining people of God for so long, would bring the assembly into the land which God had given them.  By the end of this chapter in Numbers, we read that Aaron has died and leadership passed to his son, Eleazar.  We also read that all the house of Israel mourned for Aaron for thirty days.  One ungodly reaction caused such grief to God's faithful servants as well as to the entire nation.

God is loving and kind, slow to anger, but He is also holy and just.  He means what He says.  He will not see His name or character tarnished, even by His most beloved followers.  When we allow our emotions to control us, as Moses momentarily did on this occasion, pain will result.

Talk with God about the need to hallow His name so that people around you can see Who He is.

Recognize that some of the sorrow we endure may come from our own sinful behavior.

Numbers 21                                    February 08

## Sin is Costly

In Numbers 21 we see the Lord listening to the voice of Israel and delivering up the Canaanites to them in battle. After the victory, however, the recurring pattern returns with the Israelites becoming discouraged and speaking out against God and Moses, whining about food and water once again. This time God chose to send fiery serpents to bite and kill many of the people. Again the pattern repeats itself with their confession being offered and Moses intervening for them. God's solution was for Moses to make a fiery serpent, put it on a pole, and for everyone who was bitten, to look at it and live [verse 8]. This doesn't sound like a costly remedy until we consider it as being a picture of what Jesus would do in years ahead.

The bronze serpent upon which they were to look represents Christ and future atonement being made. The cost of Jesus' death so that we might have our sins paid for and have access to God is immeasurable. The Father had to watch His Son, His perfect Son, take on our sin. We glide over that with little thought as to what that would be like for the loving Father. We glide over it because it is too much for us to contemplate, too much for us to understand or bear, because He did it for us. He had to if we were ever going to be reconciled to Him. Jesus had to leave the Father and present Himself in the most humble of ways to the world where He would eventually suffer the cruelest of deaths by their hands. Most of the people for whom He died would reject Him and the life He offers. We see the agony of this in Luke 22:39-46 as He awaits the taking of our sin on Himself. As hideous as was the physical torture, it was the bearing of our sin and the separation from the Father that were the most grievous to bear.

Sin is costly.

As you sit with Jesus today, talk with Him about what your sin cost Him.

Worship Him as He deserves.

Numbers 21:4-9 February 09

## Take Away the Pain

The Israelites once again, as was their pattern, spoke out against God and Moses as they continued on their journey. Verse 4 says their soul became very discouraged. What makes a discouraged soul? How did their soul become discouraged when the very God, the Lord of the universe, had personally called them to Himself, made them His Own and shown Himself to them repeatedly? They were not looking at Him, but had their eyes only on themselves and what was around them. They complained about "this worthless bread", the manna, which God faithfully provided for them every single day. Calling the bread "worthless" was an indication of how they viewed God, since He was the One Who gave it. It was also an indication of their gross lack of thankfulness.

So, God had to bring them back to the truth of Who He is and who they were, for their ultimate good, so He sent fiery serpents which bit them, causing pain, agony, and even death to some.

The people went to Moses and said, "We have sinned, for we have spoken against the Lord and against you." That is a great start, recognizing their sin. Next, however, instead of being interested in learning in their pain, they immediately asked Moses to pray to the Lord to take away the pain, the serpents. While it is a natural tendency to want the pain to go away, we short-circuit what God can teach us only when we are in pain. The Israelites missed it as they had done so many times previously and so would have to repeat the process again, many times, in their case.

Do you look for the easiest exit from pain, or is your goal to learn what God has for you in it?

Numbers 27:12-23                                    February 10

## Losses Due to Aging

It is safe to say that loss begins at birth. We are forced to leave the familiar, safe environment of our mother's womb to enter a world of lights, noise, poking and prodding... From then on we have to cry for sustenance [we saw the Israelites do a lot of this], figure out ways to get what we want, not always succeeding, and give up things on a regular basis. As we grow older, the things we give up become more plentiful. We begin to lose some physical abilities: can't move as quickly, can't read the fine print, can't hear as well [I personally think people mumble more than they used to] , can't remember where we put the keys, can't open that jar.... Eventually it affects our ability to drive, to live alone...Difficult losses.  We fight against them for as long as we can, but eventually we have to figure out a way to accept them and to deal with the biggest loss of all, death.

Moses is presented with this loss in Numbers 27 when God tells him to prepare for his death, reminding him of his failure at Meribah when he rebelliously struck the rock instead of speaking to it.

Moses could have made an attempt to defend himself, telling God of all the times he got it right or reminding God of the people with whom he had to deal, but he did neither of these. Instead he asks God to send a man to take his place in leading the people. The humble, interceding heart of Moses continues his work right up to the end of his life. His concern is not for himself but for God's people, that the work God gave him will continue. Verse 23 tells us that Moses laid his hands upon Joshua, his successor, and gave him charge to continue the work. He approached the ultimate phase of aging, not considering himself, but others, just as he had lived his life.

As we grow older, instead of lamenting what we are losing, what do we need to do to see that God's work continues?

Ask God to begin to develop in you the kind of heart that Moses had.

Numbers 33:50-53                                   February 11
Deuteronomy 9:1-5
Joshua 7:10-13

## Failure to Eradicate

The Israelites suffered a great deal because of the inhabitants and their idols that remained in their land. They were instructed in Deuteronomy and various other passages to completely get rid of the evil of their idols and their high places of false worship. God used words to them like destroy, demolish, and dispossess. They did not obey.

Today I saw what happens when we fail to completely get rid of something that is not good. I have a nice stand of bee balm in my yard, and today when I went to see how it was coming along, I found that the whole center of the circle where it is planted was overcome with weeds, and these unwanted plants had crowded out the desired flowers. I know how it happened, and it made me think of God's admonition to Israel: Drive them out, demolish their high places, and dispossess them. Like Israel, last fall I didn't completely eradicate the weeds. I pulled some of them out, but when it got too difficult, I quit. It hurt my hands. It was uncomfortable so I stopped, enabling the left over weeds to infiltrate and crowd out the good plants. What problems could these few little weeds cause, I asked. Now I know: My good plants were decimated while the weeds thrived.

Besides the difficulty of the work involved, why else did I fail to take care of those weeds? They blended in, and I was unaware of some of them. That is what happens as we get used to the sin around us. We don't see it as such. We become unaware of it until it grabs us and takes over.

God knows us. He knew what would take place in the lives of the Israelites if they failed to get rid of the sin around them. That is also why he warns us to not just cut back on the things that lead us away from Him, but to completely get rid of them, lest they take over and control our lives.

What do you need to remove from your life to prevent yourself from being overcome by the "weeds"?

Deuteronomy 4:27-40                                    February 12

## Remedy from the Pain of Separation from God

As we move into the book of Deuteronomy, we see Moses giving a review of Israel's history, particularly their failures and conflicts as they wandered in the wilderness. In 4:27 Moses warns the people that they will be scattered among the nations, worshiping their gods, and be left few in number. Then verse 29 says they will seek the Lord their God and will find Him IF they seek Him with all their heart and with all their soul. Verse 30 goes on to say that He is a merciful God and "He will not forsake you nor destroy you, nor forget the covenant of your fathers which He swore to them." "If you seek Me, you will find Me" is what He is saying to Israel. In their tremendous pain of being separated from Him and scattered among the nations, there is a place for them to return. Their sorrow becomes an opportunity for them to see Him and to see the condition of themselves. God waits for them, but in the meantime, they suffer.

He waits for us also, just like the Father awaited the prodigal son in Luke 15. "If we seek Him, we will find Him." Whatever pain or sorrow we are enduring at the moment, is a reminder of how much we need Him. Oswald Chambers writes in his first entry of My Utmost for His Highest, a life-changing daily devotional: "God's order has to work up to a crisis in our lives because we will not heed the gentler way". It seems we cannot have His utmost in our lives without crisis. In crises we are forced to seek Him.

Can you embrace your present crisis as something He is allowing in your life to bring you closer to Him?

Are you going to choose seeking Him or seeking another way in the midst of your crisis?

Deuteronomy 6:5-25                                   February 13

## The Sorrow of Having Disobedient Children

Throughout the years of my counseling ministry, I have seen the sorrow that results from having children who choose to go their own way and not follow the Lord. Not surprisingly, difficulties arise on a regular basis in their lives, and pain is a constant companion to their parents as they watch the natural outcome unfold.

In Deuteronomy 6:5 Moses reminds the people of their greatest command, "Thou shall love the Lord your God with all your heart, and with all your soul, and with all your mind". Then in verse 7 he tells them to teach these words diligently to their children- when they sit in their homes, when they walk by their way, when they lie down, when they rise up. They were to write them on the posts of their houses and on their gates. He tells them in verse 12 that even after He has brought them into their land and they are "full", that they must be on guard lest they forget Him. They must continually give testimony to their children as to what God has done in their lives, to their history with Him "for their good always", as it says in verse 24.

We have no guarantee as to what our children will choose, but our responsibility is to teach them the truths of His Word and by our lives, show them Who He is. Even if our children are presently showing signs of rebellion against God, we can, with His help, begin at this moment to fulfill what He has asked us to do in this area.

If you are grieving what you see in the lives of your children, commit them to Him and begin to teach them His Word, and by your life show them Who He is.

Deuteronomy 8:2-6                                    February 14

## A Reason for Adversity

In chapter 7 of Deuteronomy Moses reminds Israel of how God chose them to be a special people unto Himself [verse 6] because He loved them [verse 8]. Why, then, did they suffer forty years before being given the Promised Land? We have already seen their penchant for rebellion and disobedience so we know that they brought much of it on themselves, just as we so often do. Sin brings natural consequences. Deuteronomy 8:2 gives another element to suffering: "…the Lord your God led you these forty years in the wilderness, to humble you, and to test you, to know what was in your heart, whether you would keep His commandments or not." Verse 3 goes on to say He humbled them, allowed them to be hungry, made them depend on Him daily for manna so they would know that they needed to live, not by bread alone, but by His Words. Moses concludes these thoughts in verse 5 by saying that "as a man chastens his son, so the Lord your God chastens you." He brought difficulty to them purposefully "to do them good in the end" [verse 16].

He already knew what was in their hearts, what decisions they would make, but He wanted them to see themselves and how much they could survive without Him. It is an ugly thing when we are brought face to face with our own sinfulness, but a beautiful thing when we see in Him the remedy for that ugliness. In the pain of living He always wants us to see Him and what He desires for us- relationship with Him.

In recent adversities have you seen your true self- how you think, how you react?

Humble yourself before Him, submit your needs to Him.

Deuteronomy 10:12-13 & 11:8-17                    February 15

## Promised Blessings for Following God's Ways

In our sinful, fallen world, we are going to come upon much adversity, but there is no need to bring it upon ourselves unnecessarily by disobedience to God's Word.  Here in Deuteronomy 10, God once again gives His expectations to His people: They need to fear and love Him with all their hearts and souls and to keep His commandments- for their good.  He tells them in chapter 11 that if they earnestly obey His commands, then He will not only give them the land but He will prolong their days in the land, sending rain and grass for their sustenance.  That is His covenant with them: If this..., then that...  Why would we not want to submit to that- not just so life will go well for us but because He, the Creator and Savior, desires this deep, intimate relationship with us, mere, fallen creatures that we are?  He desires not just our obedience but our unending love and devotion.  I don't just want to prolong my days and to receive His blessings, I want to please Him, to love Him with all my being.  Oswald Chambers writes that whenever we receive a blessing from God, we need to give it back to Him as a love gift.  He advocates offering the blessing back to Him in a conscious act of worship.  The blessings He offers me are not just for me, but He wants to use them in the lives of others as well.

Can you name blessings you are receiving from Him because you have made an effort to obey His voice?

Talk to Him about giving them back to Him as a love gift.

Deuteronomy 29:12 -13 & 30:3, 9 &19                    February 16

## Removed from God's Blessings

Being removed from God is a recurring theme in Scripture, as we have seen. He surely must want us to understand why we experience this type of suffering since He puts it before us so often in His Word. Being in deep fellowship with Him is the reason for our being, so it stands to reason that if we are not experiencing it, we are going to be dissatisfied, unfulfilled, and remarkably unhappy.

In Deuteronomy 29 and 30, God's work with Israel, as well as His covenant between them, is once again reviewed. Deuteronomy 29:6 says all His dealings with them are so "That you may know that I am the Lord your God." Verse 9 tells them that if they keep His covenant that they will prosper in all they do. Verse 13 says God wants to establish them as a people for Himself and be God to them. In verse 26 and 28 we read that because they did not keep their part of the covenant and went and served and worshiped other gods, the Lord uprooted them from their land and cast them into another land. They knew well the pain of being apart from Him and the blessings He offered.

He offers us deep fellowship with Himself, through His Son, Jesus. Every day we have the privilege of being in His Presence and having our deepest longings and needs met, but we so often choose our own remedies, which never satisfy.

Just as with Israel, God offers us the opportunity to be brought back from captivity and to have His compassion on us, IF we return to Him. If we choose Him and His Word, He will gather us to Himself and meet our needs. Our work will abound (verse 6), and He will rejoice over us for good (verse 9). Deuteronomy 30:19 asks Israel to choose life. We need to make the same choice.

If you have not made the decision to choose life through following Jesus with all your heart and soul, you can make that determination with Him right now.

Joshua 4                                      February 17

## Stones of Remembrance

After Moses died in the land of Moab, God Himself buried Him, the people wept for 30 days, and then the Lord gave Joshua the responsibility of leading Israel across the Jordan to their land.  In Joshua 4 God instructs Joshua to take twelve stones from out of the midst of the Jordan to be set on the shore as a memorial to the children of Israel forever.  Joshua told the people they were to set them there so when their children asked their meaning, they could say how God dried up the waters of the Jordan so Israel could cross on dry land, just as He had done at the Red Sea, "that all the peoples of the earth may know the hand of the Lord, that He is mighty, that you may fear the Lord your God forever." They were to remember the works of the Lord in their lives.

It is good to remember.  I often ask people in counseling to keep a journal of what they see God doing in their lives.  I also want them to record where they began- their pain and struggles so they can see the miracle God is accomplishing.  If we don't remember where we were, we can't appreciate where God has brought us.  Philippians 3:13 says to forget those things which are behind and reach forward to those things which are ahead.  That means to not be hindered by them, to not allow them to hold us captive, but to learn from them, to rejoice in the place where God brings us and embrace what He has for our future.  He expects that we will use our journey through difficulty for our good and the good of others.  As Israel looked upon their stones of remembrance, God's intention was that they remember their years of wondering, their failures, so they would not repeat them as they looked ahead to what He had for them.

Don't be afraid to review your journey through difficult times- the good, of course, but also the painful parts of it so you can see God' work in your life.

Joshua 7                                                    February 18

## Defeat Following Victory

The sixth chapter of Joshua ends with, "So the Lord was with Joshua, and his fame spread throughout all the country". God had just enabled him to utterly destroy the city of Jericho simply by marching around it, blowing some trumpets and shouting. We sing songs today about the great triumph of that victory.

Joshua, expecting a similar victory, sent a small contingent of men to take the city of Ai. When his men were quickly defeated "the hearts of the people melted and became like water" (7:5). Joshua tore his clothes and fell on his face before the Lord, wondering why God had brought them to this land. Not only was he concerned about the defeat of his people, but he says in verse 9, "then what will you do for Your great name?" He is concerned how God will be perceived by the surrounding nations.

God's response is found in Joshua 7:10 and 11: "Get up! Why do you lie there on your face? Israel has sinned..." The sin, unbeknownst to Joshua, had been committed by Achan in keeping the spoils from their Jericho victory, when God had emphatically told them to "utterly destroy all that was in the city". Joshua, after his grand victory at Jericho, immediately was thrust into confusion and sorrow, having to follow God's command to execute Achan for his sin. How quickly the joy of victory can turn into pain and sorrow. It did for Joshua, and so it can for us. We need to pay attention after experiencing a great success, knowing it can leave us vulnerable if we are not careful to follow God's commands and stay close to Him. Continuing to seek Him is the key in the aftermath of victory. When things are going well is no time to strike out on our own. St. Thomas Aquinas writes: "Grant, O Lord my God, that I may never fall away in success or in failure, that I may not be prideful in prosperity nor rejected in adversity."

Have you experienced the pain of defeat after a huge success? Consider with God why that may have happened.

Consider with Him the remedy for that.

Joshua 9                                    February 19

## Adversity Comes from Compromise

Joshua 9 gives us the account of Israel's neighbors, the Gibeonites, who trick the men of Israel into thinking they are from a distant country and want to make a covenant with them. Verse 14 holds the key to this incident: "They (the Israelites) did not ask counsel of the Lord." The next verse says Joshua made peace with them and made a covenant with them to let them live, thus violating God's command to destroy the people in their land. Later when surrounding peoples decided to fight the Gibeonites, the Gibeonites called upon Israel to honor their covenant and help them, and Israel had no choice but to fulfill their duty to them. That is what happens when we compromise the Word of God: It leads us to future difficulty. We get in deeper. Of course, pain results. In this case God had to intercede for Israel, to the point of making the sun stand still to insure their victory for the Gibeonites (10:14 and 42), another example of God's great mercy.

Quite often I see the pain that results from compromising what God says. A person thinks, for example, that he can put a different spin on "Do not be unequally yoked". He deludes himself into thinking that his is a special case, but the result can be years of heartache and diminished use in God's work. Often our compromise can occur simply because we aren't paying close attention, as was the case with Israel. They made a quick decision without seeking the counsel of the Lord. To prevent the pain that results from compromise, we need to know God's principles. We also need to be in direct communication with Him so we have the wisdom to apply those principles to our lives.

As you sit with Him today, ask Him to show you if you are in danger of compromising any of His commands to you.

Submit your desires to His truths.

Joshua 13:1,13 &18:3-10 &21:43-45                    February 20

## Courage Thwarts Loss

From the time we meet Joshua in God's Word, two words seem to exemplify him: obedience and courage. He lays hold of God's promises and leads the people through 30 years of moving towards taking their land. He was decisive and courageous in his leadership. We read little of his talents, intellect, and abilities, but it is his courage that grew out of his knowledge of God, that fitted him for the task God gave him.

Joshua 13 says that Joshua was old, advanced in years, when God tells him there is still much land to be possessed. The people themselves were hesitant. Joshua says to them in Joshua 18:3, "How long will you neglect to go and possess the land which the Lord God of your fathers has given you?" He challenged them and made a plan with them to survey and then divide the land. His courage resulted in the Lord giving them all the land He had promised them (Joshua 21:43), with none of their enemies standing against them (21:44). Verse 45 says, "Not a word failed of any good thing which the Lord had spoken to the house of Israel. All came to pass."

Without the courage of a Joshua, the Israelites, God's people, would not have seen God's promises fulfilled, at least not at this time. His courage came from believing God. Obedience followed his knowledge of God. How many losses do we suffer and how many blessings do we forego because we lack the courage to act on what God has already promised us? I see this sad truth often in my counseling ministry.

Do you recognize that you are lacking courage to act on a specific promise God has given you?

Do you see the loss that might incur because you are not believing God?

Joshua 22:5, 23:6,8 &24:15                              February 21

## Holding Fast to the Lord Brings Blessing

As Joshua sends the people to their own tents and to the land of their possessions, he has an admonition for them: "But take careful heed to do the commandment and the law which Moses the servant of the Lord commanded you, to love the Lord your God, to walk in all His ways, to keep His commandments, to hold fast to Him, and to serve Him with all your heart and with all your soul." He also tells them in his farewell address to them in Joshua 23:6 to "be very courageous to keep and to do all that is written in the Book of the Law of Moses..." He reminds them again to hold fast to the Lord their God (verse 8). If they don't, and opt to go the way of surrounding nations, he tells them, God will not fight for them, and there will be snares, traps, and thorns tormenting them. He challenges them in Joshua 24:15 to choose whom they will serve.

Every day we have a choice to make: Whom am I going to serve in this day? To Whom am I going to hold fast? I say, with Joshua, "As for me, I will serve the Lord." I am going to hold fast to Him, not other people or things, even good things, of the world. I want His blessings, not snares and thorns.

Before embarking on this study of loss in Scripture, I thought that most of our pain comes to us because we live in a sinful, fallen world, but now I see how much of our own pain we orchestrate because we do not choose Him and His Word. We do not choose to hold fast to Him.

Will you say with Joshua, as for me, I choose the Lord? I will hold fast to Him and His ways.

Covenant with the Lord in this.

Judges 2:20-23                                           February 22

## The Problem with Peaceful Times

Since Joshua did not leave a successor, Judges tell us that "Everyone did what was right in his own eyes" (Judges 21:25). It has been called a book of defeat. God, in His mercy and grace, raised up leaders, judges, as they were needed. The pattern of seeing God give victory to the people, then not fulfilling His commands, turning from Him, then turning back to Him when oppressed, continues to be rampant in this book. They failed repeatedly to drive out their enemies, resulting in mixed marriages, alienation from God, their enemies becoming "thorns in their side", poverty, defeat in battle, lack of God's protection, strife amongst one another, and finally, failure to have the land and the blessings God planned for them.

The loss of God's protection and blessing on them had to be the most devastating part of this pattern. It is also the most devastating part of the pattern I see in many lives today: things go well, we become complacent, forgetting to consider God, become independent of Him, difficulties naturally follow, we cry out to Him (sometimes after blaming Him for our troubles), hopefully repent and refocus on Him, begin to obey His Word, and fellowship is eventually restored. Just as with the Israelites, when we begin to obey God, peace is restored. But how much turmoil we have to go through because we refuse to stay centered on Him when all seems to be well. How much growth in Him we forfeit. Oswald Chambers says that breaking this penchant for sin is "breaking the husk of my individual independence of God". This independence is in all of us. May we cease to allow it to control us.

Think of the most tranquil, peaceful time in your life that you can remember. Was it a time of seeking God and growing in Him? For most of us the answer to that would unfortunately be no.

What changes do you have to make in order to have the next untroubled season of your life be a time of growth?

Judges 3                                          February 23

## It's about Him, not Me

Despite Israel's continued pattern of sin and failure, God remained, and His attributes of love, grace, and mercy, as well as His justice and holiness, thankfully prevailed. If it were about us, there would be no hope. It is about Him, the Redeemer of our failures. I always stand in amazement of how He put up with Israel's sin and rebellion over so many years. I am equally amazed at how He puts up with mine- not only puts up with it , but stands so ready to redeem it. When I say He puts up with it, I do not mean that He doesn't deal with it. He most assuredly does.

In Judges 3 we read of three little known judges God raised up to deliver the people from their sinful patterns. Othniel led Israel's armies, and his victory resulted in 40 years of peace. Years later, as the pattern continued, the Israelites fell under servitude of Moab, and God raised up Ehud, who also led Israel to victory, ushering in 80 years of rest. Next came Shamgar who killed 600 Philistines and delivered Israel. In Judges 4 and 5 we read how God chose a woman, Deborah, to lead His people. Israel had rest for 40 years.

Judges 3:7 clearly states that "the children of Israel did evil in the sight of the Lord. They forgot the Lord their God..." They served false gods of the surrounding nations. As we have seen, this was not a one-time thing, nor is it a one-time thing with us. We repeatedly forsake Him, serve other gods, put so many things before Him. There is always a price to be paid for our disobedience and rebellion, the most grievous being our loss of fellowship with Him, but because He is Who He is, He always makes a way for us to return to His Presence. It is always about Him and Who He is. Thankfully.

Worship Him as you sit with Him today, thanking Him for His great love and mercy to you.

Judges 13:24, 14:1, 7-9, 15-17, 16:20-31                    February 24

## Loss from Lack of Discipline

At Samson's birth, we read that the Lord blessed him, and the Spirit of the Lord began to move upon him (Judges 13:24). The account ends, however, with his being blinded, enslaved, mocked, and ridiculed by the Philistines, and eventually dying with them. Judges 16:13 tells the tale, "He did not know that the Lord had departed from him." How is that possible that the Lord would depart from someone without their recognizing the departing? How did this happen to one who began so well, one to whom God had gifted with such strength and might?

We see some warning signs early on: He insisted on a wife from the Philistines, he took his Nazirite vow lightly when he ate honey from the carcass of a lion and kept that information from his parents.... His appetites controlled him. His attitude toward God is seen in Judges 15:18: "Then he became very thirsty, so he cried out to the Lord and said 'You have given this great deliverance by the hand of Your servant, and now shall I die of thirst and fall into the hand of the uncircumcised?' " While recognizing God as being the source of his strength, there also seems to be an air of entitlement. He did not seem to see God as He is and himself as he was.

Samson's downfall is greatly hastened by his love for Delilah, whom the Philistines used to get information about the source of his strength. After lying to her repeatedly about his strength, Scripture tells us "She pestered him daily with her words and pressed him, so that his soul was vexed to death, that he told her all his heart" (That he was a Nazirite and if shaven, his strength would be gone). He succumbed. He went from blessings to ruin because of his lack of discipline. He took what he wanted: food, women, Philistines.... Living on feelings rather than on God's truth never works. It didn't work for Samson. It will not work for us.

Ask God if there are areas in your life that require more discipline.

Be sure to respond to what He shows you.

Judges 16:21-22                                    February 25

## The Roots Remain

Samson's birth was foretold to his mother by the Angel of the Lord. God had great plans for this son whose mother had previously been barren. He was to be a Nazirite, set apart for the work of the Lord, which meant he would abstain from strong drink, his hair would not be cut, and he would have no contact with the dead. As we read Samuel's story in chapters 13 to 16 of Judges, we see that he broke all three of these stipulations.

Even though Samson began his life with God's miraculous intervention and expectations, we find him in Judges 16:21, bound as a prisoner of his enemy, the Philistines, blinded, and grinding grain for them. Samson was used mightily by God at times, but he also acted on his own other times, seeking to please only himself, resulting in the scene of his prison experience. He began with such blessing, yet ended with such humiliation and pain.

I often say to people who are in the midst of dire and painful circumstances, "The last chapter has not yet been written", meaning God is not finished. This is also true of Samson's days in the dark prison. Verse 22 says, "However, the hair of his head began to grow again after it had been shaven". The roots were still there, the literal roots of his hair, as well as the roots of whom God had called him to be. God's plans will not be thwarted even by our self-centered disobedience. We pay a painful price when we go our way, but God is faithful in spite of us. In Judges 6:28 Samson asked God to remember him, and God does, allowing him to kill more of the enemy in his death than in his life. No matter where we are or what we have done, if He is in our heart, He remembers us. In the dark place of the prison, God renewed Samson's strength. He will do the same for us, no matter where we are if we call on Him. Our roots remain.

If you are in a dark place look to your roots, HIM Who called you and remembers you.

Ruth 1 &2:1-2                                    February 26

## Reaching Out to Others in Our Pain

The Book of Ruth in its four chapters shows us so much about both the hardships and joys of life. It begins with the death of a husband, widowhood, exile, famine, loneliness but ends with redemption and joy.

Ruth, a Moabite and a widow, makes a choice to leave her own country and accompany her widowed mother-in law, Naomi, who decided to return to Bethlehem from Moab, where her family had gone to escape a famine in their country. Essentially Ruth left her family, gods, culture, country and nationality behind. She and Naomi arrive in Bethlehem at the beginning of barley harvest, and Ruth immediately sets to work to provide food for herself and her mother-in law by gleaning in the fields behind the reapers.

In her many losses, Ruth could have thought only of taking care of herself, but her well-known speech to Naomi shows us her heart, and is recorded in Ruth 1:16-17: "Entreat me not to leave you or to turn back from following after you, for wherever you go, I will go; and wherever you lodge, I will lodge; Your people shall be my people and your God, my God. Where you die, I will die and there will I be buried. The Lord do so to me and more, if anything but death parts you and me." Her loyalty and care for Naomi is remarkable. In her sorrow she left all she knew, stepped out in faith, worked hard, looked for the good of another and was greatly rewarded by God. She is given a husband, Boaz, her kinsman-redeemer, a picture of Christ redeeming His people. She has a child, Obed, who becomes the Grandfather of David. Ruth, then, is in the line of Jesus. Yes, God looks to redeem our sorrows.

When in the throes of sorrow we tend to focus on ourselves. We do need to allow ourselves to mourn and to take care to receive from God what He has for us in our sorrow, but from this account, we see that in our own pain, God may have plans for us to look for the good of another.

Has God brought to mind someone to whom you should be ministering, even while dealing with your own pain?

Ruth 1:5&6, 13, 20-21:4:13-17                          February 27

## Appropriately and Honestly Expressing Sorrow

I have often felt that Naomi, Ruth's Mother-in Law, has been somewhat maligned for her expression of sorrow in the Book of Ruth. In the days of the Judges in Israel, she had left Bethlehem with her family and gone to Moab to escape a famine in their land. While there, in a foreign land and with few resources, her husband, as well as her two sons, died. Ruth 1:6 tells us that she decided to return home to Bethlehem because she heard that the "Lord had visited His people by giving them bread", demonstrating that she continued to recognize, even in her depleted state, that God was the Provider. She attempted to send her two daughters-in-law back to their own families, saying in verse 13 "For it grieves me very much for your sakes that the hand of the Lord has gone out against me". That was her assessment at that point in her life, regarding her losses.

When she and Ruth arrived back in Bethlehem and were greeted by Naomi's friends, she told them to call her Mara, meaning "the Almighty has dealt very bitterly with me." In verse 21 she said she went out full and the Lord brought her home empty. She was not denying the Lord but felt like He is the One Who had afflicted her. In 2:20 she spoke of the Lord as not having forsaken His kindness to them. There is evidence throughout the book also that she had Ruth's welfare in mind. There is also evidence that, while sorrowing, she continued to have expectations of what God would do.

Would it have been better for her to hide her feelings? Some say so. I would not. God understands our sorrows. He can tolerate our emotional rantings, always with the goal of redemption in mind. In our denial, anger, depression, and confusion of mourning, He continues to work to bring good for us and glory to Himself.

By the end of the book, we see the joy that comes out of Naomi's pain. The scene in the last verses in Ruth 4 is of Naomi in the home of Ruth and Boaz, her new son-in-law, with their child, Obed, future grandfather to David, sitting at Naomi's breast, Her friends rejoice with her as she enters this new phase of life. It makes me think of the term: Beauty for ashes. Naomi had to get through the ashes to get to the beauty, the redemption-THROUGH the ashes, not around them. Naomi was real, and God redeemed.

Talk with God about being real in your sorrows- real, without forsaking Him.

Ruth 2:4-17, 3:10-13, 4                                        February 28

## The Redeemer

There is one more person to look at in the Book of Ruth- Boaz, the Kinsman-Redeemer.  He points us to Christ as our Redeemer.

The first thing we read of Boaz is that he loved God and sought God's best for those with whom he came in contact.  (2:4-17).  He offered Ruth sustenance, compassion, and protection.  He committed himself to her good (3:10-13) by going through all the proper channels in seeking redemption for her, eventually happily becoming the redeemer himself.

Even in our darkest hours, especially in our darkest hours, we have to stay centered on the truth that Jesus is our Redeemer.  He offers sustenance, compassion, protection, and life to us.  We mourn, but not without hope, for there is purpose in our sorrow.  II Corinthians 4:8-10 says, "We are hard pressed on every side, yet not crushed; We are perplexed, but not in despair; persecuted, but not forsaken; struck down, but not destroyed- always carrying about in the body, the dying of the Lord Jesus, that the life of Jesus also may be manifested in our body." We have hope because of Him.

We can feel at times like Naomi did, but we have to know that Jesus is walking with us, desiring to take our grief and use it in our lives to show us more of Himself.  He redeems our sorrows, meaning He brings good out of them.  II Corinthians 4:17 says, "For our light affliction, which is but for a moment, is working for us a far more exceeding and eternal weight of glory." Not only has He redeemed me from my sins so I was brought back into fellowship with God, but He desires to redeem all that I go through so I can know Him more deeply and serve Him more fully.  He redeems for my good and His glory.

Sit with Him and honor Him for His redeeming of you from your lost condition.

Trust Him to redeem your sorrows.

I Samuel 2:12,17, 22-36; 4:10-22                    February 29

## Pain from Ungodly Parenting

Hannah left her much-treasured son in God's house with Eli, the Priest. We read about Eli's sons in I Samuel 2:12: "Now the sons of Eli were corrupt; they did not know the Lord." They went so far as to be sexually immoral with the women who came to the Tabernacle. Eli attempted to correct them by words, at least to some degree, but we read that "They did not heed the voice of their father." Eli is described as honoring his sons more than God and taking advantage of his priestly position. I Samuel 3:13 tells us that he did not restrain them. Surely Eli suffered greatly as he witnessed his sons' rebellious behavior, but his lack of discipline with them would cost him much more grief: the deaths of both of his sons in the same day. God says he would then "Raise up for Myself a faithful priest who shall do according to what is in My heart and in My mind." Because Eli was not faithful in his own home, with his own family, he would also lose his position as priest before Israel. On the day his two sons were killed by the Philistines, the Ark of the Lord was also captured. When Eli was given the news of the Ark, he fell backward off his seat and died. His daughter - in-law died giving birth at this time also, but before her death, named her son, Ichabod, meaning "The glory has departed from Israel." Surely it had.

How different might this story have gone if Eli would have been the parent God intended, if he had disciplined his sons, and made requirements of them. This is also the cause of much grief in the lives of many people I see. God is loving and kind, but also holy and just. He means what He says. Our disobedience will cost us much discomfort.

Have you committed your parenting to Him?

Are there directives in His Word that you need to correct as you parent?

I Samuel 8                                          March 01

## God Suffers Also

While Samuel judged Israel with character and integrity, hearing the voice of God and speaking it to the people, he, like Eli before him, failed as a parent, so that when he was ready to die, the people demanded a king, citing the dishonesty and perversion of his sons. God's assessment of the peoples' demand was that they rejected Him, not Samuel (8:7).

Oswald Chambers writes how our obstinate self-will wounds God. Who else but he would recognize that? Yet, here it is in I Samuel 8. God expresses how He is being forsaken by the people whom He has claimed as His Own (verse 8). He warns them through Samuel that their lives will be much more difficult under a king. Their response in 8:19-20 says it all: "No, but we will have a king over us, that we may be like all the nations…" They will have what they will have despite the fact that their loving Father so longs to give them all that is good. The picture here of God being rejected and forsaken is beyond heart-breaking.

Yet, don't we do the same on a regular basis? God tells us to put Him first and all else will be added to us. We say, however, that we have so much else to attend to that we can't spend the time. We say, "but God, Your Word doesn't apply to my situation. This is a different time, a different society. Surely You can't expect me to follow what the Bible says here. I think I have a better way to do it." And on we go, rejecting Him, wounding Him. May it not be.

God shows Himself suffering here, but Israel will suffer also under their demand for a king.   Just as they did not know best, neither do we. God says what He says to us for our protection and provision. Let us behave in such a way that we do not wound the One Who is so ready to give us His best.

Sit with Jesus today and let Him lovingly show you where you may be causing suffering in Him.

I Samuel 10:9, 13:13-14, 15:10-11, 34-35                    March 02

## A Good Beginning, Not a Good Ending

Saul, Israel's new king, began well.  In I Samuel 10:9 we read that when Samuel anointed Saul, "God gave him a new heart".  That sounds like what God does for us when we receive Christ as our Savior.  When God enters our heart, we then have the capacity to know Him and have a growing relationship with Him.  The growth takes place day by day as we spend time with Him, reading His Word, applying it, talking and listening to Him, even sometimes just sitting with Him and enjoying His Presence.  The new heart, salvation, is just the beginning, the opening of the way to the deep, intimate relationship He has planned for us.   He wants us in heaven with Him, but He also wants us now.   For Saul, the new heart opened the way for him to be a great king to God's people.  While God gave Saul the capacity to know Him deeply and rely upon Him unreservedly, neither was to come to pass.  Throughout I Samuel, we see Saul lacking courage and trust in God.  He made unlawful sacrifices, he did not utterly destroy the Amalekites as God commanded, he blamed his people for his own failure to obey... because of Saul's unwillingness to grow in the Lord, Samuel warns him that his Kingdom will not continue.  It will be given to a man after God's own heart (I Samuel 13:14).  I Samuel 15:35 is a particularly sad verse: "And Samuel went no more to see Saul until the day of his death.  Nevertheless Samuel mourned for Saul, and the Lord regretted that He had made Saul king over Israel".

God gave Saul all that he needed to be a great King, right down to a new heart, but Saul would not submit to Him and trust Him.  With our new birth, He gives us everything we need to be who He has always intended, everything we need to be used by Him in a wonderful, unimaginable way.  It just requires our submission to Him day by day.

Are you submitting to Him on a day by day basis?

Are you farther along with Christ today than you were a month ago?  If not, what do you need to do?

I Samuel 13:1-14                                                    March 03

## Saul's Journey to His Lost Throne

In just his second year as King of Israel, Saul was faced with the onslaught of the Philistines, his own people being scattered, and Samuel being delayed in arriving, so Saul took it upon himself to take on the priestly role and offer a burnt offering, testifying to his thinking that God might not be trustworthy, and also possibly thinking of himself more highly than he ought to think. When confronted by Samuel, instead of acknowledging his sin and repenting of it, he made excuses. Later we see his disobedience in not destroying their enemies as commanded. We read in I Samuel 16:14 that the Spirit of the Lord departed from Saul and that a distressing spirit from the Lord troubled him. I believe this is a direct result of his refusal to deal with his sin. He continued his downward slide to losing his throne and becoming jealous of David's successes to the point where he sought to murder him. He feared David, it seems, because he recognized God's Spirit in him.

Sometimes we can look at a loss we have suffered and see how the steps we have chosen have led directly to that loss. Just as in the case of Saul, we may be able to point to wrong thinking , which then resulted in those missteps. "As a man thinks in his heart, so is he," says Proverbs 23:7. Saul allowed his insecure thoughts about himself and his lack of trust in God to drive his behavior, beginning with the unlawful sacrifice and culminating with his attempts on David's life. If we think correctly, according to God's Word, correct behavior will follow. We will never have to look at a loss in our lives, like Saul did, and know we have been the cause of it.

Spend time with God today , and let Him show you any wrong thinking you may have in your life.

I Samuel 13:13 & II Samuel 12:13 & Psalm 51        March 04

## The Enigma of David

David is called "A man after God's own heart". He was God's choice to succeed Saul as King. He was the writer of many Psalms. He is in the line of Christ. Yet we know that he sinned mightily: infidelity, cover up, murder, disobedience to God in numbering the people which demonstrated his lack of trust in God, irresponsible parenting, resulting in a myriad of problems with his children… Why did God choose such a flawed man to be used in such a remarkable way?

Unlike Saul, when faced with his sin, David mourned it, repented, and asked for God's forgiveness. He was as I Samuel 13:14 says, "A man after God's Own heart". There are numerous passages in I and II Samuel where we see David inquiring of the Lord and then doing as he was commanded. Even though Saul continually sought to take David's life, David would do no harm to Saul, even when the opportunity lay right in front of him. The reason David gave was because Saul was God's anointed. After Nathan confronted David after his grave sin with Bathsheba and the events following, he readily admitted that he had sinned against the Lord. Psalm 51 shows us his broken and contrite heart in relationship to his sin. He cries out for God's mercy and asks to be washed. He says his sin is ever before him. He doesn't say anything in this Psalm about the consequences he went through because of his sin. It is not about asking to be released from the pain. What he dwells on here is how he sinned against God. He agrees with God. He wants a clean heart and a right spirit within him. He pleads that he may not be cast from God's Presence or that the Holy Spirit may not be taken away. He wants the joy of his salvation restored. It's all about his wanting his relationship with God made right., nothing about reprieve from the consequences. Right there is why God used David in such extraordinary ways- It was always about his staying in relationship with his Lord.

Can you say that right relationship with God is the most important thing to you?

When you sin, is it your main desire to have fellowship with your Lord restored?

I Samuel 17:4-7, 42-44. 48-50                                    March 05

## Goliath's Loss

Seemingly, Goliath had all he needed to succeed, but he lost, even down to his very life. He was the Philistines' champion, had great physical attributes, as well as all the weapons necessary for victory. He also had great confidence in himself. However, we know that he was quickly slain by the young David, armed with only a sling and a stone.

Goliath's monumental defeat came about because of where he placed his confidence- in himself. It makes me think of Psalm 8:4: "God, what is man that you are mindful of him?" When we consider Who God is- and who we know ourselves to be- how can we place all our trust in ourselves? How can we place ANY trust in ourselves, apart from Him? Yes, God has shown that He values us. He allowed His Son to die for us so that we can come into relationship with Him and spend eternity with Him, but left to our own devices, we have no hope. While Goliath trusted in himself, resulting in his death, David came in the name of the Lord of hosts (17:45), knowing that the Lord would give him the victory.

How much sorrow do we endure because we insist on trusting ourselves, rather than our Savior and Lord? That independence we are so prone to is the very heart of our sin nature. We grasp hold of our possessions, money, abilities and even other people, to avoid being in subjection to God. We lose. We lose our peace, the opportunity for victory, sometimes the very things we are counting on for our success, but mostly the blessed opportunity to be in deep fellowship with Him. We lose the very reason for our being and then suffer so needlessly.

Let God show you where you are placing your trust.

What do you need to do to put that trust back where it belongs?

I Samuel 25                                                    March 06

## An Evil Husband

I Samuel 25 tells us the story of Abigail, a beautiful woman with good understanding who was married to Nabal, a rich but harsh and evil man. Nabal not only refused to feed David and his men, even though David had protected his interests, but instead treated them with disrespect and insolence. As a result David's intent was to kill all the men who belonged to Nabal. Enter the beautiful wife with good understanding. She made haste, without telling Nabal, and prepared a feast for David and his men. She rode with the feast to David, fell on her face before him and pleaded for the lives of her husband and their people, even while she acknowledged that her husband was indeed a scoundrel. She quickly intervened to prevent bloodshed, and David relented.

When Abigail returned home, she found her husband drunk, so told him nothing of what transpired until the next morning, at which time his heart died within him. Nabal died, and Abigail later became David's wife. Obviously God put His stamp of approval on Abigail's approach to protecting her family.

I have seen many women suffer with less than ideal husbands. Some could even, like Nabal, be classified as foolish, if not disrespectful and offensive. Like Abigail, these women need to take personal responsibility and behave as God directs. Surely they suffer much with such husbands, but God stands ready to offer them His love and security, if they are willing to accept it. He stands ready to meet every need that they have, and usually there are many. In their sorrow in such a marriage, there is opportunity to know God in a deeply intimate way, as he meets their needs in a manner that only He can.

I am so glad God gave us this account of such a courageous and forthright woman. What hope and encouragement it gives to women who are in difficult marriages with difficult men. Submitted to God, He can use them mightily.

If you can identify with Abigail's situation, will you put yourself under God's Lordship to use you anyway He desires?

II Samuel 1 &2:1                                          March 07

## David Mourns

When David hears about the death of his beloved friend, Jonathan, and his King, Saul, he mourns deeply, tearing his clothes and fasting (II Samuel 1:11). He writes a song about his feelings and instructs his people to teach it to their children. In his song he extols the virtues of both men, citing their victories as warriors, calling them beloved and pleasant. He praises Saul, the one who, out of his own jealousy, persecuted David, by reminding the people how he, as king, brought prosperity and provision for them. That he would extol one who made him such an enemy shows us more of David's character. We see more of his heart when he wrote how distressed he was about Jonathan's death, calling him his brother, saying how their love for each other surpassed the love of women. He mourned deeply, showing us that mourning is a natural outcome of loss. God made us with the ability and need to express how we feel when someone or something close to us is gone. Knowing the relationship David had with God, we can picture God mourning right along with David.

The very next verse after David's song says that David inquired of the Lord, asking Him where he should go. That is so consistent with mourning being the process for our going from the "Why?" to the "What now?" I doubt that David was finished mourning, but he was ready to say, "What do you have for me now, Lord?" When we find ourselves asking that, we know we are making progress in moving through the mourning process.

Are you ready to say, "What now?" to the Lord? "This has happened, and I sorrow about it, but what do You want me to do now?"

II Samuel 1 & 2:1-21                                    March 08

## Trusting God with our Sorrows

I Samuel begins with an issue we have seen before in Scripture- infertility. This time it is Hannah who longs for a child. She also has an adversary, Peninnah, also a wife of her husband. Peninnah relentlessly provoked her to make her miserable, I Samuel 1:6 says, because "The Lord had shut up her womb". Verse 10 says Hannah "was in bitterness of soul, and prayed unto the Lord, and wept bitterly." One version says she wept in anguish.

I have sat with women in counseling who were unable to conceive, and I saw the depth of the pain they experienced. It is one of those sorrows that has no end. Throughout life there are reminders of the child who never was. In Hannah's society, infertility was also looked on with scorn, explaining even more so the depth of her anguish.

In her sorrow Hannah's response was to go to the Lord and ask Him to remember her plight. She made a vow to give back to Him a child He might choose to give her. Before the chapter ends, we see Hannah giving birth to a son, naming him Samuel, "because I have asked for him from the Lord". We also see her taking Samuel to the House of the Lord and leaving him there with Eli, the Priest, thus fulfilling her promise to God.

How difficult that must have been for her, but we read nothing of that, only her praise to the Lord, saying, "My heart rejoices in the Lord", "There is none besides You", "He brings low and lifts up". She knows Him well.

In her pain of infertility she prayed specifically and directly. Her prayer changed her life and had a major impact on all of Israel. Her son, Samuel, became a prophet and was greatly used in the life of King David. By being faithful, even in great sorrow, she experienced great blessing, and brought great blessing on others.

The story continues to get better. I Samuel 2:21 says, "And the Lord visited Hannah, so that she conceived and bore three sons and two daughters. Meanwhile the son Samuel grew before the Lord." God is indeed a Master at redeeming our pain.

Do you see God as Hannah did in chapter 2:1-11?

Do you trust Him in your sorrows as she did?

II Samuel 6:1-15                                    March 09

## Being Displeased with God

After David finally became King over all Israel, he gathered together 30,000 men of Israel and they went to bring up the Ark of God. They set the Ark upon a new cart and played various sorts of instruments in celebration as they travelled with it. One of David's men, Uzzah, reached out his hand and touched the Ark to steady it. We read that "the anger of the Lord was kindled against Uzzah, and God smote him there for his error, and there he died by the Ark of the Lord." II Samuel 6:8 tells us that David was displeased because of the Lord's anger against Uzzah. Once again this reminds me of Beth Moore's expression of "God misbehaving". He doesn't do what we expect, or He does what we don't expect. He doesn't live up to our expectations.

When that happens, we need to review Who He is and who we are, realizing our thinking needs a major readjustment. Apparently it took David three months to get his thinking in order, for we read that he was afraid of God, and so instead of proceeding with the Ark, he carried it aside to a house where it remained for three months. When David saw how God blessed the owner of the house, he brought the Ark to his city "with gladness". He gave an offering to God and danced before the Lord with shouting and with the sound of the trumpet. Now that he had done business with Who God is, he was finally ready to rejoice in the Lord again.

The touching of the Ark was something God had forbidden. He was teaching a major attribute of Himself to His people, His holiness. He is God. We are not. He owes us no explanation. David had to go from anger, to fear, and back to trust and joy through this incident. He now had a fuller knowledge of his God.

Is there something that has displeased you about God? Is it keeping you from Him?

What do you think He may be trying to show you about Himself?

II Samuel 6:16-27                                    March 10

## A Spouse's Rejection and Disdain

After David became angry with God because of His outbreak against Uzzah, he saw the blessing of God poured out onto the house where the Ark was, so he brought the Ark back to his city and sacrificed to the Lord. Scripture says he was so filled with joy that "He danced before the Lord with all his might". There was shouting, the sound of the trumpet, and much celebrating as Israel brought the Ark of God home. David's wife, Michal, looked through a window and saw David "leaping and whirling" before the Lord as he was wearing a lined ephod. II Samuel 6:16 says, "She despised him in her heart". Most women I know would be delighted to see their husbands abandoning themselves in worship to the Lord, but not this woman. Apparently she was concerned with what his subjects would think, so she rebuked him, the King of Israel, saying disdainfully, "How glorious was the King of Israel today, uncovering himself today in the eyes of the maids of his servants, as one of the base fellows shamelessly uncovers himself!" She mocks him, her husband, and also God's anointed.

David was King. He could have had her put to death. He could have been angry and resentful as many men would be in our society. He may have taken on her shame and stopped his worship, but no, this is what he says, after reminding her that he is God's anointed: "I will play music before the Lord. And I will be even more undignified than this, and will be humble in my own sight. But as for the maidservants of whom you have spoken, by them I will be held in honor."

Nothing was going to keep David from worshipping his Lord, not even the disdain of his wife. His relationship with God caused him to celebrate. We see his confidence and steadfastness here, a model for us not to allow others to keep HIM from the center of our lives.

While having a critical and disdainful spouse is a painful thing, God honors our steadfastness in keeping our focus on Him.

II Samuel 11 &12                                                    March 11

## The Pain of Deliberate Sin

Several times in II Samuel it says that God preserved David wherever he went. God gave him many victories and extended his kingdom. All was going quite well, maybe too well for David to stay dependent on the Lord. In Chapter 11 we find that while David sent his army out to war, he tarried at Jerusalem, and as it happened, in the evening he rose from his bed and walked on the roof of his house. There he just happened to see the beautiful Bathsheba. I write it like that because I have never thought it "just happened". It seems to me that David had not gone where he should have (out to war as the other kings did at that particular time} and was looking for something, or someone. Unfortunately, as is so often the case, he found it. You probably know the story: he commits adultery with Bathsheba and when she becomes pregnant, attempts to cover his sin by having her husband, the very noble Uriah, killed in battle. Then he marries Bathsheba, and all would have been well, except for verse 27: "the thing displeased the Lord". God has Nathan go to David and confront him with his sin.

God's great disappointment is seen in II Samuel 12:7-9: He had given David so much and yet he "despised" God's command. The relationship between God and David suffered. God Himself felt despised by David. But there were more consequences and pain from David's actions. God said the sword would never depart from his house. There was to be turmoil for the entire nation. It gave occasion to other nations to blaspheme. Lastly, the child who was conceived was to die. Later there would be additional distress in David's family that could be traced back to this sin.

The pain that resulted from David's sin is incalculable.   However, his repentance is evident, as well as God's forgiveness. Nathan says in II Samuel 12:13 that the Lord had put away his sin. Relationship with God would be restored, while the consequences would remain. Our own sin brings us much sorrow. Here we see that it brings others pain as well. But do we consider how much grief it brings to our Lord?

Talk to God about some of the pain you have brought to yourself and others from your sin. Confess and repent of it and receive His forgiveness.

Consider the pain God experiences from your sin.

II Samuel 13                                                    March 12

## The Sins of the Father

There is a very distressing story that God gives us in II Samuel 13. David's son, Amnon, longed to have a sexual encounter with one of his half-sisters, Tamar, so he tricked her and then raped her. Immediately after the attack, Scripture says the hatred he felt for her was greater than the love he had had for her, so he sent her away, causing her even more distress than the rape did. Clearly this was a very troubled young man. Tamar's brother, Absalom, sought to console her, harbored hatred in his heart for Absalom, and began to devise a plan to avenge her. David, on the other hand, was very angry with the situation but did nothing. He is to suffer mightily for his inaction.

Absalom waited two years and then carried out his plan to kill Amnon. As a result he had to flee from David and his home. David lost two sons in one day. Verse 36 of II Samuel 13 records how David and all his sons and their servants wept bitterly. We also read in verse 37 how David mourned for his absent son, Absalom, every day. He longed to go to him but it would be several years before Absalom could return to his Father's house and even then, Scripture tells us, he did not see the king's face for several more years. Even though there was a measure of forgiveness and reconciliation between the two, this entire situation set up future rebellion in the heart of Absalom, resulting in his death and leading to David's great outburst of grief in II Samuel 18:33, "O my son, Absalom, my son, my son Absalom! Would God I had died for thee, O Absalom, my son, my son!"

While great and anointed by God in so many ways, David proved to be a colossal failure as a family man. The entire nation was greatly impacted, his family suffered much, and David himself records the depth of his own grief. God also mourned. Our sinful choices bring widespread suffering.

Talk to God about your relationships in your own family. Are they what He desires for you?

II Samuel 22                                                    March 13

## Praise for God's Deliverance

II Samuel 22 shows us why David is called "A man after God's Own heart", despite his many failings. In this chapter he speaks in song to his Lord after being delivered from Saul and his enemies. He calls God his rock, his fortress, his deliverer, his shield, the horn of his salvation, his stronghold, his refuge. God is the One to Whom David always turned in his distress, and he had plenty of that. He sings about how God drew him out of many waters, how He enlightened his darkness, how He set him on high places, how He enlarged his path, how He subdued his foes, how He delivered him from the strivings of his own people and preserved him as King. Take a moment and meditate on what each of these actions of God mean and how he desires to do similar things in your life. He so desires to be our refuge. He desires to protect us. He desires to set us on high places and enlarge our paths.

David gives us the answer as to why God delivered him so faithfully: because He delighted in him. The concept of our Lord and Savior delighting in us has been life changing to me. We know that we need to spend time with Him for our own good and growth, but the fact that He desires to spend time with us and meet all our needs, just because He delights in us, is an awesome thought. David sings in verse 7 about how God heard his voice and how his cry entered His ears. He hears our voices and our cries as well- because He is Who He is. I say with David: "He lives! Let Him be exalted, the Rock of my salvation! I will give thanks to Him and sing praises to His name."

Can you accept the truth that the Creator, our Lord and Savior, delights in you?

Reread this chapter and offer Him praise for Who He is.

II Samuel 24                                                    March 14

## The Pain of Consequences

II Samuel ends with David once again falling into sin.  God had warned him about numbering the people because He didn't want David trusting in human might, but only in Him.  Apparently Satan moved David to disobey, and he succumbed .  Verse 10 of II Samuel 24 records David's feelings after spending nearly ten months in finding that there were 800,000 military men in Israel and 500,000 in Judah: His heart smote him, and he went to the Lord, acknowledging his foolishness and sin and beseeching God to take his sin away.  God offered him the choice of three consequences for his sin.  First, the land could suffer through seven years of famine, and secondly, David could be pursued by his enemies for three months, or third, there could be three days of pestilence in the land.  All were distressful to David, but his answer in verse 14 once again gives us more insight into his relationship with God.  He said he would rather fall into the hands of his merciful God, rather than into the hand of man.

God sent a pestilence resulting in the deaths of 70,000 men.  Then God, in His mercy, said it was enough.  Again in verse 17 David acknowledged his sin and regretted that his innocent people had to die as a result.  David then brought offerings before the Lord, and the Lord averted the plague.

God is holy, and as such, requires a payment for sin.  He is also merciful and responds to our deep felt sorrow for our sin.  How glorious it is to present ourselves before Him, agreeing with Him about our sin and knowing that He is ready to receive us and forgive.  We need not build an altar and present an offering as David did since Jesus already paid the price for us.  When we have confessed our sin, God no longer sees it but sees only His Son's blood covering it.

If there is sin standing between you and God, tell Him about it and receive the forgiveness and restored intimacy.  He is waiting to forgive.

I Kings 3:1-14, 5:5, 8:63 & I Kings 11:6,11     March 15

## Disobedience in Only One thing

After David's death, his son, Solomon, became King. He started off so well- loving the Lord, walking in the statutes of David, recognizing his need for God, and when God asked him in a dream what He should give him, Solomon's answer was for an understanding heart to judge his people. God was pleased with Solomon, and not only gave him a wise and understanding heart, a largeness of heart, "even as the sand that is on the seashore"{4:29}, but riches and honor as well. God also gave the nation a time of peace so Solomon was able and willing to turn his attention to building a house for Him, which he did. It took him seven years, culminating in the dedication of the house and Solomon's sermon, filled with praise for God and admonitions to the people in I Kings 8.

So what could possibly get in the way of Solomon's deep dedication to God? Actually we saw it when Solomon was first introduced to us as King in I Kings 3:1: "And Solomon made a marriage alliance with Pharaoh, King of Egypt, and took Pharaoh's daughter as his wife." After the monumental task of building God's house, we read in I Kings 11:6 that Solomon did evil in the sight of the Lord and went not fully after the Lord, as David did. He built places for his foreign wives, of which there were 700, as well as 300 concubines, to sacrifice to their gods. The consequence? Adversaries were stirred up against Solomon, and after his death his kingdom was to be divided. God had told him that his kingdom would be taken away after his death and given to his servant, Jeroboam.

Once again we see a great man of God failing in one area of life and the suffering that follows. We can start with great intentions but if we refuse to recognize an area of life that is a weakness for us and we do not completely give it over to God, it will cause us great amounts of grief. Every day we need to be before God, asking Him to check our ways to see if they are all in line with what He has asked of us.

Let God show you any areas of your life that you haven't brought under His command.

I Kings 17                                    March 16

## Giving Whatever You Have

After Solomon's turning from the Lord and his eventual death, the
Kingdom was divided. Jeroboam reigned over Israel while Rehoboam
reigned over Judah, just as God had said. They were followed by a series
of kings, all of whom forsook the Lord. While a particularly evil King, Ahab,
reigned over Israel, God brought the Prophet, Elijah, on the scene. When
we first see Elijah, he is being fed by ravens provided by God and being
given water from the brook Cherith. The brook dries up from a three-year
drought so God sends Elijah to a widow, who with her son has only a
handful of meal and a little oil for one more meal. After eating that, she
was prepared for them to die. She gives what little she has to Elijah and
finds that the handful of meal and oil that she has is never used up. God
sustains her just as He had Elijah by having birds bring him bread and
meat. Even in the widow's destitute state, she gave what she had and was
greatly used in the life of Elijah. God had plans for Elijah. Later he would
be used to raise up that same widow's dead son. He would also be used
mightily by God in the life of Israel. Giving what little she had, led to God
performing miracles in both her life and the life of Elijah.

Usually when we are depleted and have what seems like little for
ourselves, our tendency is to encircle it and protect it for our own use. In
our deprivation we rarely think of giving out, either in a material,
emotional, or spiritual way. Yet when we do, we see God take the little we
offer and multiply it, much as He did in this widow's life. When what we
give is a real sacrifice for us, God lovingly takes it and uses it in ways we
cannot imagine. Our job is to simply offer to Him what we have, even if it
seems like only a handful of meal.

Will you offer God whatever little you have- to be used by Him in ways you
can't even imagine?

I Kings 19                                                    March 17

## Receiving God's Encouragement

Elijah finds it necessary to flee from the evil Jezebel and King Ahab after he had killed their prophets of Baal. He had just witnessed the great power of God in consuming those false gods with fire. The people who witnessed it fell on their faces and recognized the Lord as God. God had just promised rain to end the drought, and I Kings 18:46 says the hand of God was on Elijah. So, it would seem that Elijah would be encouraged and ready to take on whatever came his way. However, we are told in I Kings 19:4 that after a day's journey of fleeing from the wicked pair, Jezebel and Ahab, he sat under a tree and asked to die. "It is enough!", he said. Is God angry with Elijah's discouragement? Apparently not. He sends an angel to feed him- twice, telling him to eat because the journey is too great for him. After that, Elijah traveled 40 days and nights, in the strength of that food, to the mount of God. There Elijah pours out his feelings two times to God about the peoples' forsaking of God and how only he is left. What does God do? Before, He sent an angel, but this time He sends wind, an earthquake, fire, and, finally, presents Himself in a still, small voice. "The Lord passed by", Scripture tells us. In Elijah's great need, God visits him. God then tells him whom to anoint as kings and as the new prophet to succeed him, that being Elisha.

What a wonderful picture of God's gracious dealing with despair. He knew His servant and ministered to him. None of us have been in Elisha's shoes, having been ministered to by an angel and by God's passing by us, but His Word and His Spirit communing with our spirit are there constantly waiting to minister to us in our despair. I have experienced it many times. He gives us what we need in order to continue on. He knows us intimately and knows what we need and is so ready to provide it for us.

If you are experiencing despair or discouragement, listen for that still, small voice He gives you through His Word and through His Spirit. He longs to minister to you.

II Kings 2                                                March 18

## What We Leave Behind

It is difficult, as we age, to think about leaving behind the things we have always held so dear, whether it be our work God has given us to do, people with whom we have invested ourselves, our material things we have accumulated, or dreams that have not been completed. God has to do a work in us if we are to be at peace with leaving all that we know, even if He has given us the grace to know beyond a doubt that eternal life with Him awaits us with all its glory.

In II Kings Elijah finds himself in this position of leaving things behind. He had been to the place of wishing to die earlier when being relentlessly pursued by Jezebel and Ahab, but God in His grace revived him and gave him hope again in allowing him to throw his mantle on Elisha, as a picture to him that his work would continue after he was gone. Later, just before God took Elijah to Himself, He and Elisha have a moment where Elijah asks his successor what he can do for him. Elisha asks for a double portion of Elijah's spirit just before God takes Elijah in a whirlwind to heaven. Elisha had seen enough of his mentor to know that he wanted what he had- and actually more of what he had seen in Elijah. He also desired to serve His God and their nation. Three times he said to Elijah: "As the Lord lives and as your soul lives, I will not leave you!" He wanted to be with his mentor until the last possible moment to get from him all that he could. What a compliment to Elijah. He had negotiated "the leaving behind" well, leaving a legacy that would continue in a manner pleasing to God.

Are you considering what God wants you to be leaving behind?

II Kings 4:1-7                                    March 19

## Emptiness

In II Kings 4 we see a woman, a widow with two sons, destitute and in debt, and her sons are about to be taken away from her to pay the debt. She was completely empty of material possessions except for a jar of oil. Elisha tells her to borrow vessels from her neighbors, as many as she can, and to bring them home, shut the door, and to begin pouring oil into them from her only jar. She does that, filling all the pots she had. It was enough to pay the debt and to sustain her and her children.

This woman recognized her emptiness- she cried out to Elisha concerning her need. She had no food for herself and her children nor did she have a source of income. She was empty. Like loss, emptiness can be a wonderful gift. We see ourselves as we really are and God as He really is. Then we can cry out to Him, as this widow did to Elisha, and have our emptiness filled. If we had "stuff" we wouldn't see the need to cry out.

In this story, the woman continues to get oil until all the containers are filled. She gets as much oil as she has empty vessels to fill. If we only recognize a little bit of emptiness, perhaps that is all that God will fill for us. If we recognize just how empty we really are, He will fill that. He longs for us to come to Him so He can provide our deepest need. He won't do it, however, as long as we think we can depend on ourselves. Like this woman, we need sustenance, material things to live, but most importantly, we need HIM. Only He can fill our true emptiness, and He is so waiting to do that in our lives.

Let Jesus show you your real emptiness as you spent time with Him today. Let Him fill you.

II Kings 17:5-23                                                    March 20

## Sin Results in Captivity

II Kings is a very sad chapter as it recounts the children of Israel's sin against God, particularly how they actually feared other gods and walked in the statutes of other nations, the very nations that God had cast out before them. Verse 9 also says that "Israel secretly did against the Lord their God things that were not right." They set up high places to gods, burned incense, and served idols. God, through His Prophets, warned them to turn from their evil ways, but verse 14 says, "They would not hear but stiffened their necks." They rejected God's commands and went after the nations around them. Another very sad verse, verse 20, tells us that the Lord then rejected them, afflicted them, and delivered them into the hand of plunderers, "until He had cast them from His sight," and verse 23 says, Israel was carried away from their own land to Assyria. To be cast from God's sight is an appalling thought.

Think what they gave up because they refused to put God in His proper place and themselves in their proper place. He asked for their love and obedience in exchange for His calling them His children and bestowing on them all that that entails. Their "stiff necks" cost them their land, their homes, but mostly their relationship with their Father God.

This allows us to contemplate what our own "stiff necks" cost us today. Israel went into actual captivity. We go into a sort of captivity also when we reject God's ways. We become captive to sin and Satan. God hasn't left us, but we have gone away from Him, and put ourselves in a place where we can no longer hear His voice. We read His Word but it doesn't move us. We pray, but our words feel like they are bouncing off a wall. We are indeed captive and apart from Him when we reject his commands.

Are there words from God that you are rejecting? Think what you are relinquishing by doing that. Consider how you are hurting Him as well as yourself.

II Kings 18:1-8                                            March 21

## Results of Clinging to the Lord

In II Kings 18 we read of a good king , Hezekiah, who comes to reign in Judah.  Verse 3 tells us what characterized him as good: "he did that which was right in the sight of the Lord, according to all that David, his father did." We also read that he removed the high places and broke the images, cut down the idols.  The reason behind his doing these things is found in verse 5: "He trusted in the Lord God of Israel, so that after him was none like him among all the kings of Judah, nor any that were before him". Verse 6 says he clung to the Lord and departed not from following Him." The result is given in verse 7: "The Lord was with him and he prospered wherever he went." We find later in Scripture that when in distress he went into the House of the Lord.  Another time he received a letter and took it to God's House and spread it before Him and prayed to Him about it.  At what appeared to be the end of his life, he prayed to the Lord and wept, prompting God to give him fifteen more years of life.

What is the pattern we have seen?  Disobedience to God's truths results in things that cause us pain, such as captivity, while obedience results in a close, loving relationship with God, and in Hezekiah's case, prosperity and even years added to his life.  That's not a hard choice.  Jesus says if we love Him we will obey Him.  If we love Him we will cling to Him and follow Him as this King did.

Do you know what it is to cling to God as Hezekiah did?

Do you have a habit of taking things, like Hezekiah did his letter, and spreading them before Him?

II Kings 22:1-11 & 23:1-4, 25                                  March 22

## Restoration of God's Word and His House

After a series of bad kings, bad because they returned God's people to idol worship and other grievous sins, and brought great suffering, we read of another good king who did right in God's eyes, turning not aside to the right or to the left as it says in II Kings 22:2. King Josiah first repaired the House of the Lord. When the Book of the Law was discovered while the House was being restored, he was distraught and responded with brokenness, realizing that they had not been following God's statutes. So, then, he read the law to all his people, the great and the small. He made a covenant before the Lord to walk after Him, to keep His commands with all his heart and soul and then to act on them, which he did. His people joined in the covenant. They got rid of idols and the idolatrous priests, reinstituted the Passover, as well as other directives of the law. II Kings 23:25 says Josiah "turned to the Lord with all his heart, and with all his soul, and with all his might."

The two things that Josiah turned his attention toward are two things that deserve our attention as well, if we are going to be pleasing in God's eyes: His Word and His House. If we are to follow Him and know Him in a deep way, we are going to have to know what His Word says. He has written us a very long letter, telling us all kinds of things, wonderful things, about Himself. If we love Him, we are going to be searching every day to know more about Who He is. After Jesus' resurrection He went back to the Father, but not before leaving His Church behind as a means of growth, ministry, fellowship, service, and evangelism. We need it as a means of knowing Him more completely. We are not meant to do it on our own but with a body of believers. In His great love and concern for us, He has graciously given us His Word and His people for our good and His glory.

Is your first desire, like Josiah, to do right in God's eyes?

Thank Jesus as you spend time with Him for His Word and His people. Value them as a means to know Jesus more deeply.

I Chronicles 17                                    March 23

## Humility in Disappointment

David was concerned because he lived in a house of cedar while the ark of the covenant, which they had just brought back to Jerusalem was housed under tent curtains.  Nathan, the Prophet, spoke quickly in response to David's concern, telling him to do all that was in his heart, for God was with him.  That night, however, God spoke to Nathan, telling him to tell David that he was not to build Him a house.  God told Nathan to remind David of how He had been with him and that in the future He would establish his seed after him, but that his son would build God's house and his throne would be established forever.

Here is David's response in I Chronicles 17:16, "Then David went in and sat before the Lord…" In his great disappointment he humbles himself before God and remembers all that God has done for him and with him.  He sees himself as he is, having been honored and used by God despite his sin.  He praises God for Who He is.  "There is none like you.  You are God" is his assessment.  He wanted to build God's house, but more importantly, he wants God's will and for His Name to be magnified forever.  It was not about David- it was about God.

David went in and sat before his God.  There is the key to how he handled his disappointment and again, why he is called a man after God's Own Heart.

What do you do when God says no to something you have your heart and mind set on?    Follow David's example and go in and sit before the Lord, seeing yourself as you are and Him as He is.

I Chronicles 22:13 & 19                                      March 24

## Setting Our Heart and Soul on Him

I & II Chronicles present many of the events already seen in I & II Kings. In I Chronicles 22:13 we see David's charge to his son, Solomon, telling him that if he looks to fulfill the statutes and ordinances which God gave to Moses, he will prosper. It is impossible to miss that truth as we go through Scripture. He also instructs Solomon to have courage, to not be dismayed or to dread anything. Before he talks to Solomon about building God's Sanctuary, he tells him to set his heart and soul to seek God (verse 19).

Set your heart and your soul to seek the Lord your God. How much unnecessary pain we would avoid if we would just follow that admonition. How do we set our heart and soul to seek Him? It sounds quite purposeful and intentional. It is a decision, not a feeling, and we have to determine to do it. When we think correctly, our actions follow that, and then our emotions eventually catch up. How we think is our engine, and our feelings are the caboose. So, we make a determination to set ourselves on the truth of God's Word and on Him. We are going to give Him the best part of our day, and are going to make Him part of everything we do. I used to think of Him as number one in terms of priorities, but I have come to think of Him as being over and in everything I do. I need to consider Him as most important, whether I'm in a counseling session, talking to someone about Him, playing with a grandchild, or cleaning my house. We do this because He has asked us to bring Him into our entire lives. He deserves it, and we need it. Setting our heart and souls to seek Him is why we were created. He desires it, and it is what fills our emptiness.

Can you say you are purposefully setting your heart and soul on Him?

If not, let Him show you how you need to think and act differently about it.

I Chronicles 28:20-21                                    March 25

## No Reason for Dismay

When David was charging his son, Solomon, with the task of building the Lord's temple, he tells him to be strong and of good courage, to not fear nor be dismayed. Then he gives him the reason not to fear or be dismayed: "For the Lord God, even my God, will be with you; he will not fail you nor forsake you, until you have finished all the work for the service of the house of the Lord". Also God's people, it says in verse 21, would be supporting him in the work. How could he fail when God Himself would be with him and would also be supplying support staff?

How can we fail when God directs us to a work? We just need to do what verses 9 and 10 of I Chronicles 28 says: Serve Him with a perfect heart and willing mind, be strong and do it. We fear and become dismayed when we dwell on all the obstacles to the work or when we allow the attitudes and actions of other people to discourage us. I have seen cases where well-intentioned people of God have become dismayed, discouraged, and doubted the work that God had clearly given them to do, maybe even abandoning the work because of their disappointment. God says to serve Him with a perfect heart and a willing mind- to take care of the sin in our lives, to desire to serve Him before all else, to seek Him, then to be strong, have courage, and do it, knowing He is with us and will supply the support we need. It is HIS work, not mine. I just have to accept the charge willingly, take courage in His Presence, and do it. He will not fail me. What occurs to discourage us with other people is never really the issue. What occurs is always meant to be between Him and us. He always has much in mind to teach us about Himself and to use in our lives.

Is dismay something you frequently experience? Grasp onto the truth that He is with you and will not fail you, often sending others as support. Don't miss what He has for you about Himself.

II Chronicles 6:24-31                                    March 26

## Spreading Our Pain Before the Lord

After Solomon's work of building the temple is completed, he offers a prayer of dedication in II Chronicles 6. He presents various scenarios that may happen in the lives of the Israelites: If they are defeated by an enemy (verse 24), if there is no rain (verse 26), if there is a famine (verse 28), followed by what they need to do when these situations take place. He acknowledges to God that these things happen because they sin against Him. He also acknowledges that if in their affliction, they return, confess His name, pray before Him in this house, turn from their sin, then he knows God will hear, forgive them, teach them the right way to walk, and bring them again to the land which He gave them. There will be sin in their lives, which brings misery and sorrow, but God stands ready to receive them back when they repent.

Verse 29 says that whatever prayer a man offers when he knows his own burden (some versions say "his plague" or his own "sore") and his own grief, and he spreads his hands in this house they are dedicating, Solomon asks that God will hear and forgive. Solomon is asking God to hear a man's pain as he presents it to Him. It requires that he spread it before the Lord, tell Him about it. Once more here is the concept of intimacy with God. He desires our deep interaction with Him, and He desires that we go into His Presence and spread our "sores", our "plagues", our "burdens" before Him. Then He will hear, forgive, and direct. Verse 29 says that everyone shall know his own burden, meaning we have to be honest with ourselves before we can be open and honest with God. We have to know our own pain before we can present it to Him. Intimacy with ourselves is necessary if we are to be intimate with God and others, as God desires.

Do you recognize and acknowledge your own pain and grief? Spend time with God, asking Him to help you access it. Then spread it before Him.

II Chronicles 10                                       March 27

## Rejecting Wise Counsel

Rehoboam, Solomon's successor as King, was told by Jeroboam and all Israel that his father had made their burden very heavy, and they asked for it to be lightened, saying they would serve him if he would listen to them. King Rehoboam asked his father and the elders of Israel for advice on how to answer the people. They advised kindness and good words to the people. Verse 18 tells us that he rejected their advice, choosing instead to listen to his peers who advised him to take a much harsher line with them than even Solomon did. The results of his failure to follow wise counsel is found in verses 18 and 29: when he sent his aide in charge of revenue to collect taxes from them, they stoned him to death. Rehoboam had to flee Jerusalem and ended up losing half of his kingdom.

"In the multitude of counselors there is safety", is the message in Proverbs 24:6. The best counsel we are going to get is in God's Word. That is why we need to be in it every day, trusting God's Spirit to help us understand it. Then we must be discerning in how to live it out. God also is faithful in sending people into our lives to give us direction. We will know if their counsel is good if it is consistent with God's Word. Then other criteria will help us know if their advice can be trusted: Are their own lives consistent with what they are saying? Do they have a heart for God? Are they hearing Him? Are they out for my good and the good of God's people? Are they willing to tell me what I don't want to hear? Do they have the wisdom to see all sides of an issue? Do I believe God has sent them into my life?

Failure to listen to Godly advice had major negative repercussions in Rehoboam's life. Let it not be true in ours, Lord. Give us the humility to discern and to listen to those you have allowed in our lives. Save us from unnecessary suffering because we refuse to listen.

Think of people of God He has put in your life to give you advice and direction. Make a determination to be open to them.

II Chronicles 15:17-19 & 16                                    March 28

## Remaining Loyal to Him

King Asa of Judah had made great strides with the lord, having sought Him in his troubles, learning that God was with him when he was with God, having gotten rid of idols in his nation, and having made various other reforms.  However, Scripture tells us that the high places were not taken away.  Then we see in chapter 16 of II Chronicles that he relied on an earthly king instead of the Lord.  God sent him a prophet to warn him of his sin, but instead of heeding the warning and turning from his sin, he became angry and imprisoned the messenger.  The result is found in 16:12: he developed a severe disease.  Even in that he did not seek the Lord, but physicians.  So, he died, having begun well but not having finished well.  He did not stay the course.

Once having seen the Lord and being given direction by Him, how do we get off track?  There will be times when God doesn't reveal Himself so directly, and we don't sense His Presence.  It is in those times that we have to rely on what He has already told us about Himself.  Oswald Chambers calls that "the steady persevering work in the unseen".  When we are not seeing Him as clearly as we have in other times, we rely on the truths He has given us in the written Word.  We rely on what He has shown us about Himself in the past.  Remember.  We keep looking to the Risen Jesus, and when God is ready for us to see Him more clearly, He will again reveal Himself, and how glorious that revealing will be.  We will know him at a deeper level than we ever did before.

II Chronicles 16:9 says, "For the eyes of the Lord run to and fro throughout the whole earth, to show Himself strong on behalf of those whose heart is loyal to Him".  We must remain loyal to Him even when we can't see very much.  Again, if we keep seeking Him, He will be found.

Think what you typically do in those times when you don't sense God's Presence so clearly.

Decide with Him what He would have you do.

II Chronicles 15:4                                    March 29

## Turning to God in Troublesome Times

King Asa came to reign in Judah in the days when Judah and Israel were warring against each other.  We read that the Lord sent the Prophet Azariah to Asa, telling him that "the Lord is with you while you are with Him; and if you seek Him, He will be found by you, but if you forsake Him, He will forsake you." How many times has God repeated that truth in these books of the Bible?  Israel had been without the true God, without a teaching priest and without law, verse 3 tells us.  They were indeed in trouble.  The next verse says that when they turned to God in their trouble, and sought Him, He was found by them.  In their adversities, they entered into a covenant to seek God with all their heart and soul (verse 12).  The chapter ends by showing how Asa restored things to the House of God, got rid of idols and had a "perfect" heart toward God.  As a result there was no war during the first 35 years of his reign.  That continued only a as long as he sought the Lord and followed His ways.

When we seek Him, He will be found.  How can we miss that principle?  People sometimes tell me they never hear from God.  When I hear that, I have to wonder if they are seeking Him to get something or if they are seeking Him because of Who He is, the One Who desires their fellowship with Him.  I also must question if sin is in the way.  Perhaps we want Him but don't want to give up our sinful ways.  In this portion of Scripture, Asa made reforms early in his reign, getting rid of idols and the altars to them.  God doesn't tolerate sin.  When He shows it to us, it has to go, or a close intimacy with Him is not possible.

Do you hear Him?

Are you seeking Him because of Who He is?

II Chronicles 20:1-30                                   March 30

## Eyes on the Lord in Affliction

Asa was succeeded by his son, Jehoshaphat. We are told that he sought the Lord and "his heart was lifted up in the ways of the Lord". In II Chronicles 20 he offers a prayer to God in His house before the people of Judah, asking God that when evil comes to them by way of the sword, judgment, pestilence, or famine that they would stand before Him and cry unto Him in their affliction and that He would hear and help (verse 9). He tells God how their eyes are upon Him as they enter into battle with their enemies.

God's answer to Jehoshaphat's prayer is found in verse 15: "Be not afraid nor dismayed by reason of the great multitude, for the battle is not yours, but God's". God told him they didn't even need to fight but to just stand still and see God's salvation. At that response Jehoshaphat and all his people fell on their faces and worshipped the Lord. Then they went out to battle, having appointed singers to praise the Lord as they went. Needless to say, God gave them victory.

As the great multitude of his enemies approached to war against him, Jehoshaphat, in his fear, sought the Lord. He gathered his people and together they called out to God and then listened to God's direction. In his hour of great crisis for his people, his eyes and his peoples' eyes were upon God. Later, like so many of the leaders of this period, we find that he did not finish well, as he succumbed to the idols and alliances of other nations, but here we see a great example of trusting God in the face of what seemed like impossible odds, and God responding with a marvelous victory. "Our eyes are upon You", says II Chronicles 20:12. That is where our eyes need to be in our seemingly impossible battles. Then we will see what God will do.

Whether you are in a battle right now or are enjoying rest and peace for a time, turn your eyes to Him.. Let Him show you Himself.

II Chronicles 34                                        March 31

## Death is Better

Josiah was one of the best kings of Judah. He was only 8 years old when he succeeded his evil father, Amon. Josiah began seeking the Lord when he was 16, purged Judah of its idol worship when he was 20 and began restoring the house of the Lord also when he was 26. In the process of that restoration the Book of the Law was discovered, and when Josiah saw how far off the mark his nation was, he was so sorrowful that he tore his clothes and wept. He had some of his servants inquire of the Lord and then made a covenant before the Lord to follow him and keep his command (35:31). He made all the children of Israel diligently serve the Lord, which they did all of Josiah's days.

At the beginning of II Chronicles, Scripture says Josiah reigned 31 years, and since he was 8 when he began, that meant he died at 39. I wondered why that would be the case when he stood above all the other kings in seeking the Lord. Then I read in verses 24-28 what the Lord said regarding their neglect of His Word: "I will bring calamity on this place...because they have forsaken Me and burned incense to other gods..." He goes on to say that His wrath will be poured out and not be quenched BUT because Josiah's heart was tender and humbled before Him, He would take him to his grave in peace before his eyes would see the calamity God would send. God was protecting Josiah by taking him to Himself at age 39. Death was a gift, far surpassing what he would have to witness were he given a longer life.

Do you see the goodness of God in this passage, so far beyond our abilities to understand?

Ezra 8:21-23 & 9-10:8                                    April 01

## Mourning Over Sin

Because of their continued rejection of their God, the Israelites had been carried into captivity by Nebuchadnezzar, King of Babylon, where they remained for 70 years. Ezra records their return and his own God-given role in reconstructing the Jerusalem Temple so true worship could once again take place.

The reconstructing of the Temple was not without adversity and difficulty. There was great resistance from surrounding leaders who wrote letters to the King in protest, suggesting that the Israelites would not pay taxes to him, that they would incite sedition, and that the King would ultimately lose power. They asked that the King cause the building to cease, which is what happened for a time. Later, however, God caused it to go forth and even orchestrated that their treasure, which had been in Babylon, be restored to the Temple. The House was completed and dedicated, and that is when the scribe, Ezra, comes on the scene. He proclaimed a fast that he and his people might humble themselves before their God, to seek Him for direction.

Ezra became aware that the priests and Levites had not separated themselves from the people around them, particularly in the area of inter-marriage. His reaction to this is recorded in Ezra 9:9: He tore his clothing, plucked out the hair of his head and beard, and sat appalled. In verse 5, in his heaviness of the peoples' sin, we read that he fell on his knees and spread out his hands unto the Lord. Verse 6 says he was ashamed to lift his face to God. Even in their great and continued sin, he says, God delivered them from their captivity and restored their place of worship. While he continued to recognize God's mercy and their grave sin, the people also joined in confessing their sin and agreed to separate from it.

We see Ezra's great sorrow as he contemplates the sin of his people. Have we ever had that kind of response when we are brought face to face with our sin or the sin of our people?

Let God show you where there is sin in your life. Look on it, appalled, as Ezra did.

Confess it and turn from it.

Nehemiah 1-2:8                                                  April 02

## Quieting Our Hearts in Our Sorrow

While the Temple had been rebuilt, and Ezra led the returning people back to the true worship God desired, Nehemiah was given the task of rebuilding the ruined walls surrounding Jerusalem. The walls were broken down, and the gates had been burned. When Nehemiah, a cup-bearer to King Artaxerxes, heard how his people were afflicted and under reproach by the surrounding people because of this condition, he sat down, wept, and mourned, fasted and prayed for many days, perhaps four months, confessing his and the children of Israel's sins. In his prayer he also praised God and reminded Him of His covenant to restore Israel when they finally returned to Him. He also prayed specifically that God would give him favor before the King, and that he would be allowed to visit Jerusalem and rebuild the walls. The King agreed. Then Nehemiah respectfully but boldly asked for letters to guarantee his safe travel and another letter that would assure his being given lumber to do the building. "And the King granted me, according to the good Hand of my God upon me", Nehemiah says.

In his great sorrow over the condition of God's City, Nehemiah first fasted and prayed. He was so overcome with grief that the King noticed it on his face, which caused Nehemiah some fear. He quieted his heart in order to get direction from God. He sought Him, seeing God as He is and himself and the people as they were. He prayed specifically about his plan to rectify the situation, knowing it would not be his plan, but God's. While he had great respect for the King, he approached him with confidence, being sure that God was with him.

So, from this account the lesson for us in our grief is to first quiet ourselves before the Lord, seeing both Him and ourselves as we are. Then commit the situation to Him, asking Him specifically for His direction.

In the throes of grief, what do you typically do first?

Talk to God about what He would have you do,

Nehemiah 2:9-20                                        April 03

## Allowing Sorrow to Result in Constructive Action

In his great burden of knowing the walls and gates of Jerusalem lay in ruin, Nehemiah, after expressing his grief and pouring it out to God for a period of four months, acted. He went to Jerusalem and after three days, went out with a few men in the night to survey the shambles. Only then did he approach the leaders and workers of his people, telling them what God had placed on his heart and how the King supported him. He was given a burden, spent time with God, mourned the situation, assessed it, and shared his plan with others so that they said, "Let us rise up and build."

In our sorrow or loss it is easy to become immobilized. Depression is part of the recovery process when dealing with loss, and depression by its very nature slows us down. If in our "slow down" we are sitting with God, we will be ready at some point to move in the direction He has planned for us. It is important to take the time to mourn, but eventually we need to move. God has a plan for our sorrows.

Sometimes people want to bypass the four months where Nehemiah, in his grief, sat with God. The weeping, mourning, fasting, and praying that he did can be a lonely, painful time, but oh, so necessary and valuable. The great work he did in rebuilding the walls and gates resulted from those four months of pouring himself out to God. Surely he knew God and himself so much better.

It took only 52 days to rebuild what had lain in ruin for 120 years. It is important to note that from the time Nehemiah first heard about the conditions in Jerusalem until he spoke to the King, about 120 days passed. He spent those 120 days with God.

Pour out your pain to God, but also listen to Him, and be ready to act on it when He directs.

Nehemiah 4 & 6:15-16                                              April 04

## The Pain of Opposition

Nehemiah had a clear vision of what he was supposed to do in rebuilding the walls and gates of Jerusalem, and he set about the work with diligence, enlisting and organizing God's people who had a mind to work. A man named Sanballat, along with some others, became angry and indignant and conspired to attack Jerusalem, creating confusion in order to stop the work. First, he tried mocking and ridiculing the workers, and when that failed to work, he tried fear, intimidation, conspiracy, rumor and threats. His motive was for Jerusalem to remain as it was as far as commerce and political power were concerned since, of course, that would benefit him. None of these oppositional tactics worked on the one who remained faithful to his calling. Nehemiah would not even take time from his work to go and talk to the detractors (Nehemiah 6:3). He developed a plan with his people to complete what God had given them to do.

In addition to the outward resistance, there was opposition from within. Chapter 5 tells of disputes among the people regarding taxes, food, and property. Again, Nehemiah handled it all and would not be deterred from the task to which God had called him. Nehemiah 6:15 presents the outcome: "So the wall was finished on the twenty-fifth day of Elul, in 52 days. And it happened when all our enemies heard of it, and all the nations around us saw these things, that they were very disheartened in their own eyes; for they perceived that this work was done by our God." The work was finished and the opposition defeated.

When we determine to be centered on the Lord, we can be certain there will be opposition and distraction in the work He has given us. It is not pleasant, but we should do as Nehemiah did: not entertain them, continually review the vision God has given us, look to the work and to Him who gave it to us, knowing He will give us what we need to finish it. It is, after all, HIS work.

Can you identify with Nehemiah as he was opposed in what God had given him to do?

Sit with God and review with Him His calling on you.

Nehemiah 8:1-3, 9-11                                    April 05

## A Time for Joy and Celebration

After the temple, the walls, and the gates were restored in Jerusalem, the people assembled together "as one man" while Ezra read from the Law of God. They worshiped the Lord "with their faces to the ground".
Nehemiah spoke to the congregation, telling them not to mourn or weep. They had already done that when seeing what had become of God's House and His City. God had enabled them, in their sorrow, to rectify it all so now was not a time to mourn but a time to rejoice. He told them to go, eat, drink, and share with others, not to sorrow, for the joy of the Lord is their strength. The Levites' message to the people was, "Be still, for the day is holy; do not be grieved." The people understood and went out to celebrate. They then re-instituted the Feast of tabernacles where they made booths and sat under them for seven days, having the Law read with very great gladness.

This portion of Scripture caused me to pause and consider whether I rejoice enough after a work is completed. There is a time to put our hands to the plow, there is a time to mourn, but there is also a time to celebrate what God has done. Perhaps we need to do more of that.

We see as the Jews continued with their convocation in the eighth day following the Feast of Tabernacles, that they assembled with "fasting in sackcloth and with dust on their heads." The celebrating was over and now was a time of confession and remembering their history of transgressions before God.

There is a time to mourn. There is also a time for joy and celebration. Both have a part in our relationship to God, and we need to listen to Him about which He would have us do at a given time.

Do you need to devote more time to joy and celebration in what God has done in and through you?

Esther 2:5-4:4                                                    April 06

## Refusing to Bow

Esther, a Jew, raised by her older cousin, Mordecai, in the land of Persia during the Jewish captivity, finds herself in the unlikely position as Queen to king Ahasuerus. During her reign, a man named Haman, somewhat like the Prime Minister to the King, felt disrespected by Mordecai because he would not bow down to him, and discovering that Mordecai was a Jew, got the King to sign a decree that all the Jews be destroyed in one day, both young and old, little children and women. When Mordecai heard of this, he was in such distress that he tore his clothes, put on sackcloth and ashes, and went into the midst of the city, crying loudly and bitterly. There was also quite naturally great mourning among all the Jews with fasting, weeping, and wailing. Queen Esther was also deeply distressed when told of the situation.

In all the drama that takes place in the Book of Esther, it is possible to pass over the cause of the death threat to the Jews: Mordecai refused to bow down in reverence or worship to a mere man, Haman. The result was the possibility of the annihilation of all of God's people. Even in the midst of Mordecai's great pain, seen in Esther 4:1, he continued to refuse to compromise and dishonor his God. He would rather endure the anguish he was in than succumb to that.

In the face of certain death, what would we do? Would we compromise a command that God has given us? Mordecai did not. We already know he was a man of principle, having taken in and carefully taught his orphaned cousin, treating her like his own daughter. When she was taken into the palace, Scripture tells us that everyday Mordecai paced in front of the palace, trying to learn of Esther's welfare. This man of integrity is an example of one who continued to make righteous decisions throughout his life. When it came to bowing down to a man, instead of God, there was no doubt what his choice would be, even though the consequences brought much grief.

Do the possible, difficult circumstance of a righteous choice cause us to compromise God's Word?

Consider with God the consequences of that.

Esther 6-10                                        April 07

## If I Perish, I Perish

In his distress concerning the pending death of his people, Mordecai turned to Esther, asking her to appeal to the King. The problem was that if Esther would enter the King's presence without his invitation, she herself could face death. She agreed, however, taking in Mordecai's challenge to her: "Who knows whether you have come to the kingdom for such a time as this?" She asked Mordecai and the Jews with him to fast for her. She and her maids did the same. Then she uttered her famous words, "I will go to the King, which is against the law; and if I perish, I perish."

To quickly sum up the outcome of both Mordecai's and Esther's courage, King Ahasuerus not only received Esther but gave her leeway to orchestrate the death of the evil Haman, the honoring of Mordecai, and, of course, the saving of the Jews. God used these two to turn the tables on evil intent. Not only were the Jews protected, but they actually overpowered those who planned to murder them, and many of the people of the land became Jews, because of their fear of them. Mordecai became second in command to the King, and Esther was given great authority.

Esther went from orphan to Queen, from thinking she might die for entering the King's presence uninvited, to being received and given opportunities to right great wrong, from being the target of evil intent by a murderous man, to being in the position of deciding his fate, from grieving the potential loss of all of her people, to helping them prevail and enter a time of feasting and gladness. Again, we see the pattern of pain and distress followed by joy and gladness.

God's name is not mentioned in the book, but His Hand is so clearly seen. He took an unlikely young girl and placed her in a position to save His people, knowing her character would cause her to say, "I will do it, and if I perish, I perish".

Are you willing to say to God, "I will do whatever you ask of me, and if I perish, I perish?"

Job 1                                                    April 08

## Maintaining Perspective in Loss

When we think of pain and suffering no Scripture comes to mind more quickly than the Book of Job. To summarize, Job, an upright man who feared God, had a wife, ten children, and much wealth. He was the greatest of all people of the East. He prayed regularly for his family. Even though everything about Job was blameless, Satan accused him before God as only following Him because he was so blessed. Satan maintained that if tragedy were allowed into Job's life that he would curse God to His Face. God accepted the challenge and gave Satan freedom in the life of Job, only up to attacking his person.

In just one day Satan let loose with the powers of hell to take away all of Job's wealth, his livestock, his servants, and finally, his ten children. Job's response is found in Job 1:20-22: He tore his robe, shaved his head, fell on the ground and worshiped his God, acknowledging that it was God Who had given him all that he had, and it was God Who had taken it away. "In all this Job did not sin nor charge God with wrong." How disappointed he must have made Satan with that response.

How does one maintain that kind of perspective in such a time as Job was enduring? He obviously had had a long and deep relationship with God. We know from verse 5 that he rose early in the morning to spend time with God. In this moment of abject tragedy and loss beyond understanding, he was able to see the One with Whom he had spent so much time. He had no answers at this point, so all he could do was to look at the one Who did.

What has been your initial response in times of loss?

If it has not been to see God as He is, how can you change that?

Job 2                                                                    April 09

## Two Responses to Job's Pain

When God commended Job's response toward his losses to Satan, Satan insisted that if his person were attacked, Job would curse God to His face. God gave Satan permission, only up to taking his life, so Satan struck him with boils so painful that Job had to scrape himself while he sat in the midst of the ashes. What a troubling picture.

Enter Job's wife. Her admonition to him was: "What good is your integrity now. Curse God and die!" In defense of her, we must remember that she too has lost all of her ten children and all of her material possessions. I would like to think that over time she might come to a different place as she goes through the mourning process.

Then we meet Job's three friends, Eliphaz, Bildad, and Zophar. They came to him to mourn and comfort him and were so distressed at his appearance that they did not even recognize him, causing them to weep, tear their robes, and sprinkle dust on their heads, all cultural signs of deep grief for their friend. They begin so well, aligning with Job's pain and sitting with him seven days and nights, saying nothing to him, knowing they had nothing to offer that would relieve his tremendous grief. They could not have ministered to Job in a better way. What intimacy, to just sit with a friend for days and let him grieve, to listen to him, offering nothing but your presence.

This is the first principle we need to understand in dealing with people who are suffering- first, just be with them and listen.

If you are suffering, go sit with God, pour yourself out to Him. He will listen.

If you are ministering to one in pain, be with them. Listen.

Job 3                                                              April 10

## Job's Mourning

Job handled his losses with grace until he became physically ill. Then we read in chapter 3 that he opened his mouth and cursed the day he was born. He had managed well until his health and physical stamina were taken away. His worst fears had come to pass (Job 3:25). He longed to die. Understandable.

The good thing is that Job expressed his grief. Later we will see that as he goes through the grief process, he searches himself to see what needs correction. He will also question God and others before coming to the place of deciding that God is indeed trustworthy. He had never abandoned his commitment to that truth, but he had to examine it. The character, integrity, and knowledge of God he had prior to his losses, remained, while he went through the depression, questioning, and anger that are a universal part of loss.

I am happy to read of Job's lament in chapter 3. Too often I see people get into the denial stage and remain there, missing the opportunity to be real with God, to come out of the mourning process, knowing and being known at a much deeper level than ever before. Not being real in our mourning of losses opens up the chance that we will carry a low level of anger and depression with us, never being freed from it. Every aspect of our life can be impacted and our intimacy with God and others most definitely will be limited.

Here Job pours out his pain, and we will see later what God does with it.

When you have pain or loss, are you real with God, or do you hide?

Job 4:1-11, 8:1-7, 11:1-6, 42:7-10                    April 11

## Three "Friends"

It is time to meet Job's friends more closely. They all had a belief as to why Job was suffering so greatly, and after a week of sitting quietly with him, they just had to tell him. Basically Eliphaz's message to Job was that he was suffering because he sinned and was being chastened by God. Bildad and Zophar both said he needed to repent. Their lack of understanding caused them to accuse Job and actually add to his burden of pain. They lacked some of the truth about what was going on, and they completely missed the emotional and spiritual connection that Job needed in his sorrow. Job recognized this, as well as his friends' inability to see from the eternal perspective. It was Job who said, "For I know that my Redeemer lives, and He shall stand at last on the earth" (Job 19:25), essentially saying that he didn't understand what was happening or why, but one thing he did know and that was Who God is and that He lives!

The three friends, on the other hand, thought the answer to suffering simply lay at the feet of Job's bad behavior. Job rightly calls them "miserable comforters", and so they were, so ready to give their righteous answers to questions that had no quick and easy answers. They were simply looking to what made sense to them, not to Who God is and what He might be doing eternally. We know that God was not pleased with them, for after nearly forty chapters of their condemnation of Job, God says to Eliphaz in Job 42:7, "...my wrath is aroused against you and your two friends, for you have not spoken of Me what is right, as my servant Job has". He then tells them to take a sacrifice, go to Job and have him pray for them. They had done Job a grave disservice and had also maligned God, speaking of what they did not know. Lord, help us to tread carefully as we seek to comfort those in pain. Let us be vessels of Your love and truth, not "miserable comforters".

Allow God to show you the pain of another, and let Him teach you how to be the comforter He desires.

Job 6:24, 7:11 & 13:15                                                    April 12

## Job's Questions

Despite attacks from Satan, his wife, and his three friends, Job searches himself for the truth of his tragedies: "Cause me to understand wherein I have erred", he says in 6:24. He also continues to pour out his grief, not "restraining his mouth, but speaking in the anguish of his spirit, complaining in the bitterness of his soul"(6:11). In chapters 9 and 10 he pleads with God. In chapters 12 and 13 he answers the criticism of his three friends, recognizing their failures and telling them how he sees God: "Though He slay me, yet I will trust in Him". He is saying in his pain that he doesn't understand it, but he knows Who God is and that He is perfectly trustworthy. We are privileged to see the progression of his mourning as he goes through it. As he is trying to make sense of what is happening to him, he moves from, What did I do to cause this? to pouring out his anguish, to declaring that even in all the pain, he will continue to trust the Lord.

He questions "Why? Why, Lord?" That is one of the first things that comes to mind when tragedy strikes. Job's questions included, "Why was I born? Why do you hide your face from me, Lord? Why do the wicked prosper? Where are you, Lord?" I have heard many of these same questions, even have asked some of them myself when in the depths of the mourning process. It is part of the journey as we work our way through grief. Its purpose is to bring us to the place where we say, "I've asked the whys, so what now, Lord?" We may never get answers to the whys, but if we stay centered on Who God is, as Job surely did, we will know Him so much better. God never answered Job's questions but He showed him Himself. Job said, "I used to hear You, now I see You." While God did not answer his questions, neither did He condemn him for asking them. He only rebuked him for doubting His righteous character. Job was brought to the place of confessing Who God is and was now ready to receive His blessing.

Are you honest with God about your feelings when you are in pain?

They will serve to bring you to a more complete understanding of Who He is.

Job 38:1-4, 40:1-5, 42:5-6 & 10-16                    April 13

## Job's Response to God's Majesty

God remained silent for many chapters as Job questioned, expressed his grief, and worked through his confusion. Finally in Job 38 and 39, the Lord answered Job out of the whirlwind, asking him where he was when God laid the foundation of the earth and prepared all of creation. Job's response to God's revealing of His Own Majesty begins in Job 40:4: "I am vile. I lay my hand over my mouth for I have no answer". He sees God, and he sees himself. Right there is one thing God plans to accomplish as we move through the mourning process: To see Him as never before and to see ourselves as we really are. God continues to reveal Himself in chapters 40 and 41, and Job responds again in chapter 42:5 and 6, confessing, "I have heard of You by the hearing of the ear, but now my eye sees You. Therefore I abhor myself and repent in dust and ashes." When Satan petitioned God to attack the most righteous man he could find, little did he know what God planned to accomplish through the attacks in Job's life. God has plans to use our pain for a good that will go so far beyond our understanding.

Having gotten from his grief what God intended, now Job was ready to receive more blessings from God. After God had him pray for his three friends, He restored Job's losses, giving him twice as much as he had before, giving him the comfort and companionship of family and friends, and eventually ten more children. He lived to be 140 years old and saw his children and grandchildren for four generations. He died "old and full of days".

Look to your sorrows, whether large or small, as an opportunity to see God as He is and you as you are. Get ready to receive the blessings from that knowledge.

Psalms 1                                                   April 14

## The Contrast of Two Lives

The Book of Psalms begins with a contrast, telling of two men, two ways of living and two outcomes.  The man who walks in the counsel of God delights in His law and meditates on it continually will bring forth fruits, and its leaves will not wither.  He will prosper.  In contrast, a man who does not do these things will come to nothing, like the chaff that the wind drives away.  He will not be with God but will perish.  The contrast between the two types of men could not be clearer.  If we do what God created us to do, we prosper.  If we go our own sinful, independent way, we perish.  The ultimate in loss.

Verse 2 tells us how to walk with God: by getting counsel from His Word.  We are to meditate on it day and night, not just give it a cursory read, but to sit with it, with Jesus there with us, and examine what it says to us.  Someone has said that the Bible is the only Book where the Author is sitting with us as we read.  When He puts His Word in us, then we grow and bloom like a tree that has all the nutrients it needs.  It refreshes us.  It produces fruit that lasts.  The fruit comes forth in its season, just as it is supposed to.

The loss of not taking counsel from God's Word is indescribable.  One cannot grow, be nourished, or produce fruit without it.  When I meet with people who remain immature, make unwise, destructive decisions and produce no fruit, there is always a common denominator- no time in God's Word.  What a loss for them, and what pain and sorrow result.

Determine with God to meditate on His Word every day before anything else.  You will find yourself delighting in it.

Psalm 4:4                                                      April 15

## When We refuse to Feel

When we refuse to acknowledge our emotions we forfeit the opportunity to experience God's comfort and see, on a deeper level, Who He is. Every emotion carries with it the opportunity to deepen our relationship with God, which is why we were created. Our emotions often show us ourselves, our sin, and that is something we attempt to avoid. They also show us the world in which we live and the degree to which it has fallen, again something on which we would rather not dwell.

God intends that we pay attention to the feelings He has allowed us to experience. He intends for us to listen to them. When we refuse to listen, we are essentially running from Him. In the throes of the death of his son, David's heart was breaking. He fasted and wept [II Samuel 12] but when the child actually died, David went to the house of the Lord and worshipped Him. Many of the Psalms are written by David, telling of his pain. Tightly knit with his sorrow are his struggles with God. We are privileged to see his raw emotions of anger, doubt, and fear. We are also privileged to see, in his struggles, his coming to an understanding of the character of God. Then he worships, truly worships.

Psalm 4:4 invites us to commune with our own heart upon our bed and be still. David, the one whose life knew a great deal of pain, wrote that, knowing the value and necessity of acknowledging and working through our pain. It presents us with the glorious opportunity to commune with God in a way we never have before.

Consider with God whether there are emotions that you have been unwilling to recognize- to yourself and to Him.

Ask Him to reveal them to you so He will have the opportunity to show you what He plans to do with them.

Psalm 6                                                          April 16

## Groaning Before the Lord

David says in Psalm 6:7 that his eye is consumed because of grief. It grows old, he says, because of his enemies. He further says that he is weary of his groaning, but he also knows the Lord has heard his weeping and his calling out to Him and that He will receive his prayer.

This man who has been described as "a man after God's Own Heart", King David, the writer of many of the Psalms, is in distress. The overriding emotion we see here is one of humility. He enters God's Presence, asking not to be rebuked, but to be received in his pain. His very bones and his soul are troubled, and he describes himself as weak. He cries out for God's deliverance, drenching his bed with tears.

After he has poured himself out to God, and been with Him, he begins to show some confidence, knowing the Lord has heard him and will receive his prayer and that his enemies will turn back.

That is exactly what time in the Lord's Presence, pouring ourselves out to Him, will do- take us through the suffering and bring us to a place where we can move ahead with confidence in Him.

The enemies in our lives are different from David's, but just as troubling to our bones and souls. There are times in our lives when we also get weary of our groaning, sometimes causing our beds to swim with tears. If in our pain we go after God's Own Heart, we will also go from being unable to move, to confidence that He has not only heard but is giving us what we need to move ahead with Him.

Do you humbly approach Him, honestly declaring your suffering, knowing He hears and will take you through it to a place where you can begin to move again?

Psalm 22 April 17

## The Suffering Savior

Psalm 22 is written by David. In it he is prophesying about the crucifixion of Jesus, the good Shepherd giving His life for His sheep, as well as presenting his own lament in his distress of what was required in God's deliverance of him. Here is the deepest of pain revealed, beginning with Jesus' separation from the Father: "Why have You forsaken Me?" Why are You so far from helping me, from hearing my pain, Jesus cries out as He is completely alone.

David himself feels alone, but he is also spanning the thousand years before Jesus' crucifixion and prophetically describing what Jesus would feel. David, as he expresses Jesus' agony, returns to "But You are holy". You are the One Who delivered Your people. He sees God as He is: The Creator, His God. Then in verse 6 he sees himself as a worm. There it is once again, seeing God as He is and ourselves as we are, a requirement for being rightly related to God.

Verse 14 begins the graphic picture of crucifixion which Jesus would be enduring: the pulling of the bones out of joint, His heart melting within Him, His strength exhausted, the extreme dehydration and thirst, the piercing of His hands and feet. David goes on to present other circumstances that would accompany the death of Jesus, including the parting and casting of lots for his clothing. Again, this writing takes place 1,000 years before the actual event. Consider also that crucifixion was a Roman means of death, unknown to the Jews at this time of David's writing.

Verse 22 makes the shift from crucifixion to resurrection: Jesus proclaims the Name of the Father to His people. Through Jesus' death all people would have the opportunity to be reconciled to God and to worship Him, putting Him in His right position and themselves in theirs.

Jesus had to suffer the unspeakable, as prophetically recorded in this chapter, in order for us in our sin to have a chance to come to reconciliation with the Holy God. Jesus, for a time, had to bear His affliction alone in order to take on our sins, but it was only for a time before He would be resurrected, reunited, and glorified by the Father.

Perhaps this is why God sometimes allows us short periods of feeling alone in our pain and sorrows, to give us a tiny inkling of what Jesus endured for us. "Weeping may endure for a night but joy comes in the morning".

Meditate with Jesus on what He endured for you.

Psalm 23:1-6                                                   April 18

## Distressing Times

Being in the valley of the shadow of death mentioned in Psalm 23:4 would certainly be one of the more distressing times in our lives. In that valley there may be great physical suffering, as well as emotional distress, concerning what is pending, the death of our body. What is about to happen is unknown to us. We have to give up what we have always been familiar with and enter into something we have not previously known. We generally are not good at that. At that point we are going to have a clear picture of where we are in Him. Do we really believe what we have always said we believe concerning Him? David did. He said, "Even though I walk through the valley of the shadow of death, I will fear no evil; for You are with me; Your rod and Your staff, they comfort me". When you contemplate the end of your life, do you fear no evil, knowing HE will be there with you, offering everything you need, His very comfort? Even in that most stressful of times, we need not fear anything bad, for HE is there and will provide the comfort that we need.

The reason for walking through the valley of death, or any other valley, is for us to come out of it where He wants us to be. He wants to change us in that valley by showing Himself to us. He wants us to experience His comfort. He wants us to experience HIM.

Picture Him standing with you in your valleys, using His rod and staff to guide, protect, and comfort you.

Psalm 23                                                                                      April 19

## The Great Shepherd caring for His Sheep

What does the Shepherd caring for His sheep have to do with pain and suffering? As sheep we are vulnerable, prone to wander away from the other sheep and their Shepherd. We, on our own, can be prey to others who do not have our good in mind. Our wandering can lead to various disasters, even including our death. Sheep are not particularly smart and have little means of defense. They desperately need a Shepherd.

"The Lord is my Shepherd. I shall not want." In our vulnerability there is One Who is willing and able to care for us. In Him we will have no real need that is not met. He meets our physical needs: green pastures, still waters. He meets our spiritual needs: He restores our souls, directs us, and He leads us in right paths. In times of great crises in our lives, even when death lurks around us, He walks with us and we need not fear, for His rod and staff bring comfort to us. Our enemies will not have victory over us. His Spirit covers us so that our life in Him will be one of abundance. Finally He is preparing eternity for us. We will live with Him forever. Our vulnerabilities as sheep will no longer plague us. In Him and with Him we will find peace and rest. He is indeed our Shepherd.

Think of your Shepherd waiting to meet all the needs of your life as you go through today. Submit to Him.

Psalm 30                                                    April 20

## From Weeping to Joy

David was one who knew the depths of suffering and the depression and despair that accompany it. In the 30th Psalm, however, he praised God for deliverance and answered prayer. He begins the Psalm acknowledging how God lifted him up against his enemies, how He healed him when he cried out, how God preserved his life. There is a time to cry but through our tears we can still see God and acknowledge that it is He Who is keeping us alive in our mourning. He is there.

Three times in this Psalm David expresses the truth of God's turning our mourning into dancing (verse 11). In verse 5 he says, "Weeping may endure for a night, but joy comes in the morning". The irony seems to be that the deeper the mourning, the greater the joy. In our lives we will have occasion to weep, but we will not weep forever- because of Him. Verse 11 talks about putting off our sackcloth and being clothed with gladness. Only God can accomplish that in our lives. That is why we must not deny our pain. It must be recognized if we are also to recognize the joy that God longs to give us. In the process of mourning, we get to see Him, to walk with Him, to know Him in a different way than at any other time. Then we can praise Him as David does here, "O Lord my God, I will give thanks to You forever'.

Have you seen God turn your night of weeping into morning joy?

Consider how it is only He Who is able to do that.

Psalms 30:5 &77 April 21

## The Grief Process

As we have seen, the purpose of grieving is to get us beyond the debilitating pain to face our loss and work, with God, on adapting to it and allowing Him to use it for our good and His glory. We need to change our relationship with whatever it is we have lost, develop our own life to encompass that change, and invest in new things that God will give us. Philippians 3:13 says, "Forgetting those things which are behind and reaching forth..." In the grieving situation we don't forget what we lost, but we let go of it so we can have free hands to reach for the things which are before us- other things that God has for us in this new season of our lives. We can do this if our identity and significance are in Christ and not in the people or things in our lives. HE is why we are here. Yes, He gives us people and things to enjoy, but we are to hold them lightly for now. We can do this if our thinking is in line with Scripture: II Corinthians 4:18 tells us that our afflictions are temporary, "but for a moment", Psalm 30:5 tells us that weeping endures for the night but joy comes in the morning. After our period of mourning, God stands ready to restore joy to us. The truth is that not only will God restore, but He will reveal Himself to us in our suffering. That is a theme through the Book of Psalms. Psalm 77 begins with Asaph being so troubled that he cannot speak [verse 4], then he remembers the days of old, wonders if God has abandoned him, but after working through some of this, he remembers the works of the Lord [verse 11]. As he is ready to move ahead and reinvest, he meditates on God's work and talks of His doings [verse 12]. We see his getting through the mourning process and coming out the other side.

Meditate on Psalm 77 and see how the Psalmist moves through the grief process.

Do you see yourself in any of these stages?

Psalm 31                                                            April 22

## In Trouble

Trouble will naturally find us at some points in our life. I remember reading James Dobson, probably 35 years ago, where he said either we are coming out of trouble, are in trouble, or will be in trouble. I have found that to be true.

In Psalm 31 David is in trouble, just one of the many times in his life. It is causing him such grief that he says his eye wastes away, his strength fails, his bones waste away. He says people avoid him, are repulsed by him, while he is in his pain. Fear is all around him, and his years are spent with sighing. He certainly is not whitewashing how he feels, nor is he denying the trouble in which he finds himself.

Now here comes the good part. Even in his condition, in the depths of his adversity where pain seems to be consuming him, he knows that underneath him is a Rock and a Fortress Who will strengthen him. He calls out to his Rock to lead him and guide him, knowing his Rock can and will. He knows he is redeemed, is glad and rejoices in Him, even in the depth of his trouble. His trouble is real, but so is his God.

The greatest comfort is found in verse 7: "You have considered my trouble; You have known my soul in adversities..." God knows exactly where David is and what trouble is upon him. He knows his very soul. He knows he will be hidden in the secret place of His Presence (verse 20). Nothing is happening in David's life that hasn't gone by God first. Not only does God know every detail of what David is suffering, but He also hears his cries (verse 22), even though for a while David felt cut off from Him. In his weakness, resulting from his trouble, David knew it was God Who was strengthening him.

Meditate on the truth that God considers your trouble. He knows your very soul.

Psalm 34                                                        April 23

## A Broken Heart

I have a client today who has a broken heart. Her 27-year-old son, her only child, whom she raised alone as a single Mother, just died of leukemia. She sat by his side for many months as the reality of what would eventually happen became more evident as each day passed.

My son has a broken heart. The anniversary of the death of his best friend and business partner was last month. He was 26 when killed in a car crash. My son also lost his beloved brother-in-law and mentor on September 11th and his dad before he was even two years old. His young heart has been broken many times. As they have remembered their son, Brian's family has had a broken heart for the past several years and will continue to feel the pain of their broken hearts for the remainder of their lives.

In Psalm 34:18 David writes that the Lord is near unto those who are of a broken heart. I am certain His Own Heart breaks as He stands beside this mother in her devastating sorrow, as He looks on a not-yet-two-year-old whose father has died, as He surrounds him when he loses his brother-in-law and mentor, as He walks with him to the grave of his best friend. He is there.

Verses 15 and 17 say His ears are open to our cries. He is there. He hears. We never walk alone, especially in those darkest of hours when no one else can bring comfort. He is there to fulfill His purpose in grief: That we might see Him, experience Him as never before. In verse 22 it says, "The Lord redeems the soul of His servants and none of them who trust in Him shall be desolate". I know this to be true.

Take your broken heart to Jesus and let Him redeem it.

Psalm 38                                                          April 24

## Sorrow for Sin

Our adversities and sorrows come to us from various sources, often simply because we live in a world where the fall has wrecked all kinds of havoc. All of us have seen where our own sin or the sin of others brings sorrow. Satan constantly looks for ways to bring us to our knees. Then there is God's discipline for sin, discipline meaning teaching, so that we are brought to a better place which He desires for us.

In Psalm 38 David described what he is experiencing as a result of his own sin: The piercing of God's arrows, God's Hand pressing him down, no health in his bones, wounds that are foul and festering, a burden over his head that is too heavy to bear. He goes on to say that he mourns all day long, is bowed down and troubled, there is turmoil in his heart, no peace. He is feeble, broken, there is no light in his eyes, no strength. His loved ones have abandoned him, and his enemies look for his destruction. He is paralyzed in his sorrow, cannot hear, cannot speak.

What a picture of the depths of sorrow. It is all going on in David's life because of his own sin. God is allowing it for a time in David's life for his good- so that he will present himself before God, be forgiven, and once again see and hear God. Amongst all his sorrow, we see him doing this. Verse 9 says all his desire is before his Lord. He knows God hears his sighs. His hope is in Him, and he knows He will hear (verse 15). He declares his sin in verse 18 and cries out for God's Presence to be with him once again (verse 21), and that is why God allows us to suffer in our sin- to bring us back into His Presence.

Sit with the Lord and let Him show you any sin that may be in your life. Declare it to Him so He may allow you once again to be fully in His Presence.

Psalm 40                                                                    April 25

## In the Pit

David describes himself in Psalm 40 as having been in a horrible pit, in the miry clay. That sounds like depression. In verse 12 he also talks about the innumerable evils that have surrounded him and his own iniquities that have taken hold of him so that he can't even look up. The evil of the world, more, he says, than the hairs of his head have weighed him down so that his heart fails. He is stuck in miry clay and in a pit so he cannot move, and he is so burdened with his own sin and the world's evil that he cannot lift his head to look up.

That is where he was, overcome with depression and despair, paralyzed, but he didn't stay there. Verse 2 says God brought him up out of the pit and actually put a new song in his mouth. God had thoughts towards David. He did not forget about him when he was in deep despair (verse 5). David was in trouble, some of which he brought on himself, but God thought about him, inclined to him, heard his cry, and did wonderful works in him, so many, David says, that they cannot be numbered.

After his experience in the pit, David says that God opened his ears (verse 6) so that his despair turned to delight, delight to do God's will, after hearing Him and seeing more of Who He is. His turnaround from depression to exhilaration in the Lord was so great that he had to declare it to those around him. He also asks for God's continued mercies, truth and deliverance in his life, knowing his circumstances would probably not change that much. He recognizes his need and knows his only answer is to magnify the Lord.

Have you ever been where David was- stuck in the miry clay, in a pit, burdened down with sin around you and in you? Magnify Him.

Psalm 42                                                        April 26

## Thirst for God

Do you know what it is to be thirsty? I remember going fishing with my Dad as a little girl, being out in a hot rowboat on the water, and being so thirsty I thought I might die. My Dad's response was, "You should have gotten a drink before we left home." I was left to deal with my thirst alone. When I read verses about being thirsty for God I think of that day and how much I desired water. I want to desire Him even more than that.

In Psalm 42 David describes his longing for God being like a deer panting for water in a brook. He is searching for God but can't seem to find Him. He remembers times of joy with Him but now he is cast down, in sorrow, has no peace, and continues to long. Even in the depths of these feelings, however, he knows that at some point God will once again reveal Himself. He will see His loving-kindness and have His song within him. Even though David is not sensing Him at the moment, He calls Him his Rock and continues to hope in Him and continues to praise Him, based on Who He is as well as what he has experienced with Him. Even though his soul is cast down, his countenance will change when he sees God once again.

The times when God is quiet and not so revealing of Himself in our lives are painful times, just as David describes, but they are valuable times, times for us to realize how much we long for Him, how much we need Him. They are opportunities to exercise our faith, remaining committed to what we cannot see.

Talk to God today about your thirst for Him, how much you need Him.

Psalm 51                                                        April 27

## A Penitent Heart

David's sin was great but so was his sorrow concerning it, and we are privileged to see what he does with it.   Psalm 51 expresses his pain in having not only sinned against Uriah, Bathsheba, his family and his nation, but mostly against his God.  He agrees with God about his sinful condition as well as the specific evil he has committed.  He recognizes that his nature is one of sinfulness and therefore, needs to be cleansed by the Only One Who can do that.  He asks that God, out of His mercy, wash him so that he can know the joy that results from right relationship with Him.

Until the cleansing of his sin takes place, David feels the pain right down to his bones, describing them as broken.  He feels the separation from God, the ultimate in pain.  Only this brokenness of spirit and the penitence of his heart will bring him to God.

When he receives God's forgiveness, not only is his heart clean, his spirit right, but his joy is restored as he is in the Presence of his Lord.  He can then praise God once again and even bring others to God.   So here in Psalm 51 is God's plan of salvation.  We are sinful in our very core and need cleansing.  Only He can do that.  Our sinful nature brings great suffering into our lives because it separates us from God.  We can do nothing about that sinful nature.  No sacrifice or offerings of ours will suffice.  His cleansing through Jesus' blood allows us to come into God's Presence which results in unspeakable joy.

Does sorrow for your sin drive you to God's Presence where you can receive cleansing?

Psalm 57                                                              April 28

## In the Shadow of His Wings

As I write this I am aware of several people this very day who are in the shadow of His wings, taking refuge in His care and protection. What a glorious place to be. Picture it as David presents his experience in the shadow of God's wings.

David wrote this Psalm as he ran from the jealous Saul who was intent on killing him. David, absorbed with fear for his life, found himself escaping to the mountains and caves of Israel. He asks for God's mercy as he seeks refuge in the shadow of His wings until the calamities facing him have passed. He understands the power of his adversity, like a lion intent on the kill, whose teeth are spears and arrows, whose tongue a sword. The adversary is seeking to ensnare him at every step. Naturally there would be a great deal of anxiety and fear in David's life. Those are his emotions, how he feels, but this is a perfect Psalm to see one who acknowledges his emotions but who lives on the truth of God. While he is being hotly pursued, he fears for his life, but his thinking is centered on God. He knows in the shadow of God's wings will be protection, no matter what is going on in his environment. He knows God is able to perform all things, that taking care of the enemy is not a problem for Him. He steadfastly exalts and praises God, singing to Him of His glory. His triumphant conclusion to this Psalm, "Be exalted, O God, above the heavens: Let Your glory be above all the earth", shows us his mind set. It is one of God's truths. He may feel out of control, but he acts on the basis of Who God is.

In the midst of turmoil can you say with David, "This is how I feel, but what is the truth? I will acknowledge how I feel, but I will behave on the truth of Who You are."

Psalm 71                                                   April 29

## The Sorrow of old Age

The Psalms cover a multitude of sorrows, even that of old age, as seen here in Psalm 71. The Psalmist has trusted God from his youth, knowing it was He Who formed him in the womb, was present at his birth, and taught him and used him throughout his life. He is asking God now, as he is advanced in years, to make him a testimony of what God can do in a life. Not only does he plan to praise God more and more as he goes through some of the infirmities of old age, but he wants to pass down what he has learned of God. He desires to bring honor to Him Who has done such great things in his life.

As he becomes old and gray-headed, he asks that he will never be put to confusion, that he won't be cast aside due to lack of strength, that he not be overtaken by enemies. On the contrary, he asks that he can be revived and use the experiences he has had with God, even the great and severe troubles, to instruct the next generation about Who God is and what He does. He desires to take what God has taught him and pass it on, make it count for God's honor and glory.

There are various developmental tasks that we negotiate as we go through life. One of them as we age is to look back on our life and either be satisfied with how we have lived or be regretful. While aging brings many losses to every area of life, this Psalmist is so satisfied because his life has been one of knowing God, and his desire is that others will have what he has had. He is so satisfied because of his redemption that he can only talk of God's righteousness all the day long. The losses of old age are not a problem for him because he draws comfort from the One Who has been with him since before he was born, the One with Whom he has had a relationship throughout life and the One Who continues to use him, even as he enters the last years of life.

Do you have the attitude of the Psalmist as you age, that your desire is to leave a legacy of Who God is, what He has shown you about Himself?

Psalms 77                                                    April 30

## What Is Good Grieving?

Grieving is allowing ourselves to feel our feelings, think our thoughts, lament our losses and protest our pain. It is being real, which is what God has called us to be. We are to know and be known, first with Him and then with others. Easy clichés will not get us through to the other side of grief where we can see God and ourselves in a way we never could before. Joy awaits us there, but the pain must be embraced before we can get to it. Suffering IS going to come. I Peter 4:12 tells us we shouldn't be surprised that we are suffering. The key to remember is God doesn't want us to waste it. He intends for it to be a gift, a gift that will teach us so many things about Himself that we cannot learn when all is well. I have heard Beth Moore say in one of her DVD's, "The greatest work you will do, will be on the other side of your pain." I know this to be true for me. Neither my counseling ministry nor this writing would be taking place if I had not had a parcel of pain to take to Him. We need to walk through the offenses we encounter and see Him. To see the pain as a gift that God wants to use in our lives is correct thinking. If we get that down, our behavior will follow and our emotions will follow that. Our emotions are telling us we hurt. We pay attention to them, we even share them with others, and we certainly share them with the One Who is so waiting to offer comfort to us. Our emotions, however, are not the engine. Correct thinking, God's thinking, is our engine. We may feel abandoned, alone, and frightened, but God's Word tells us the truth. We need to go with that.

Asaph writes in Psalm 77 that he was so troubled he could not speak in the day of his trouble, but he sought the Lord. He meditates on God's works. He says then that God gave him ear. Asaph feels his pain but remembers the truth: Who God is as he works his way through.

As you are working your way through some suffering in your life, express it to Him and remember Who He is and what He wants to do with your suffering. Let Him help you see something of the bigger picture.

Psalms 77                                                    May 01

## Our Emotions Reveal Who We Are

Just as emotions will reveal God to us when we acknowledge them, they also reveal our sinful nature. I see the heart of our sinful nature as being independence and pride [Genesis 3]. We feel a negative emotion, and we go about trying to fix it in our own stumbling way. It shows just how opposed to God we really are. The emotions I see every day in people, and too often in myself, are anger and fear. What reaction do these two emotions elicit from us? Anger puts us on the offensive while fear puts us on the defensive. We attack or we flee. We are not sure that God can rectify the situation or, in the case of fear, that He can protect us, so we go with our penchant for independence and do battle or run away. When we truly look at our anger or fear, we see how we have dethroned God and put ourselves in His place. We make it about us when it should be directing us to Him. When we see what we are doing in our negative emotions, God's intent is that we come to Him and really see Him. In Psalm 77 Asaph begins by expressing his grief and pain. He says his soul refused to be comforted. He sought his own way out of the difficulty. Of course, that didn't work. It never will. Then he says his heart made diligent search- he examined himself. Only then does he remember Who God is, His works [verse 11]. He meditates not on his pain and how he will get out of it, but on his Lord [verse 12]. In verse 14 He calls God the God of wonders. He sees God as the One Who knows what to do in trouble. His plan is always to redeem it.

Let God show you your attempts to deal with your pain on your own, and acknowledge your sin in these attempts.

Give whatever your pain is to Him. You can trust Him with it.

Psalm 130                                                    May 02

## Waiting for the Lord

Have you ever spent a long night waiting for the light of sunrise, immersed in sorrow or anxiety? The minutes are agonizingly slow, the darkness engulfing, the fears growing in intensity. The worst is the feeling of being alone, separated from others as you endure your grief. When morning finally comes, the problems remain, but there is hope, in the light of the day, that you can endure. Light brings promise. You are less conscious of being alone.

In Psalm 130 the Psalmist is expressing his feelings about waiting for the Lord. He says he waits for Him more than one who watches for the morning. Then he repeats that phrase, emphasizing how his soul longs to reconnect with his God. He cries out of the depths for Him, begs Him to hear him and be attentive to his voice.

While he waits he finds hope in God's Word. Perhaps he is remembering what God has shown him in the past. How blessed we are to have the written Word of God. When we are in a period of not sensing God's Presence, we have truths on every page to remind us that He will never leave us or forsake us. We have no excuse for allowing our emotions to tell us that He has abandoned us when He has given us the truth that we can access every day. The truth always supersedes our feelings. While we wait to hear from Him or sense His Presence once again, we live on the truth of the Word of God.

Treasure the truths of His Word. Thank Him for always speaking to you through them, no matter what your feelings are.

Psalm 143                                                    May 03

## Help, Lord!

Psalm 143 shows us David's feelings and thoughts as his soul has been persecuted by the enemy. He says that Satan has smitten his life down to the ground and has made him to dwell in darkness, like a dead person. His spirit is overwhelmed, and his heart is desolate so he cries out to his Lord, knowing in himself there is no righteousness. He is completely dependent on God's faithfulness and righteousness in order to be heard by Him. There is nothing in himself that he should expect God's answer. So, he acknowledges Who God is and who he is, which is the foundation from which we can rightly relate to God.

In his desolation he begins to remember and meditate on what God has done in the past, and he longs for Him. He cries out for God to show him His face. He wants to see Him as well as to receive direction as to how he should walk. "Teach me to do Thy will; for thou art my God." He ends the Psalm by proclaiming himself as God's servant.

David's soul has been made desolate by the persecution of the enemy. In his darkness he remembers God's work in the past and goes after Him, seeking His guidance, knowing in Him he will be revived and his soul brought out of its trouble.

Do we thirst after God when our very souls are brought low, or do we look for other means to revive ourselves, other people, activity, various addictions perhaps? The dark times are opportunities to seek Him and find Him at a level we never have before. Hopefully we will not waste these opportunities.

Are you approaching God from the right foundation, knowing Who He is and who you are?

Are you remembering that you were created first and foremost to know Him and be known by Him?

Proverbs 1                                                    May 04

## Lack of Wisdom Brings Suffering

What causes us to lack wisdom? Isn't it by being called by God and refusing? Proverbs 1:24 says God has stretched out His Hand, and no one regarded it. People disdain His counsel and have none of His rebuke. He lets Himself be known by people, but they will not hear. The result is terror, distress, and anguish at some point in life (verse 27). Verse 28 is one of the saddest verses in Scripture: "They will call on me, but I will not answer. They will seek me diligently, but they will not find me." God had given them a choice earlier, but they did not choose Him, demonstrating instead their hatred for knowledge. Therefore they shall have what they desired, the fruit of their own way, but it will bring destruction.

How different that image is than the one presented in the final verse: "But whoever listens to me will dwell safely and will be secure, without fear of evil". To be secure and safe in Him! Lord, may we choose You.

I have seen individuals who God called throughout their lives, but in their pride, they would not bend their knees to Him. Later in their lives I saw no evidence of God's pulling them to Himself anymore. To receive Him requires the knowledge of Jesus' payment for their sin, the Holy Spirit's pulling them, and then their response. God's Word says He will not always strive with man. I cannot imagine anything more fearful than that.

Be careful to respond to the Lord when He pulls you to Himself, whether for salvation or for direction in a certain area of life.

Proverbs 12:17-19, 13:3-5, & 15:1-2, 23          May 05

## Destruction from our Mouth

Proverbs, with good reason, is full of admonitions about our speech. How many times we have all seen a person's mouth get him in trouble. Just today I had a client whose family has been literally torn apart by uncensored words spoken in anger about one another. Maybe it has even been our own experience. James 3 addresses the power of the tongue, saying how it can be like a fire, an unruly evil, full of deadly poison. We can use it to bless or to curse. Proverbs 15:1 & 2 shows how our words have power over others; we can calm another's anger by using gentle responses. Verse 23 says how good is a word spoken at the appropriate time. That we would choose to make that choice as opposed to increasing another's anger by not allowing God to control our words.

Not only does what we say greatly affect others but Proverbs 12:18b tells us that it affects us as well. "The tongue of the wise promotes health", others and ours. Lack of discipline with our words can actually bring destruction says Proverbs 13:3, while guarding our words preserves life.

How much pain and destruction seen in the counseling office come not from actions, but words, words that do not come from one who is allowing God to have control over them. We have the power to bring reconciliation or destruction by what we say and how we say it. Sometimes I sit with a couple and silently pray that one of them will allow God's Spirit to give them just one word that is so sorely needed to begin the healing process between them. Just one word at the appropriate time- sometimes that is all that is needed for God to be able to begin His mighty work in a heart. Proverbs 12:18 says our words can be like the piercing of a sword or they can heal and promote health. Guarding our mouths preserves life while "opening wide our lips" brings destruction. Being intimately involved with the Lord enables us to choose words that are from Him and will bring health.

Consider with God the words that come out of your mouth. Do they promote health or destruction?

Proverbs 19:21 May 06

## Broken Dreams

At one time I had a client who, after years of living out of the will of the Lord, had made decisions to begin to submit to Him and was making progress in getting her life back on track, going to school, planning for a career, taking in God's Word and getting rid of the things in her life which did not please God. Then "out of nowhere" a major accident shattered many of her dreams. Education was put on hold, her planned career would no longer be feasible, just taking care of her basic needs stretched her to the limit. In reality she had to depend on other people to make life work for her. There was also a sense of loss for what she had previously given up in her quest to be who God wanted her to be. This pattern of determining to move ahead and follow the Lord and then having unexpected obstacles stop her in her tracks, bringing with it, not only physical pain, but emotional distress and spiritual confusion and doubt, was to be played out several times in her recovery.

Why? Her dreams were finally good ones, but I believe God has even better dreams for her. Sometimes He has to allow our good dreams to be taken away so we go for the BEST dream, HIM. It is not just about lifestyle. He wants us to yield up ourselves so we can see that only His Presence will give us what we really need. Sitting with shattered dreams allows us to look at Him and really see Him. That is the best one and the new one that He desires to give us.

Are you sitting with a shattered dream? Let Him give you a new one, the best one, the one that is HIM.

Proverbs 20:1                                          May 07

## The Pain of Addictions

Many of the addictions that people fall prey to today are not specifically addressed in Scripture, mainly because they didn't exist then as they do today. Drugs, pornography, smoking, excessive working, compulsive exercising, compulsive eating, co-dependence with people, perfectionism, etc., while common in our society, are not presented in Scripture, but there are principles that most definitely can be applied to them. Alcohol and sexual addictions are two that we do see quite often in Biblical times. Here in Proverbs 20 Solomon wrote about the power of wine and strong drink and how we can be deceived by them. That is what addictions do: they deceive us. They deceive us into thinking that the substance or activity we are seeking will take away our pain and emptiness and meet our need. We turn to an addiction in an attempt to feel better. We are empty, in pain, because we have unmet needs. The greatest need we have is the fulfillment for which we have been created. Why am I here, we wonder, so we go about trying various things, even good things, such as careers, education, family, friends- good things, but not THE Thing. We are created to know God intimately, and nothing else can give us the satisfaction of that. So, after we see that even the good things don't work, we may turn to some of the addictions that are not good, such a alcohol, as mentioned in Proverbs 20:1. It deceives us into thinking that we will feel better and have our needs met. It may calm us or help us forget our pain for a time, but in the long run will cause us greater pain. The worst part is that we will not find what it is that truly satisfies. We are deceived. What our souls long for is a deep relationship with God through Jesus. Nothing else, no addiction, will ever suffice.

Talk with God about any addictions (something you look to in order to make you feel better, be more in control, or to take away your pain) you may have in your life.

It may even be something that on first glance seems good, but it takes the place of intimacy with God.

Proverbs 22:6,15 & 23:13                                        May 08

## Lack of Discipline in Parenting

If you are in the midst of child rearing, what would you hope the child would be like in 10, 20, 30 years? Whatever that vision is, you need to make preparations for it now by the decisions you make as a parent. That vision will not come to be by accident but will take your cooperation and submission to God as you follow His Word. His Word regarding child rearing is not very popular in today's child-centered society. Yet we need to remember that He knit our children together while they were still in the womb, He planned for them before they were conceived, He loves them far more than we, as sin-ridden parents, are able to, and His plans for them are not to harm them but to give them a future. He has a vision of who He desires them to be. We know that His desire is that they would love Him beyond all else and know Him intimately, that they would serve and obey Him. What do we need to do now to help them get there?

How can we help our children avoid so many of the sorrows we see going on around us? The answer is by following His Word regarding our parenting of them. Proverbs 22:6 says to train them up in the way they should go. They need to be taught His Word. Just as we have a basic nature of sin, so do they. Verse 15 says they are innately foolish, as we are, so they need correction. There is not a lot of that going on today, and I see the results of that lack regularly in my counseling office. Parents are afraid or not willing to discipline. I love that word, discipline. It means teach. We are given the responsibility to teach our children the way they should go, so they can become the people God intends. How much pain and sorrow would be avoided if we would obey God in this.

Do you really believe that God loves your children more than you do, that He has their very best interest in mind? Covenant with Him to follow His Word in your parenting.

Proverbs 23:29-35                                        May 09

## The Ravages of Alcoholism

Proverbs 23:29-35 paints a vivid picture of a person who is suffering from addiction to alcohol. According to this scripture, alcoholism brings woe, sorrow, contentions, complaints, wounds without cause, redness of eyes, hallucinations, thoughts and behaviors not characteristic of the sober person, including the inability to feel, and coming to the point of looking forward to waking up only so he can seek another drink. Nothing else matters to him. He did not set out to abuse alcohol or to be addicted to it, but when he started down that road he left himself open for that possibility. What other substance, besides drugs, can bring such pain into a life and into a family? This portion of Scripture says it looks pretty in the cup, it even sparkles, but it bites like a serpent and stings like a viper.

My grandfather was a full-blown alcoholic, and my dad, who did not drink, had the personality of one. Holidays were invariably ruined, anger was rampant, and pain was evident in many of the lives in the family. I have seen the destruction alcohol abuse has caused in the lives of many clients as well. Even the most basic of needs go by the wayside to support the habit. Women with alcoholic husbands often spend their time and energy focused on his alcohol problem. Children grow up with a sense of shame, often turning to the substance themselves to cover their pain. The most tragic part is that an alcoholic looks to the alcohol to meet his needs, missing the One Who can truly meet the emptiness inside of him. He cannot serve two masters, and until he can give up his dependence on alcohol, God will never have first place in his life as He desires. Alcohol is indeed a master but only promises what it cannot fulfill.

Is there anything, including alcohol, that you look to to meet your need, instead of allowing God to do it?

Ecclesiastes 1                                              May 10

## All, Including Wisdom, is Vanity

Solomon, known for his wisdom, shares it with us in Ecclesiastes when he says that all is vanity. Apart from God, that is absolutely true. Solomon himself attained greatness, knowing and understanding more than all who were before him in Jerusalem, but he says in Ecclesiastes 1:18 that it only brought him much grief. "He who increases knowledge increases sorrow", he says.

When Solomon, as a youth, was about to succeed his Father, David, he requested knowledge from God (I Kings 3), and God was so pleased with his request that He gave him a wise and understanding heart above all others, as well as riches and honor above all the kings of his day. God's covenant with Solomon was that if he kept His commandments, then his days would also be lengthened. We know that Solomon lost his focus in keeping God's commands and allowed his many wives to turn his heart after other gods. He had wisdom, but he didn't apply it to himself as he went on with life. Thus we see his pessimism in Ecclesiastes. Wisdom, while a good thing, by itself is vanity.

In our society we see well-educated, even wise people, who in their knowledge, do not acknowledge God. They eschew His Word, thinking they know better. Their arrogance is astounding, sometimes even to the point of mocking God. Just as Solomon came to see that wisdom did not fill the God-shaped longing in his heart, so will they at some point in life. While wisdom is meant by God for good, apart from Him, it can actually keep us from Him, deceiving us into thinking that we can run our lives, that we have all the answers and can be independent. There again is the root of our fallen state: we don't want to need God. We think we have what it takes to be our own god. This is vanity in all its ugliness.

Do you see that wisdom apart from God leaves us empty, depressed and without hope?

Ecclesiastes 1:9-10                                    May 11

## When Work Consumes

I was attempting to think of issues I have seen in counseling that don't seem to be presented in God's Word. When I think of one, or think I am thinking of one, I quickly realize that God has given direction about it under a larger principle, showing us there really is nothing new under the sun. He knew exactly what each one of His people would be facing in life and, ahead of time, He wrote to us concerning how to deal with it.

One major area that I deal with quite often and can find little about in Scripture specifically, is when work consumes. God presents work as a good thing. Back in Genesis, even before the fall, He gave Adam and Eve work to do. It is in our being to want and need to produce. It is a good thing. When it becomes too important in a person's life, however, it destroys marriages and families. The ramifications of it can travel through generations. How often have I sat with a wife as her tears flowed, relating to me how her husband's first love is his work, how she feels unloved, and how her children are feeling neglected. If not corrected, I might sit with the family later as the children are out of control, in rebellion when young, turning to destructive addictions when older, in an attempt to cover their pain. It would be a good guess that they themselves later would seek to avoid intimacy, since they were not familiar with it, and become workaholics as adults- or perhaps even worse. It is an area of life, while not specifically seen in Scripture, does have principles that apply. The verse, "Put Me first and all else will be added unto you" gives direction about the place of everything else, including work, in our lives. Scripture says husbands are to love their wives, not to love their work first and foremost. God's Word says to bring up our children in the way they should go, requiring time and attention. In the Old Testament there were many of God's laws designed to see that rest was a part of the Israelites' lives.

There are many teachings in Scripture, which speak to this very common and potentially destructive area of life. There really IS nothing new under the sun. God has already given us answers to cover all that we face. He thought of everything since He knows us so well.

Do you need to make any changes as you look at your work in relationship to other areas of your life?

Ecclesiastes 2                                                              May 12

## Pleasure is Vanity

Just as Solomon acknowledges that wisdom alone does not give him the real meaning of life, he discovers the same concerning pleasure. He tried gratifying his flesh with wine and laying hold on folly, even while guarding his heart with wisdom, but his assessment of that approach to finding the meaning of life was- "madness"! He built houses, planted vineyards, made gardens and orchards, constructed pools, acquired servants, herds, and flocks, gathered silver, gold, and treasures of kings, acquired musicians and instruments, all in search of finding satisfaction in pleasure. It was vanity, grasping for the wind.

His assessment in Ecclesiastes 2:12-26 is that even though wisdom excels folly, both end with the same result: both the wise man and the fool die just the same. He began to find his work distressing and came to hate it, knowing he would be leaving it behind. Even his labor was proving to be vanity.

At this point all that Solomon pursued in an effort to be satisfied and find meaning in life were the wrong goals. They are the same goals men seek today: acquiring lots of things ( I think of it as "the bigger, better, more" approach), using food or substances to assuage the emptiness, hoping diversions such as music or sports will bring us enough enjoyment that we can stave off the constant feeling that something is wrong. Vanity. Something IS wrong, and it will continue to be wrong until we agree with the One Who created us that it is He Whom we need. He is the only One Who can fill the emptiness in our hearts and souls. We must be brought into relationship with Him through the work of His Son, Jesus. Nothing else will ever suffice.

Have you been looking to the wrong things to satisfy the emptiness in your heart?

CS Lewis said, "We are halfhearted creatures, fooling about with drink and sex and ambition when infinite joy is offered us, like an ignorant child who wants to go on making mud pies in a slum because he cannot imagine what is meant by an offer of a holiday at the sea. We are far too easily pleased." How about you?

Ecclesiastes 3                                                    May 13

## God's Timing

Solomon, in his wisdom, tells us in chapter 3 of Ecclesiastes that there is an appointed time for everything under heaven. We don't orchestrate the timing. God does. We just need to recognize His timing, accept it, and get from it what He desires. I have often said to God, "I don't like this, but don't let me waste it". I want to get from whatever is going on, whatever He desires.

Our society is not good at looking into a painful time in life and saying, "This is a sorrowful time for me. I am in pain. It is appropriate to mourn". Our belief is that we should get rid of the pain as quickly and as efficiently as possible. Move on and grasp hold of whatever makes us feel better. There are plenty of things to help us do that, but we then deprive ourselves of the opportunity to learn what God wants to teach us. We won't learn it when all is well, when it is a time to laugh. We will learn it when we are in a time of weeping. It is necessary to embrace a time to mourn. When we do that successfully, we will recognize later when God gives us a time to dance, and we will be able to embrace that more fully as well.

There is a time to weep and a time to laugh, a time to mourn and a time to dance, a time to gain and a time to lose, a time of war and a time of peace, a time to be born and a time to die. God knows whatever time we are in. He has allowed it, maybe even orchestrated it- always for our good. His first desire for us is that we know Him deeply. We need to cooperate with Him in every season of our lives so that that will be the outcome.

Do you accept that in your life there is a time to weep and a time to laugh, a time to gain and a time to lose? Will you trust God to show you His good in both?

Ecclesiastes 4:9-12                                      May 14

## Value in Friendship

The Book of Ecclesiastes continues to express Solomon's frustration about the emptiness, the vanity of life. The word "labor" is used 23 times, "evil" 22 times, "vexation of spirit" 9 times. The words grief and mourning are also present quite often. He seems to take a brief respite in chapter 2 verses 9-12 when he presents the value of friendship. He writes that "Two are better than one". They can work together and have some satisfaction in what they have accomplished together. If one falls, the other can lift him up. There is comfort in that. Two can lie together and be kept warm. They can meet each other's needs to some degree. They can join forces and stand together against an enemy. That sounds like a good marital relationship, what God intended when He made Eve for Adam. It is the second purpose for which we were created: an intimate, deep sharing of ourselves with another person, and he with us, the loving of another person as we love ourselves. We should find satisfaction in that, and Solomon in his pessimism, acknowledges that.

However, this deep relationship with another person, as satisfying as it can be, is not the first thing. The first thing is a deep, intimate relationship with God, like Adam had before he was given Eve. If these two relationships are in place in the order which God commands, the emptiness which Solomon cries out about will not occur. I believe he alludes to this when he speaks of "a threefold cord not quickly broken" in Ecclesiastes 4:12. There is the answer to all the emptiness Solomon rails against throughout the Book.

Do you see the emptiness of all else in light of our need for God and our desire for other people?

Ecclesiastes 12 May 15

## The Conclusion of the Whole Matter

So, Solomon finds that nothing in our lives, even the things that we would call good, serve to meet the needs of our heart. They alone do not satisfy. Only in relationship to God does life make sense. Only a life lived with God and in obedience to Him meets that need inside us. Solomon, in the last chapter of Ecclesiastes, cautions us to "remember our Creator in the days of our youth" before the difficult days come. It is only through, and with, Him that we can keep from saying, "All is vanity." He gives the conclusion of the whole matter in Ecclesiastes 12:14: "Fear God and keep His commandments, for this is man's all. For God will bring every work into judgment, including every secret thing, whether good or evil." We are here for HIM. We are here to relate to Him in such a way that we can hear and know what He has for us to do. Then our responsibility is to do it. We are not responsible for the work itself but to stay in constant, concentrated touch with Him so He can do the work through us.

We can have careers, education, families, relationships, people, homes, recreation as we go about living our lives, but the center has to be HIM or all will be vanity, emptiness, as Solomon says. It is our all to fear Him and keep His commandments. One day we will give an answer to Him as to what we have done with the life He has given us.

Is there vanity in your life or have you made it about Him?

Song of Solomon 2:15                                      May 16

## The Little Foxes

Solomon's Song shows God's love for His people, His church, His Bride, even while proclaiming a husband's love for his wife. It is a joyous description as we see the husband enjoying and cherishing his wife in an intimate God-ordained relationship. We see her responding to Him also. When we consider that God uses this account as an allegory of His love for us, His chosen, we want to respond to Him with the same passion He has for us. This is such a positive, delightful book, how can we find any adversity in it? There is one small verse, 2:15, that suggests a problem: the "little foxes". The brothers of the Shulamite woman, the beloved, speak about the little foxes. They spoil the vines and need to be caught, the brothers say, or they will ruin the tender grapes. So, amidst the wonder and beauty of all that is loving and pleasant, they are suggesting that lying in wait can be those things, the "little foxes" which can bring turmoil and ruination. They are to be caught, but first we need to be aware of them, to be on guard against them. Satan loves to catch us basking in pleasantries and then attack us unawares. As we center on Jesus, the "little foxes" are waiting to pounce, and we need to know that to not be taken by surprise. We need to expect and prepare for those things that can spoil our intimacy with Him or our intimacy with others. They are often little things at first, maybe even good things. We are to be vigilant for them.

Can you identify the "little foxes" in your life that want to spoil your intimacy with Jesus?

Isaiah 5:20-21                                          May 17

## Calling Evil Good

The Prophet Isaiah writes in a day when Judah was invaded and Israel carried away. He looks forward to a time when there will be a new heaven and a new earth, but in the meantime, he warns Israel of their behaviors. He says "Woe unto them who call evil good, and good, evil, who put darkness for light and light for darkness; who put bitter for sweet and sweet for bitter." This reminds me of the pressure we face in our world to accept and even embrace what God has clearly called evil. We as Christians are called rigid, narrow-minded, unloving, and worse when we refuse to compromise what God has called sin. Sometimes we succumb because we begin to think that we are wrong. We can never be wrong in following what God gives us in His written Word. What He says is good, is good, and what He says is evil, is evil. Compromising to be accepted by the world brings pain and heartache.

Isaiah also says "Woe unto them who are wise in their own eyes, and prudent in their own sight." This propensity for exalting ourselves and attempting to diminish God goes back to the beginning of man and is at the very heart of our sin. It brings emptiness now and death later. In chapter 2, verse 12 Isaiah says, "..The day of the Lord of hosts shall be upon everyone who is proud and lofty, and upon everyone who is lifted up, and he shall be brought low." In Isaiah 2:17b he writes that "The Lord alone shall be exalted in that day." It is He Who determined what is evil and good, and it is He Who will bring the arrogant low and exalt Himself. Woe unto them who will not listen , hold onto and live His truth.

Think of how we are tempted regularly to follow the world's pressure to call evil, good, and good, evil.

Isaiah 6:1-9                                                                May 18

## Seeing God

Isaiah had a vision. He saw the Lord as He is, sitting on a throne, high and lifted up, His robe filling the temple, surrounded by seraphim who were praising Him, saying, "holy, holy, holy is the Lord of hosts; the whole earth is full of His glory." His voice caused the door posts to be shaken, and the house was filled with smoke!

Why would we include this in a study about pain and suffering? Look at Isaiah's reaction to his vision of God in verse 5: "Woe is me for I am undone!" We are going to be undone when we see God as He is because it also causes us to really see ourselves: "men of unclean lips, dwelling in the midst of people of unclean lips." If we are not undone when we see Him and then ourselves, something is wrong. Isaiah's eyes have seen the King and he is forever changed. It brings suffering as he contemplates his situation, the huge distance between God and himself, but then he is touched by one of the seraphim of God, is cleansed and responds to the call to serve God. How could he not, after this experience? God wants someone to send to tell His people about Himself. Isaiah responds, "Here am I! Send me." After the pain of seeing the holiness of God and the vast difference between Him and his own sinfulness, he submits himself to the holy One. He is ready to serve the One Who has just revealed Himself to him.

Seeing God as He is and ourselves as we are should bring sorrow and pain to us, but sorrow and pain that can be used to rightly relate us to the Lord. We see the need to accept His cleansing, then we can do nothing else but ask to be sent to do His work and His will.

Do you see Him, really see Him? Do you see yourself, really see yourself? Let the sorrow of the contrast propel you to fall before Him and say, "Here am I! Send me."

Isaiah 13                                                    May 19

## Coming Pain

While Isaiah prophesies concerning what will befall Babylon, it is also a picture of what will befall anyone who does not accept God's way of salvation through Jesus. Isaiah 13:6 says to "Wail for the day of the Lord is at hand. It will come as destruction from the Almighty." Wailing suggests the ultimate in expressing sorrow. Isaiah goes on to say that hands will be limp, hearts will melt and every man will be afraid. Pangs and sorrows will take hold of them, like the pain of a woman in childbirth.

When the day of the Lord comes, Isaiah says, the land will become desolate, there will be no light from the stars, sun, or moon. God will shake the heavens, and the earth will be moved. Death will reign.

Man's arrogance and pride that is so evident in our world will be halted, while he will finally acknowledge who he is and Who God is. I sometimes wonder how God is able to put up with some of the things people say about Him and themselves, the attitudes they have towards Him and themselves. The day is coming when He will avenge all of that, when His long suffering will end, and his anger and fierce wrath will burst forth.

I mourn as I consider not only the condition of man but his treatment of the One Who has provided him with everything he needs, the main thing being the opportunity, despite his sin, to be reconciled to Himself. It cost Him His Son. He had to cut Himself off from His beloved Son and watch Him take on our sins. He did it out of His great love for us, and yet so many of us refuse Him. That separation from God is what will cause the ultimate in pain and suffering.

Talk with Him once again about the price He paid for your salvation.

Covenant with Him to tell others so they will never know the sorrow described here.

Isaiah 24 & 25                                                      May 20

## Wiping Away Tears

As Isaiah describes the Babylonian invasion, he also presents a picture of the distress of the coming tribulation. Our earth will experience God's judgment for sin. He describes the emptiness and waste. It will be turned upside down, and the people will be scattered. All people, in their haughtiness and sin, will be affected. Few will be left. The music and wine that once distracted men from their sorrows will no longer do so. Desolation and destruction will reign. No one will escape as the earth reels to and fro and is thoroughly dissolved. Isaiah's prophecy can't begin to be touched by any sorrows we have experienced in our lives. No horror movie can depict what Isaiah presents in this chapter.

Thankfully chapter 25 follows with Isaiah praising God, exalting Him for the restoration He will bring. He will swallow up death forever and wipe away tears from all faces, he says in 25:8. Those who waited for Him will be saved and will rejoice in His salvation. He has a plan for His people, those who know Him and have accepted the salvation He offers for sin. It stands in stark contrast to the future awaiting those who refuse Him. Chapter 24 and 25 could not present two more different pictures: abject destruction verses the celebration we can have in Him. To think that there will be no more death, and that He Himself will wipe away tears from our faces. That truth alone can sustain us through anything we will endure. This life makes us very familiar with pain and suffering, and surely there is more to come, but knowing what He has planned for us not only gets us through but helps us to rejoice in it. Isaiah 26:3 says we will be kept in perfect peace when our minds are stayed on Him.

As you spend time with him today, talk with Him about that day when He will wipe all tears from your face.

Isaiah 29:9-16                                                    May 21

## Blindness

If a person is handed a sealed book and told to read it, he cannot do it, just as an illiterate person cannot read a book handed to him. Men are like that concerning God's Word when they approach it with arrogance, or when they refuse to obey Him. Sometimes when I am talking to certain people, particularly about receiving Jesus, there seems to be a veil covering their eyes. They are unable to receive it. They are blind. It is a distressing thing to see because if the veil is not removed they will not come to a saving knowledge of Him. I also see this sometimes when presenting a believer with Scripture regarding something in his life. He does not want to take it in. He is blind... Isaiah 29:10 characterizes it as being in a deep sleep with closed eyes. If God's Word cannot penetrate, the person has no chance to change. He is headed for much grief and sorrow. Isaiah says, "Woe to those who seek deep to hide their counsel far from the Lord, and their works in the dark." Woe is not a word that portends anything good coming their way.

This passage suggests that a person enters this state of blindness because he has esteemed himself higher than the One Who created him. The arrogance of questioning God about His ways and suggesting that God had nothing to do with His being, prevents God from imparting His truths into that life. To be spiritually blind, not able to receive the truth of God, is a frightful place to be.

Talk to the Lord about any pride or disobedience in your life that may be preventing you from hearing the truth.

Isaiah 38                                                        May 22

## Facing Death

Hezekiah, a good King of Judah, who had served the Lord well, became sick unto death. Isaiah told him to put his house in order for he would die. Isaiah 38:2 gives us his reaction to this news: He turned his face toward the wall and prayed unto the Lord, asking Him to remember how he had served Him with truth. He wept bitterly. God's response is seen in verse 5: He heard his prayer, saw his tears and said He would give Hezekiah an additional fifteen years of life. God saw his tears, just as He sees ours.

Hezekiah recounts in the remainder of the chapter how he felt when he was expecting death to come. He lamented the leaving of his people. He also dreaded the being cut off because of his sickness. He describes his mourning, his eyes failing with looking upward, being oppressed and asks God to undertake for him. He says, "I shall go softly all my years in the bitterness of my soul."

In his recovery he praises God. He appears to see how God even used his illness for good, saying in verse 17 that "it was for my own peace that I had great bitterness." He says he will sing songs to the stringed instruments all the days of his life in the house of the Lord. He also says how God has cast all his sins behind His back. What an image- that God casts our sins behind His back, a place where He does not see them. Hezekiah clearly loved and served God, yet he was not ready to face his illness and let it claim his life. He mourned the prospect of it. That is part of our human nature. God heard him and responded to his cry. While trusting God, we, like Hezekiah can mourn when our bodies fail and we face the prospect of leaving behind what we have always known. He hears. He responds.

Do you have a relationship with God where you can tell Him the depths of your pain, how you feel about what is going on in your life?

Isaiah 40:6-31                                                    May 23

## Our Insignificance

"All flesh is grass...like the flower of the field...the flower fades because the breath of the Lord blows upon it...the people are grass...the grass withers. The nations are like a drop of a bucket, and are counted as the small dust of the balance. All nations before Him are as nothing, and vanity. The earth's inhabitants are like grasshoppers...The judges of the earth shall not take root in the earth, and He shall blow upon them, and they shall wither and the whirlwind shall take them away like stubble." That is who we are, as painful as it is to contemplate. We, who in our sin, are born thinking we are the center of the universe and who battle that belief throughout our lives, experience pain when we realize the truth of Isaiah 40.

Then there is the truth about Who God is: "He feeds His flock like a shepherd; He shall gather the lambs with His arm and carry them in His bosom, and shall gently lead those that are with young...He measured the waters in the hollow of His hand...It is He Who sits upon the circle of the earth...He brings princes to nothing...The everlasting God, the Lord, the Creator of the earth does not faint nor become weary. He gives power to the faint..." That is Who HE is.

In the pain of seeing who we are in relation to Who He is, there is boundless joy, for in our insignificance and helplessness He chooses to feed us, to gather us to Himself and gently lead us. He renews our strength. In Him and only in Him, "we shall mount up with wings like eagles; we shall run, and not be weary; and shall walk, and not faint"- all because He has chosen, in our insignificance, to make us significant, to make us His beloved.

As you ponder your insignificance, do you rejoice that despite it, He, the Creator, the Savior, has chosen you to come to Him and know Him intimately?

Isaiah 43                                                        May 24

## Passing through the Waters

Just as Israel was in need, so are we, in grave need. Israel needed Someone to make a path through the waters so they could escape their Egyptian captors. They needed Someone to protect them from the flames as they passed through the fire. They needed a Redeemer. So do we.

In Isaiah 43 God says these things to His people: I have redeemed you; I have called you by your name; You are mine; You are precious in My sight; You have been honored; I have loved you; I am with you.; I have formed everyone who is called by My name; I made him; I have created you for My glory; You are My witnesses; Besides Me there is no Savior; I make a way in the sea and a path through the mighty waters; I give waters in the wilderness and rivers in the desert; the people whom I have formed for Myself shall declare My praise. Think of it: He promises to be with us as we pass through the waters and the fire. He Who calls us by our name, Who specifically created us to bring Him glory, He Who made us to declare His praise and witness for Him, He will walk with us through whatever life brings.

Even in all these truths God says through Isaiah that Israel has burdened Him with their sins. They grew weary of Him, did not bring Him offerings or honor Him with sacrifices. Yet it is He Who stands ready to blot out their transgressions, to remember their sins no more.

What a God! He knows my name and calls me by it as He walks through the waters with me. When I fail Him He doesn't remember it. Thank You, Lord!

See Him walking through the waters with you, calling you by name, forgetting your sins as you confess them. Praise Him!

Isaiah 44                                                          May 25

## His Help

Verses 9-20 of Isaiah 44 once again show us ourselves in our natural state of attempting to be our own god. A man cuts down cedars for himself, plants a pine, uses it to warm himself or to bake bread. He makes a god and worships it, all in a vain attempt to meet his own needs. It does not work. Verse 20 says, "He feeds on ashes; A deceived heart has turned him aside; And he cannot deliver his soul…" At some point he realizes his emptiness. His eyes are shut and his heart cannot understand, says verse 18. What a deplorable condition.

We are helpless to meet our own needs. We were never intended to do so. Verse 2 says we were formed from the womb by the One Who will help us. He will pour water on us when we are thirsty and flood the dry ground for us. He tells us in verse 8 not to be afraid in our helplessness for we are His witnesses. Not only has He formed us but He "blots out like a thick cloud, our transgressions, and like a cloud, our sins". He hides them.

Trying to live our own lives apart from Him brings nothing but pain and misery. Not only do we make a mess of things, but our inner needs are not met. We are empty, lonely, always thrashing around looking for something to fill us, when all the time it is He Who waits to be invited in to do the filling. We are helpless without Him.

Do you truly understand and accept your helplessness? Do you see Him as the only One Who can help you?

Isaiah 48                                                    May 26

## The Furnace of Affliction

While much of our affliction comes because our world is fallen and full of sin, not at all the world that God created, and we as inhabitants of the world bear the natural results of the world, that is not the whole answer to why we suffer. Our own sin, others' sin, and Satan also contribute to our pain. Then there is affliction that God directly sends, tests, for His Own sake, as He says in Isaiah 48:10-11. In His testing, He is actually restraining Himself so that we are not cut off. It is also for our good as well as His glory. He is refining us in the furnace of affliction.

God is speaking of Israel in Isaiah 48 but, oh, how it applies to us as well. We are obstinate, our necks being like "iron sinew" and brows like "bronze", immovable, set on our own way. We don't hear, we don't know, our ears are not open to Him. We are transgressors from the womb. Our sin causes affliction to come into our lives. God allows and sometimes even prepares it to bring us to Himself, that He might be glorified. Even when He does this, He is most definitely holding back. If He were to pour out on us what our obstinance deserves, we would not have a chance.

The second half of this chapter declares Who God is, the First and also the Last. His hand has laid the foundation of the earth, and He commands the heavens. He loves His people, protects them and prospers them, even while bringing affliction when necessary. He sent His Son, our Redeemer, that we might live, that we should be led in the way we should go. Just as He sent the waters to flow from the rock for Israel, He pours His Spirit upon us that we might flourish for Him. Sometimes it takes affliction for us to really flourish.

When affliction comes, do you look for ways that God can use it in your life to refine you- for His honor and glory?

Isaiah 53                                                    May 27

## He Bore Our Grief

Our grief, sicknesses, insecurities, weaknesses, turmoil, pain, and sins have been exchanged for joy, health, security, strength, peace, wholeness, and forgiveness.  Only through Jesus can that happen.  He gave up all that He had with the Father in heaven so all of that exchange could occur.

Isaiah wrote about the birth, deity, ministry, death and future reign of Christ 700 years before Jesus' birth.  This 53rd chapter is amazing in its detail of what Jesus would endure in bearing our grief: despised and rejected of men; a Man of Sorrows and acquainted with grief; not esteemed; carrying our sorrows; wounded for our transgressions; bruised for our iniquities; given stripes so we could be healed; having the Lord lay on Him the iniquity of us all; oppressed; afflicted, yet not defending Himself by words or actions; cut off from the Father and everyone He knew; dying with the wicked; pouring out His soul as an offering for sin; interceding for us...

We pass over these truths quickly, too quickly, so as to avoid the pain of knowing what Jesus had to do to provide for us, to bring us into reconciliation with God.  Without what He did for us, there would be no hope.  We would be forever lost in our sins.  It is because of Him that I can sit with people and offer them hope as they fight the ravages of disease, the fear of impending death, the grief of a child in the clutches of devastating sin, the death of their closest relationship on earth, the grip of addiction, or whatever it is they are facing.  It is because of HIM that we have hope.  He bore our grief.

Whatever grief you are in today, Jesus bears it for you.  As you sit with Him, talk to Him and praise Him about that truth.

Isaiah 55:6-13 & 64:6-8                                         May 28

## The Potter and the Clay

Isaiah so clearly contrasts the differences between God and us. Our righteousness, our very best, are like filthy rags. We get carried away with our sins. We fade away as a leaf. Despite all the self-centered pride and arrogance of humans, that is who we are. We are as clay in His hands. He is the potter; we are the work of His hands. Without Him we are nothing, and our lives have no meaning. Humbling, yes, but glorious to think that despite being in filthy rags, He chose to clothe us with His righteousness. His desire is that we come to Him.

Despite who we are, He, the Holy One, can be found by us if we humble ourselves and seek Him. He has provided times for us that He can be found, times when He is near and we can call upon Him. We need to give up our ways and our thoughts and go to Him on His terms. We go to Him as we are but not any way we want.

His thoughts are not our thoughts nor our ways His ways. The first step to having a relationship with Him is to recognize that. I am in need, and only He has the answer to that need, Himself. The very heart of our sin, our pride and arrogance in ourselves, must be seen in light of His holiness and glory. He is the Potter; I am the clay being formed by Him. My very breath is provided by Him. Anything I accomplish is contingent on His allowing it and giving me the ability to do it. Anytime I approach Him, it is only because He has made it possible. He is God, and I am clearly not. That is the basis of our relationship.

Do you really see yourself as He does? Do you see yourself as the clay in His Hands?

Isaiah 64:4b &8, 65:17 &24, 66:18 May 29

## To Be Gathered by Him

Despite who we are and Who He is, God calls us to Himself to be redeemed by Him and to relate deeply to Him. He desires us to know Him through intimate fellowship, not just now, but in eternity. Isaiah 64:4b says that we have not heard or seen what He has prepared for those who wait for Him. Even though our righteousness is as filthy rags, as it says in verse 6, He has chosen to be our Father and to mold us for Himself. We are the work of His hands, both here and in eternity. Part of His plan for us is His creation of a new heaven and a new earth. We all have a tendency to cling to this life we know, but He tells us that we won't even remember it or think of it when He gathers us to the new one with Him. The things that are so troublesome here will not be present there. What WILL be present will be HIM, and He says before we call, He will answer, and while we are yet speaking, He will hear (Isaiah 65:24). We, as well as all nations and tongues, will come to see His glory. Imagine it.

We need to imagine it as we go through the pain and sorrow of this life. This truth of what is being prepared for us enables us to go on with courage and joy. When we are in the throes of mourning whatever it is that we have lost, we need to see Him in that day when He will gather us to Himself, to be with Him forever and enjoy all that He is. That truth will sustain us as we allow our pain to be used by Him in any way He chooses.

Picture that day when He will gather you to Himself and wipe away all your tears from your eyes.

Jeremiah 1                                                    May 30

## A Tough Call

Jeremiah, called "the weeping Prophet", was attacked by his own people for telling them of their impending captivity. Jeremiah 1:5 shows us God's call to Jeremiah: "Before He formed him in the womb, He knew him, sanctified him, set him apart, and ordained him as a prophet to the nations". He put His words in Jeremiah's mouth. He also tells Jeremiah that as he speaks the words to the people that he should not be dismayed at their faces- they aren't going to like it when he is telling them God's message of change and repentance. In verse 19 He further tells Jeremiah that they will fight against him but will not prevail because it is God Who has sent him. As he ministered to them, Jeremiah would weep profusely over the hardness of his people and the consequences of it in their lives.

This tough call to Jeremiah scared him. In verse 5 he cited his inability to speak because of his youth. God would have none of it, saying in verse 7: "You shall go to all to whom I send you and whatever I command you, you shall speak." He could say this to Jeremiah because He wasn't going to leave him to do it alone. "For I am with you to deliver you", He said. The Lord Himself touched his mouth, put in His words, and called him to "root out, to pull down, to throw down, to build and to plant (verse 16). Yes, a tough call, but Jeremiah would not do it alone.

When God calls us to difficult tasks, we do not do them alone: He will be there to deliver us, to empower us. Like Jeremiah, we SHOULD feel inadequate because we are. He is not.

Do you feel like the circumstances where God has placed you are too tough? If you said yes, that is a good thing. Then he can do His work through you. Let Him.

Jeremiah 2:8,13,32,35 & 5:3b,12,25b                    May 31

## Things that Do not Profit

The Israel to whom Jeremiah was called to minister was in big trouble. It is not difficult in these verses to see why. Jeremiah 2:8 says, "They walked after things that do not profit", not after the things of the Lord. The problem was that they knew better. God had given them, just as He does to us, everything they needed to live their lives for Him. In their case they were directly led by God. He gave them their land and the law. In our case we have His written Word and the Holy Spirit within us. Yet, we, like Israel, often insist on walking after things that do not profit. Jeremiah 2:13 says Israel forsook God, "the fountain of living waters," and made their own cisterns, broken ones that hold no water. How could trouble not ensue?   Jeremiah 2:32 is a very sad verse, "My people have forgotten Me days without number". May this not be said of us. Even in this state the children of Israel defend themselves, saying they are innocent, that there is no sin in them (2:35), and they have the audacity to plead their case before Him and question why He is angry with them. Again, do we see ourselves?

Jeremiah 5:3b says, even when God disciplines His people, they refuse to receive correction. They will not admit that when evil comes upon them that it is from the Lord, and due to their own sin (5:12). Scripture says they lied about Him. Jeremiah 25b says their sins have not only brought trouble to them but have caused the withholding of good. May it not be said of us.

See in these verses how God's people open themselves to unnecessary pain by walking toward things that do not profit and away from what a loving Lord wants to give.

Jeremiah 7:23, 6:10b &16, 8:6,12,15,18 June 01

## That It May Be Well With You

There is a very simple formula, found in Jeremiah 7:23, for your wellbeing: "Obey My voice, and I will be your God, and you shall be My people, and walk in all the ways that I have commanded you, that it may be well with you." He also tells us in 6:16 that when we walk in His way, we will find rest for our souls.

What we see in these passages, however, is a people who have no delight in His Word (6:10b), who turn to their own way (8:6). What is the result? Jeremiah 8:12 says they will look for peace but it will not come, for health, but they will receive trouble instead.

Jeremiah witnesses this in his people and so is sorrowful, and his heart is faint (8:18), knowing what lay ahead for them. They were a people so lost in their refusal to surrender to God that they no longer even blushed over their sinful ways (8:12). Jeremiah mourns because the people had been given all they needed to live lives of peace and contentment under their God, but they would not.

This reminds me of parents who give their children all they know so they can live productive and satisfying lives, but the children will not have it. Instead they choose ways that lead to chaos and trouble. How I see the pain etched on the faces of parents with these rebellious children. While the children of Israel caused much sorrow in the life of Jeremiah, how much more they caused to the Holy God, the One Who provided everything they needed for lives of joy and peace, but they would not.

Lord, may it never be said of us that we hurt You by refusing Your ways and choosing our own.

Jeremiah 9                                                    June 02

## Jeremiah's Lament

Jeremiah describes himself in Jeremiah 8:21 as being in mourning, being hurt for the hurt of his people. He wonders if there is no chance of recovery for them. He continues in chapter 9 to mourn as he contemplates their condition: adulterers, treacherous men, liars, going from one evil to the next, not knowing God, deceivers, slanderers. He is so distraught that he could weep day and night for them.

As I sit with people every day who are in various forms and stages of pain, God gives me compassion for them, but I find it difficult to "weep with those who weep" when they continually bring trouble on themselves because they will not bend to the Lordship of God. Jeremiah shows me here what it is to mourn for a stiff-necked people. As we look at people who know the truth and are not following it, there has to be something other than impatience and anger if we are going to help lead them to the place where God wants them to be. As we look at people who don't know the truth and are heading for not only lives of destruction here on earth but an eternity apart from God, there must be a sorrow so deep that we risk our own comfort and safety to tell them the truth. Jeremiah would suffer opposition and rejection, he would be beaten and put in stocks, he would be disgraced and imprisoned, he would have assassination attempts made on his life, he would be denied a wife and family, yet he persevered in the call God had given him because of his great love and compassion for the people. He saw them as God did. May we see those around us as He does.

Do you mourn as Jeremiah did over the condition of people around you? Will you talk to God about how He wants you to minister to them?

Jeremiah 15:15-21                                          June 03

## God Lifts Up

Jeremiah expresses how dejected he is in chapter 15 of his writing, regretting that he was even born. He is at odds with the whole earth, totally alone. While false prophets have told the people what they want to hear, Jeremiah has told them the truth and has therefore been rejected. Even in his pain of being lonely and mistreated, he remembers how God has called him (verse 16). He knew that it was God Who gave him the words to speak and those words, while not accepted by the people, were a joy and cause of rejoicing to him, because they were from God. While he sits alone, however, his pain is also real. It continues and seems incurable to him. He knows the truth that God has called him to this difficult task of telling people what they won't accept but at the same time, in his loneliness, he is feeling abandoned, even by God, even asking Him in verse 18 if He too will fail him.

Just as with us, God knew every thought and emotion that was going on in Jeremiah. He knew he needed to be lifted up, and lifting up is what God does with him, reassuring him in verses 19-23. First, He shows Jeremiah Himself. This is always what we need in our discouragement: to see Him. He shows Jeremiah a God Who speaks to and through him, a God Who can and will save him, Who will deliver him and redeem him. He then shows him a picture of the people, a people who fight against the truth and all that is right, a stubborn and rebellious people, a people who will not listen. He lets Jeremiah know that how he sees the people is how God sees them also. Then He shows Jeremiah victory: He can and will overcome. "I will deliver you. I will redeem you." What a beautiful picture of God giving His servant just what he needs.

In your times of discouragement, of feeling alone and mistreated, let God show you His truth- and Himself.

Jeremiah 16                                                June 04

## Jeremiah's Loneliness

Besides being rejected and mistreated by the people he longed to lead back to the Lord, Jeremiah was instructed by God to take no wife and to have no family. We can guess that they would be hard words for Jeremiah to hear. It is difficult to understand, but God was showing His love for His Prophet, protecting him from future sorrow which would encompass the people born in that place.

Being without a spouse and family is one of the great sorrows I see in people regularly, particularly young women. Unfortunately, I have seen some of them, tired of waiting on God and anxious that He may not come through in the way they think He should, make grave mistakes and pay for them for the reminder of their lives. I have seen others wait for God's best and be rewarded for their trust in Him. Then I have seen still others to whom God gave another plan, not including a spouse and family. That is painful for those who had always dreamt of family life for themselves, but in their disappointment is always the potential for growth, a greater communion with God, and an opportunity to serve Him in ways they otherwise could not. We can also assume that in some cases, it is God's protection for them. God has given me 26 years of widowhood. I can say with no hesitation that I know God at a much deeper level than I would if I had my husband to rely on. It is probable that the counseling I have done for 20 years would not have taken place, nor would I be writing this. These 26 years have been painful, sometimes full of sorrow, often lonely, on occasion frightening, but in those times was the opportunity to cling to God and see what He would do. It was always beyond my imagination.

Jeremiah 16:21 says God would cause them to know His hand and His might. I have seen it. In His loneliness and rejection, so has Jeremiah.

Whatever your marital status, and whatever it might be in the future, will you commit it and accept it from God, trusting Him that even though it may be painful at times, it is for good?

Jeremiah 17:5-18                                                  June 05

## Trusting in Man

Since God made us first and foremost to relate to Him, nothing else is going to work in bringing satisfaction and fullness into our lives. Even trusting in good things and putting them before the Lord will result in destruction.

In Jeremiah 17:5 God says that a person is cursed when he trusts in man. He is like a shrub in the desert and won't even recognize good. It is like living in a parched place in the wilderness where there is nothing.

Co-dependence is a common malady seen in counseling offices. It is a person, often a wife, attaching herself to her husband in an unhealthy way, making him the center of her life to the extent that all her thoughts and actions are about making him into what she wants him to be, while at the same time not dealing with herself. She wraps herself in him, while he himself is dependent on something else in his life. While the husband-wife relationship is one of the main blessings God has given us, even this we, in our self-centered sin, can destroy. Co-dependence can and does occur in other relationships as well and always leaves one empty and frustrated.

On the other hand the man or woman who trusts in the Lord is like a tree planted by the waters with its roots spread out. Its leaves are green, there is continual fruit, and there is no concern of drought, but God goes on to say in verse 9 that the heart is deceitful above all things and desperately wicked. There is deceit in co-dependence. It may look like a good, loving thing to care for another person, but when he or she is placed before God, it cannot be good. When it is about control and attempting to get our own needs met in the other person while neglecting our own self, it brings desolation as described in verse 6.

He is to be our praise (verse 14). If he heals us, we shall be healed. He is our hope.

Ask God today as you sit with Him if you are depending on anything before Him. Remember, we are deceitful by nature, so listen to Him carefully.

Jeremiah 20 June 06

## Jeremiah's Discouragement

In chapter 20 of his writing, we are given the privilege of seeing into the heart of Jeremiah, one of God' great servants. He proceeds from complaining to God at the beginning of the chapter, then to praising Him, and finally to cursing the day he was born. He shows us discouragement.

Jeremiah prophesies calamity for Israel because they had forsaken God. God had told him that the catastrophe would be so great that whoever heard of it would find his ears tingling. Everyone who saw the desolation would be astonished. This doom is what Jeremiah reported to his people, and because of it, we find in 20:2 that he is struck and put in stocks- simply for telling the truth in an effort to save his people. When he is released what does he tell Israel's priest? He will go into captivity in Babylon, will die and be buried there with all his friends to whom he has prophesied lies. Jeremiah continues to give out the unwanted Word of God for the good of the people, and for that, is mocked and held in derision and reproach daily. The treatment against him was so distressful at one point that he decided he would just be quiet and not speak in God's name. Of course he found that to be impossible since God's Word burned in his heart- He HAD to give it out, once again bringing on Himself the wrath of the people.

In verse 11 he moves from discouragement to praise, turning his eyes from his situation to God, seeing Him as mighty and awesome, One Who sees the heart and mind of His people. He pours himself out to His God, knowing He will prevail, no matter what he sees going on around him.

Despite his seeing God, the chapter ends with his eyes back on his situation and in his discouragement, wishing he had not been born to endure the shame he is going through. We see him being real before God. We see and understand his pain.

In your pain and discouragement, talk to God, be real with Him, but also see HIM, see Who He is and what He can do in your life.

Jeremiah 29                                                    June 07

## God's Thoughts for Us

Israel has been carried away captive into Babylon, and the captivity is going to go on for 70 years. Jeremiah 29 is a letter Jeremiah writes to them in this dark hour. They are in the position they are in because of their sin of refusing to heed God's very clear words and of carrying out disgraceful acts just like their pagan neighbors, acts such as adultery and speaking lying words in God's name (verse 23). What hope could Israel have in their situation?

Their hope lay in a merciful, loving God, albeit a Holy God whose character also demands obedience. Israel deserves all that has come before them and more, but even in this, God promises to visit them after the 70 years in Babylon, and "perform His good Word toward them" (verse 10), and cause them to come back to Jerusalem. What follows are much-loved verses, Jeremiah 29:11-14: "For I know the thoughts I think toward you, says the Lord, thoughts of peace and not of evil, to give you a future and a hope. Then you will call upon Me and go and pray to Me and I will listen to you. And you will seek Me and find Me when you search for Me with all your heart. I will be found by you, says the Lord, and I will bring you back from your captivity."

Even in their blatant and despicable sin, God's character causes Him to reach out to them once more, to offer them Himself and all the peace that He can supply. His thoughts for them have never been anything other than that. If they call on Him, He will still listen even after all they have done against Him.

In whatever captivity we are in, whether of our own making or not, His thoughts always remain for us. His desire is for peace for us, peace which can only come from Him. If we seek Him we will find Him, in whatever circumstances we find ourselves. He wants to bring us back from our captivity, to Himself.

Talk to the Lord about what is holding you captive, what is keeping you from His peace. Remember His thoughts for you, and seek Him with your whole heart.

Jeremiah 31:1-20                                                   June 08

## Joy Replaces Sorrow

God's people have experienced great sorrow, including captivity and temporary distance from God, but just like us, when we need to be disciplined for our sin, His plan is always restoration. From the time of Adam and Eve, when their willful disobedience drove them from God, He had a plan in place to bring them back to intimate relationship with Himself. That plan was and is Jesus. Jeremiah 31:3 & 4 tells us why: "I have loved you with an everlasting love; Therefore with loving kindness I have drawn you. Again I will build you, and you shall be rebuilt...And you shall go forth in the dances of those who rejoice." There will be a time of singing with gladness, a shouting of joy, a giving of praise, of God gathering His people as a Shepherd does His flock, a redeeming of His people, a streaming to the goodness of the Lord, a watering of their souls, and a time of no more sorrow. Verse 13 says He will turn mourning to joy, and will comfort and replace sorrow with rejoicing. What a picture of a loving God.

Just as Israel had to suffer much before all of this would come about, so do we, and one of the reasons is found in Jeremiah 31:14b: They, just like we, are not satisfied with His goodness. We, like Israel, go seeking other things, illegitimate things than can never meet our needs, and we, like them, bring suffering to ourselves. In that day, God says, "My people shall be satisfied with My goodness." May it be true of us today.

As you spend time with him today, agree with Him that He is Who you need. He is enough. It is for Him that our hearts yearn.

Jeremiah 32:16-44                                              June 09

## Is There Anything Too Hard for Him?

Some of the situations I see people in are such tangled webs that in myself I can see no solutions or good outcomes. How do you rectify years of alcoholism, multiple marriages, infidelities, situations where children don't know who their parents are, neglect and abuse, mountains of debt, broken health from sinful living... We cannot. God can. He says, "I am the Lord, the God of all flesh; Is there anything too hard for Me?" (Jeremiah 32:27).

Jeremiah makes the same statement of God in Jeremiah 32:17 as he prays to Him. At this point Jeremiah is in prison, and Jerusalem has been overtaken by the army of Babylon. Jeremiah was imprisoned by the king of Judah for prophesying their nation's captivity. As Jeremiah sat in prison, while God's people refused to heed the truth given by God, he prays, "You have made the heaven and the earth by Your great power and outstretched arm, and there is nothing too hard for You." He recounts Who the Lord is and what He has done: shown loving-kindness to thousands; is great in counsel and mighty in work; has His eyes open upon all the ways of men; has shown signs and wonders; has given His people a name; has brought them out of Egypt; has given them a land. Now, though, His people find themselves, due to their own sinful choices, in what looks like impossible circumstances. God reminds them Who He is and that He can handle the impossible. He will bring them out to safety once again, they will be His people, and He will be their God, just as He promised.

Whatever is going on in your life right now, remember the truth, "Nothing is too hard for God." He can unravel it and bring you to a place of safety where you can be His person, and He will be your God.

Will you let Him?

Lamentations 1                                                   June 10

## God Cries

Through the remainder of the Book of Jeremiah, the prophet faithfully continues to proclaim the Word of the Lord while God's people just as faithfully refuse to listen and follow, resulting in the fall of Jerusalem and their being carried away captive into Babylon. Jeremiah suffered greatly through all of his dealings with the people, being imprisoned and at one point being cast by ropes into a dungeon where he spent days sunk in the mire with no food or water.

Much like Psalms gives us intimate insight into the heart of David, the Book of Lamentations allows us to see the deep pain and hurt Jeremiah has for the people in their exile and self-destruction. The book is a cry for what they had brought on themselves. It can be looked on as God's lament as well. Just as Jeremiah weeps, I believe God weeps also. Like the prodigal father, God waits for His people to return to Him, but in the waiting, He must witness their suffering, brought on by their own sin.

I see the pain parents go through when their children choose sin instead of their Godly direction. How much more painful it must be for the Holy, Perfect God, Who paid so much for the redemption of the people He loves, when they refuse to receive it. Lamentations 1:16 says, "My children are desolate." What is more painful to witness than that? Jeremiah also says in Lamentations 1:12, "Is there any sorrow like my sorrow?" This very day I sat with a dear woman whose daughter is "desolate", choosing to live on the streets, rather than under the loving care of a mother who cries in pain for the condition of her daughter. This is a sorrow that God recognizes well.

Oh, Lord, let us not be a people who bring suffering to You. Let us seek Your loving Arms and Your ways.

Are you careful to bring no pain to God in your relationship with Him?

Do you lament for God's people who bring pain on themselves by refusing to obey Him?

Lamentations 3                                                    June 11

## It's About the Truth

Despite his anger at his people for their disobedience and the destruction it brought , Jeremiah intercedes for them before God. In chapter 3:22-23 we see his hope, but before that, he acknowledges and expresses his pain in verse 1-19. He feels like God's hand has been turned against him, he has aged from his grief, he feels he has been set in the dark with bitterness surrounding and filling him, his ways are blocked, his paths crooked, he feels desolate, bent low, his soul is far from peace, he has no strength or hope- until he remembers the truth about God. Until verse 20 it is about his feelings, but after that it is about his thinking, about the truth.

Even though he feels abandoned, rejected, and desolate, without hope, he knows that is not true. When he brings the truth to mind, then he begins to have hope. His hope comes from the truth of Who God is: merciful; compassionate; faithful; steadfast; good to those who wait for Him, to those who seek Him. Yes, He caused grief but not willingly, as He says in verse 30. He will not cast off His people forever. The grief He causes is for their good, to bring them back to Himself, the place of peace and safety.

Even though Jeremiah's eyes "overflow with rivers of water for the destruction of the daughter of my people" (verse 48), he has hope when he fixes his vision on Who God is: "Through the Lord's mercies we are not consumed, because His compassions fail not. They are new every morning, great is your faithfulness" (verse 22,23).

We acknowledge and express our feelings because they give us information, and we are called to share our selves, but we live on the truth of Who God is.

Are you driven by your feelings or by the truth of Who God is?

Ezekiel 3                                                                  June 12

## Leave the Results to Him

I have seen great discouragement when people give witness to God's truth but their intended recipients will not hear.   A principle I must employ in counseling is: I give the truth of God's Word to the best of my ability, as He makes it clear to me, and then I leave the outcome to Him.  That is also a principle used by Campus Crusade in their witnessing materials.  We take the initiative to present the truth, trust the Holy Spirit to do His work, and leave the results to Him.  We must do our part, but we can't do God's, and He won't do ours.  If we understand that, we may be sad if a person doesn't receive the truth, but we will not take defeat and discouragement upon ourselves, but will remain hopeful, knowing God is able.

The Book of Ezekiel begins with God giving a call to Ezekiel as he and his nation were exiles in Babylon: "Go to My stubborn and impudent people and say, Thus says the Lord God.  He who hears, let him hear, and he who refuses, let him refuse, for they are a rebellious house" (Ezekiel 3:27).  In other words, Ezekiel was to hear God's words, deliver them to his people, and that would be the end of his responsibility.  The people would then decide what they would do with the truth.  "Whether they hear or whether they refuse" is repeated several times in this chapter.  That was to be of no concern to Ezekiel.  The responsibility God gave him was to "eat the scroll", to take in God's Words and then go to the house of Israel.  God even forewarned Ezekiel that the people would not listen to him just as they would not listen to God.  He also warns Ezekiel not to be afraid of them, of their words, or of their looks because what he is giving them is from God.  If he simply fulfills the responsibility God has given him and leaves the remainder to God, he will be right before God, and there is no need for anxiety or discouragement.

How are you at doing what God calls you to do and then leaving the results to Him?

Ezekiel 7 & 11:16 & 12:15                                                    June 13

## A Sanctuary

God declares in Ezekiel 4 that He will bring judgment on His nation for their disobedient ways. He says they will not be spared nor will He have pity on them because they need to know that He is the Lord (7:4). That is why He does what He does- so that all will know that He is the Lord. Ezekiel 12:15 says "So they shall know that I am the Lord, when I shall scatter them among the nations, and disperse them in the countries". To know Who He is, is in the very best interest of every person. It is why we were created. A person who does not know that, will always remain empty and dissatisfied, apart from God. God is always about revealing Himself. Only He can fully satisfy our deepest need. He is willing to bring hurt to His people so they will be broken enough to see Him.

Verse 19 of Ezekiel 7 talks about how silver and gold will not deliver the people from their need, nor will it satisfy their souls, nor fill their stomach. Only HE can do that. Man continually seeks peace but none will be found except in HIM. He calls Himself a sanctuary where His people can come and find what they need (11:16).

Adversities and suffering come from various sources, but when God directly sends them, it is always so He can be seen, so that we will know that He is the Lord. It is an opportunity to be reconciled to Him, to know Him, our Sanctuary, from all the strivings and emptiness that surround us. It is an opportunity to see HIM.

Is He your Sanctuary?

In your next trial, will you say to yourself, "This is an opportunity to go to my Sanctuary and see Him more fully, to know that He is the Lord"?

Ezekiel 18 June 14

## Blaming Our Fathers

In Israel there was a proverb that said,: "The fathers have eaten sour grapes, and the children's teeth are set on edge." The saying was a way of blaming their problems on their fathers. In Ezekiel 18:3 God tells them He doesn't want them using this proverb anymore. Each person is responsible for how he is going to live, and the choices he makes will determine his outcome. Verse 20 says, "The soul that sins, it shall die. The son shall not bear the iniquity of the father, neither shall the father bear the iniquity of the son; the righteousness of the righteous shall be upon him, and the wickedness of the wicked shall be upon him." Verse 31 says we are to cast away our sins and have a new heart and a new spirit. For us, that means allowing Jesus' blood to cover our sins and accepting Him into our lives.

It is not unusual to see people who blame their backgrounds for the messes of their lives today. Surely, as children, they had little choice other than to be impacted by what was going on around them, and God knows every detail of it. However, there comes a time when God makes Himself known to us, and we make a choice to allow Him to cleanse us and renew us, or to continue in the pain and dysfunction. Accepting Jesus means all the transgressions we have done will not be mentioned to us, and we shall live (verse 22). We don't all begin on a level playing field, but we have the opportunity to end on one, through Jesus' work on the cross. Blaming someone else for our messes only enables us to stay in them. Jesus came that we might have life and have it more abundantly. We have a choice.

Sit with God and talk to Him about the things in your background that have negatively impacted you. Give them to Him, and let Him use them for good.

Ezekiel 24:15-27                                                        June 15

## Don't Mourn?

The message throughout Scripture has been that there is much suffering in the world, and we need to acknowledge it, express it, trust God in it, and allow Him to redeem it. Giving our pain over to Him is an opportunity to know Him at a level that we otherwise would not. Here, however, in Ezekiel 24, God tells Ezekiel that a major loss is about to take place in his life and he is not to mourn. The desire of Ezekiel's eyes, his wife, is going to die and the instructions from God are: "You shall neither mourn nor weep, nor shall your tears run down. Sigh in silence, make no mourning for the dead." Essentially he was simply to go on with life. The sorrowful prophet, whose life is a continual ball of pain as he contemplates the condition of his people, is told not to sorrow when one of the greatest losses of life assails him. Why could that be?

His lack of mourning was to be a picture to his people of what would come into their lives as they continued down their path of rebellion. God wanted to get His people's attention. It worked. When they saw Ezekiel the morning after his wife's death, going about business as usual, they asked, "Will you not tell us what these things signify to us, that you behave so?" They were ready to hear what the cause of this strange behavior was. Finally Ezekiel was then able to give them the message that the desire of their eyes, the delight of their souls, their children, would also perish, and they would not be allowed to weep either but would pine away in their iniquities (verse 23). Ezekiel was a sign to them of things to come, and that when they would come to pass "they would know that He is the Lord God."

Do you agree with God that what He allows in your life is so "that you may know?"

Ezekiel 34                                                        June 16

## The True Shepherd

The leaders, the shepherds of Israel, did not feed the flock, did not strengthen the weak, did not heal the sick, did not bind up the broken, did not bring back what was driven away, did not seek the lost, and so the sheep scattered. God tells Ezekiel that He holds the shepherds accountable for feeding themselves rather than feeding His people, and He Himself will take over the shepherding. HE will search for His sheep and seek them out, deliver them from captivity and gather them to their land, feed the hungry, give the weary rest, bind up the broken, strengthen what was sick, give the unprotected and fearful safety, and give the undirected guidance. There will be showers of blessing for them, and they will know that He is the Lord and that they are His people. Verse 31 says, "You are My flock, the flock of My pasture; you are men, and I am your God."

Because of their continual sin, God's people were scattered and had no sense of belonging. The need to belong is a basic human need. God put us in families, ordained the church community, and draws us to intimate relationship with Him to meet that need. Israel resisted. We resist. Then we wonder, as Israel did, why we feel lonely, separated, not fulfilled. There is a Shepherd longing to gather us to Himself to do all the things for us that the Shepherd says He will do for Israel in Ezekiel 34- to feed us, give us rest, seek us when we are lost, bring us back to Himself, bind us when we are broken, strengthen us when we are sick, give us safety when we are afraid, shower us with blessing, and show us that He is our God.

Will you let Him?

Ezekiel 37:1-14                                           June 17

## Dry Bones

The Lord showed Ezekiel a valley filled with dry bones, which was a picture of Israel dead in their sins, without life or breath, lost, cut off. God tells Ezekiel to prophesy, to tell the dry bones, Israel, to hear His Word. The bones come together; sinews, flesh and skin cover the bones. Then again when Ezekiel prophesies to the breath, breath comes upon them so there is life. God's message to His people in Ezekiel 37:12 is: "I will open your graves and cause you to come up from your graves and bring you into the land of Israel." What is the reason for this? Verse 13 says once again, "Then you shall know that I am the Lord, when I have opened your graves". Verse 14 continues, "I will put My Spirit in you and you shall live, and I will place you in your own land. Then you shall know…"

When we don't hear the Lord, we are like dry bones, without life, lost, cut off. It brings misery. God has provided two main ways for us to hear Him, the written Word of God and His Spirit Who comes to dwell within us at salvation. We too often neglect both. When I ask people how they spend time with God, they often say they listen to Christian music, pray when they drive to work, or watch television pastors. They neglect God's Word. How can we know Who He is and how we are to relate to Him, how we are to live, without His Word?

Many of us don't realize or draw upon the Power that is within us, the Holy Spirit. He directs, convicts, illuminates the Word, comforts, empowers. He brings life to the dry bones. We cannot be cut off or have lost hope when we have Him. We have the opportunity to live, to really live, as God intended. As we open ourselves to the Word and the Spirit, we, like Israel, will know that He is God.

Covenant with God to allow His Word and His Spirit to bring life to the "dry bones" in you.

Daniel 1 & 2                                      June 18

## No Need to Panic

When King Nebuchadnezzar of Babylon took captive God's people, Daniel was one of the choice young men who found himself in that foreign land. Because he was highly gifted, he was taken to the King's palace to be taught the ways of the Chaldeans and to serve them. Daniel quickly distinguished himself, even as a youth, as a man of principle. He was a captive but even so would not defile himself or go against his principles in the area of food and drink. Because he was respectful, as well as wise, he was able to negotiate with his captors and protect his values and convictions, even while working from a position of servitude.

Soon a second crisis entered Daniel's life. King Nebuchadnezzar had troubling dreams and demanded to have them interpreted. None of the "wise" men in the land were able to do so, resulting in some deaths. Daniel and his friends were next on the list, so Daniel asked the King for some time to find the interpretation. He went to his three companions and asked them to seek the Lord concerning the meaning of the dream, so they might live. We read in Daniel 2:19: "Then the secret was revealed to Daniel in a night vision". Look at Daniel's response to God. He praises Him, citing His wisdom and might, noting how He was the One Who removes kings and raises them up, gives wisdom and knowledge, and reveals deep and secret things, which He had just done. He said to God in verse 23: "You have now made known to me what we asked of You".

Daniel was in a very tight spot, facing imminent death, but we see nothing of panic in him. He gathers information, uses his wisdom, and more importantly, asks his friends to seek God. Right there is why he saw no need for panic- He knew God was in control of all of it. He simply needed to submit himself to Him.

In a situation that could produce panic, do you remain calm, knowing God knows every detail that is happening and is ultimately in charge?

Daniel 3                                                            June 19

## But If Not....

All seems to be going well for Daniel and his three friends after Daniel interprets King Nebuchadnezzar's dream.  The King recognizes God as "the God of gods, the Lord of kings and a revealer of secrets".  Daniel, Shadrach, Meshach and Abed-nego are given gifts and placed in positions of power.

However, we soon find in Daniel 3 that Nebuchadnezzar decides to make an image of gold and requires that all peoples, nations and languages bow down to it when they hear the sound of music.  Whoever disobeys is to be cast immediately into a burning, fiery furnace.  Since Shadrach, Meshach, and Abed-nego refuse, they are brought before the king, who asks them who the God is who will deliver them from his hands.  They tell him.  "Our God Whom we serve is able to deliver us from the furnace, and He will deliver us from your hand, O King, but if not, let it be known to you, O King, that we do not serve your gods, nor will we worship the gold image which you have set up".  "Even if He doesn't deliver us".....That is Who their God is, One whom they could trust in any situation, no matter the consequence for them.

After they are cast into the exceedingly hot furnace, Nebuchadnezzar sees four men, walking, unharmed, and recognizes One as the Son of God.  When he calls to the three to come out, not even the smell of fire is on them.  He blesses their God and makes a new decree that anyone who even speaks against their God would be destroyed.  The three young men are also promoted in the kingdom.

Shadrach, Meshach, and Abed-nego faced a crisis: bow down or die an excruciating death.  They won the victory because they knew their God, knew His capabilities, His attributes, and His character.  They also knew His sovereignty, the fact that His will reigns, so they did not presume to know what He would do.  They simply trusted Him no matter what the outcome, knowing He would act in their best interest, just as He always had.

When you expect God to do a certain thing, do you also say, "But even if You don't, I will trust in You, knowing You have my best and Your glory in mind?"

Daniel 4                                                            June 20

## Loss Shows Us God

King Nebuchadnezzar was the epitome of pride, arrogance, and self-centeredness, yet God had a plan for him, a plan that involved faithful young men like Daniel and the three who were willing to go into a fiery furnace, rather than bow to a false God.

The King had a second dream which he called on Daniel to interpret, knowing he could, "for the Spirit of the Holy God is in you," he said. The interpretation was that Nebuchadnezzar would be driven away from men, dwell with the beasts of the field, eat grass like an animal, be wet with heaven's dew until he would "know that the Most High rules in the kingdom of men and gives it to whomever He chooses". His kingdom would be taken away but would be restored when "he came to know that heaven rules." This great king had to know that God was God, and he was not.

God goes to great lengths to show us Who He is and what He requires of us. At the end of Nebuchadnezzar's time in the fields, he lifted his eyes to heaven and blessed the Most High, praised and honored Him, seeing Him as He is (verses 34 &35). This one who ruled many people had to relinquish his control and power, and submit to the One Who is in actual control. His arrogant heart had to learn humility and submission. That must have been a painful experience for him, but how great were the rewards. He saw God, recognized His awesome majesty and saw himself in need of Him. The difficulties we go through can do that for us, if we are willing to have a teachable spirit.

In your losses do you look to God?

Do you make an effort to see who you are?

Daniel 4                                                    June 21

## Nebuchadnezzar's Losses

The proud and arrogant King Nebuchadnezzar came to the place of praising and honoring God, but that only came about because God severely humbled him. God gave him a dream, which Daniel interpreted for him. The dream, which came to fruition, was that he would be driven from men and would dwell and eat with the beasts of the field. Through that experience he would come to "know that the Most High rules in the kingdom of men" and chooses whom He will. It took a season of having his kingdom taken from him as well as his very reason, to see that God is God, and he was not. He moved from creating a 90-foot-high golden "god" whom he demanded that everyone worship, to declaring, "I praise and extol and honor the King of Heaven, all of Whose works are truth, and His ways justice. And those who walk in pride He is able to put down". Nebuchadnezzar knew that well. He had just experienced it in a remarkable way.

For some people it takes a dramatic experience for them to see God as He is. God may have to remove things in their lives that mean too much to them, things that get in the way of their seeing the most important thing, their need for HIM. Loss has to occur, and it is painful but so worth the end result. For Nebuchadnezzar it was a small thing to lose all he had, including his mental capacities, and to live with the animals, in order to come into relationship with God, the reason for which he was created.

Whatever the loss in our lives, if it brings us into a saving knowledge of Jesus, and an intimate relationship with Him, it is worth the pain, worth the suffering, to get us to see our need for Him and Him alone.

Can you say that you would be willing to give up everything for a deeper relationship with Jesus?

Daniel 6                                                      June 22

## Facing the Lions

Nebuchadnezzar's son, Belshazzar, was "weighed in the balance and found wanting" so God had his kingdom divided and given to the Medes and Persians. Darius, the Mede, ruled and placed Daniel in an exalted position, causing other leaders to look for a fault in him. They found none, so their plan then became one of manipulating King Darius into making a law with which they knew Daniel could not and would not comply. The decree said that any person who petitioned any god or man for 30 days would be cast into a den of lions. It was Daniel's long established custom to kneel before the Lord three times a day in his upper room with his windows open toward Jerusalem. Of course, his accusers were delighted to go before the king and demand that he honor his own law. King Darius was upset with himself that he had been tricked into this position and sought to deliver Daniel but could not rescind what he had decreed. When he sent Daniel into the den, he said, "Your God, Whom you serve continually, He will deliver you"(verse 16). The king fasted all night and was unable to sleep, so great was his concern for the worthy Daniel. He hurried early in the morning to discover Daniel's fate, and was exceedingly glad to find him unharmed (verse 23).

While Darius spent a night of anxiety, we do not read that this was the case with Daniel. "He believed in God, " says verse 23. It would seem that he expected nothing else than to be delivered. It would also seem that he would agree with his three friends that even if that were not God's plan, Daniel would still choose to worship the true God in the way He commands, no matter the consequences.

Do you have the resolve of Daniel, Meshach, Shadrach, and Abed-nego that no matter the outcome, you will worship God?

Daniel 7:15, 8:17,27, 9:3-19 &10                                    June 23

## Truth Brings Grief

God communicated with Daniel through visions, particularly visions about what would come to pass in the end times. We may think that would be a desired experience, but it says in Daniel 7:15 that Daniel was grieved in his spirit and his body, and the visions of his head troubled him. Daniel desired insight concerning these visions and asked for an explanation of them, again something that seems like a privilege. The result of the "privilege" is found in 8:27, "And I, Daniel, fainted and was sick for days", astonished by what he saw. While he was seeking the vision and Gabriel was giving it to him, we read in 8:17 that he was afraid and fell on his face to the ground. It was a fearful thing for Daniel to receive the truth of what would be from the holy God. Daniel's response was that "I set my face toward the Lord God to make request by prayer and supplication, with fasting, sackcloth, and ashes." He mourned, prayed and confessed, seeing himself and his people as they were: disobedient, wicked, and rebellious, and God as He is: great, awesome, forgiving, faithful, and loving. He intercedes for his people before this great and mighty God Who had just shown him a vision of the end times. He was so affected by what he saw that we read later in chapter 10 that he mourned three full weeks, eating no pleasant food, only what he needed to sustain himself. While he was in a deep sleep with his face to the ground, in his state of deep mourning, he was touched by a hand and told not to fear. Since he had "set his heart to understand" and humbled himself before God, his words were heard, and he was ministered to by an angel from God. He had been overwhelmed by sorrow, devoid of all strength by what he was told would come to his people, but he was revived by the touch God sent him.

If we are listening to God, we may be overwhelmed, even dismayed at times, but also with the knowledge that He also sends us His touch and ministrations to deal with His touch.

Are you really seeking God, even seeking those truths that are troubling and cause you grief?

Lorraine Brosious

**Hosea 1:2-8, 2:13, 19-23**                                                    **June 24**

## God's Pain

The prophet, Hosea, was called by God to suffer much, both in his personal life with an adulterous wife and in his public life of delivering an unpopular message to a rebellious people. He was called to live what God was living, rejection, both by the people they so deeply loved. Hosea's experience with a harlot for a wife was a picture of the unfaithfulness of God's people in their relationship with Him. Hosea's suffering is a demonstration of God's suffering. This book shows how both continue to love and seek back the ones who have left them.

In chapter 1 Hosea is called by God to marry Gomer, a harlot, and have three children with her. What a call! Hosea nevertheless obeyed, knowing his life did not belong to himself but to God. He was willing to live a life of continual pain and rejection in order to be a living metaphor of God continuing to love His people, despite their repeated offenses against Him. Hosea 2:13b shows the hurt of God: "She went after her lovers; But Me she forgot". To be forgotten by the one you love….What is more painful than that? Yet, Hosea stayed with Gomer, just as God stayed with Israel, saying in 2:19, "I will betroth you to Me forever".

It is not difficult to envision the pain that Hosea must have felt in his situation, but we don't often think of how the Lord suffers pain. He Who is love longs to give it, yet it will not be received. He longs to protect His people, but they will not be protected by Him. Whatever He offers, while always meant for their good, is rejected.

Hosea knew God's pain. May we seek to be a delight to God, not a contributor to more sorrow for Him.

Consider how God feels pain and sorrow when we are not in the relationship with Him that He so desires.

Be aware that God, Who suffers much from His people, understands our suffering.

Hosea 4                                                                    June 25

## Destroyed for Lack of Knowledge

Hosea presents a picture of what life will be like for Israel if they continue in their adulterous ways: "the land will mourn; and everyone who dwells there will waste away" (Hosea 4:3). He says in verse 6 that they will be destroyed for lack of knowledge because they have rejected it. Their glory that God intended for them will be changed to shame. God had repeatedly given them the truth of what He expected of them through the law and the prophets, but they had refused it, not taken it in, resulting in their destruction. Hosea 4:14 says, "people who do not understand will be trampled". We also have access to the truth, through Scripture and through the Holy Spirit Who dwells within us when we are saved. Yet I see so many people living destructive lives due to lack of receiving knowledge. They do not seek it or have seen it but have rejected it. There is no way to be pleasing to God without diligently seeking Him and His truth through His Word. I often hear the excuse, "I don't understand it". And they never will until they covenant with God to sit before Him daily and allow Him to illuminate it for them. That is one of the tasks of His Holy Spirit. A book is read one page at a time. Begin to read His Word, diligently seeking His truth, and He will show you. People's lives are destroyed for lack of knowledge. It was true in Hosea's day, and it is just as true today. We can't know how to live nor can we truly know God without seeking Him through the written Word, which He so graciously gave us. After being given His truth, then we need to accept it and live in it.

Sit with God right now and make a promise to Him that you will get into His Word on a daily basis and seek His truth.

You can trust Him to make it clear to you.

Hosea 7 & 14                                                June 26

## The Pain of Confrontation

Hosea confronts.  He confronts because, despite the gross sin of the people, he loves them.  They, however, do not like being confronted.  I know few people who do.  Good confrontation has as its goal, restoration, and comes from a heart of love.  Through the remaining chapters of Hosea he continues to present the gravity of Israel's sin, using words like "lies", "the evil of their deeds", "disobedience", "loving idols", "backsliding".  In showing them the results of their sin, he says God will spread His net on them, will bring them down, will bereave them of their children, will cast them out, and make them wanderers.

Fortunately the Book of Hosea ends with Israel's restoration, always God's intention.  His goal is always reconciliation to Himself.  Despite His people's sin and the necessity of rebuke and painful consequences, HE remains a loving God.  He says in Hosea 11:9, "I am God and not man".  His sympathy is stirred (11:8).  He says in 13:4 that He is their God, and they shall know no God but Him.  There is no Savior besides Him.  Even though they suffer destruction, their help is from Him and He will be their King (13:19).  The final chapter of Hosea ends with a call for them to return to Him and also with a promise that He will heal their backsliding and love them freely.  If they return, He says, He will be like the dew to them and will grow them like a lily.

Because of Who He is, God cannot allow their sin to go unchallenged.  His character requires that it be confronted so they have an opportunity to repent of it and return to Him.  His unbounding love is shown in His unwillingness to allow them to go on sinning.  It is in their best interest to be stopped, so they can return to the only One Who can offer them all they need.

So it is true with us.  God confronts, and it is indeed painful.  He punishes sin but only out of His love and desire for us to be brought back into reconciliation with Him.  It is for our good.

How do you react to God's confrontation?

Do you recognize that it comes from a loving God, desiring that you be brought back into fellowship with Him?

Joel 1 & 2:1-14                                                  June 27

## Mourning in the Day of the Lord

The Prophet, Joel, takes an event that happened in the life of Judah to point them to the coming "day of the Lord". Their land was invaded by locusts and laid waste. Joel 1:10 says, "The field is wasted, the land mourns; For the grain is ruined, the new wine is dried up, the oil fails. There is no harvest, no food, no way to live.". He tells them to lament, to wail, to lie all night in sackcloth and to cry out to the Lord. He tells them to note this momentous event and to tell their children and future generations about it because it has great meaning. Just as the locust invasion came in an instant and was catastrophic, so the day of the Lord will come "as destruction from the Almighty" (1:15). Joel seeks to get their attention concerning the coming "day of darkness and gloominess, a day of clouds and thick darkness" (2:2). People will writhe in their pain, their faces drained of color, the earth will quake, the heavens tremble, the sun and moon grow dark. He concludes his description of that coming time in Joel 2:11: "For the day of the Lord is great and very terrible; Who can endure it?"

After that destruction, Joel then calls his people to repentance, telling them to turn to the Lord with all their heart, with fasting, with weeping, and with mourning. Instead of rending their garments, which was a way of expressing grief in their culture, they were to rend their hearts and return to the Lord their God (2:13). He says that if they repent, God will restore what the locusts have done, He will pour out His Spirit on them and they will know that He is the Lord their God. There will be a day when God will sit in judgment, and those who refuse God will know terror far beyond the locusts, while whoever calls on the name of the Lord shall be saved (2:32).

Daily our news headlines speak of disaster. Like the invasion of locusts in Joel's time, they show us what is to come, and that God has a plan to punish the rebellious and reward the obedient. He will show all that He is the Lord.

Do you recognize the things that go on in our world as pointing to Who God is and what He will ultimately do?

Amos 1-3                                                    June 28

## God's Mercy and Wrath

Amos, a shepherd, was called by God to prophesy against, and correct the injustices of his day in the surrounding nations, as well as in Israel and Judah. In chapter 1 he talks of the judgment on Israel's neighbors, probably much to Israel's delight. However, in chapter 2 he turns his attention to their failures. Amos 3:2 gives the reason for his "attack" on them, saying of all the families on the earth, they were the one God chose to know and also call to a higher standard. He had called them to be in relationship to Him and show other nations Who He is. They failed miserably. As a result "an adversary shall be around the land; he shall sap your strength from you, and your palaces shall be plundered" (3:11).

In our society, we love to think of the mercy, love, and grace of God and rightly so, for that is His character, Who He is, but that is not all He is. It is clear throughout His Word, and particularly in the Book of Amos, that He is also a God of holiness and wrath when that holiness is attacked. He expects His people to be in obedience to Him so we can be in deep relationship with Him. He provides for us in every way so that is possible. As with Israel, He always makes a way to return when we stray from Him by bringing things into our lives to show us our need to return. In Israel's case he brought lack of food, withheld rain, brought blight and mildew to their crops, sent a plague, overthrew some of them, all chronicled in Amos 4. Since they, even with all these hardships, continued to refuse Him, Amos tells them to prepare to meet your God" (4:12). In that day, His love will be seen, as well as His wrath and judgment. It is a sobering thought to consider giving an account of ourselves to God.

What comes into our lives, whether directly from Him or another source, comes as an opportunity to see Him and relate in a deeper way to Him.

Do you have a balanced picture of Who God is?

Talk to Him about His expectations for you.

Amos 5                                                          June 29

## Seek Me and Live

In chapter 5 of Amos, the Prophet offers a lamentation concerning the state of God's people, particularly their leaders and the grief they have brought. The leaders have no righteousness or justice in them (verse 7), they abhor ones who speak the truth (verse 10), they tax the poor for their own gain (verse 11), they afflict the just, take bribes, and deprive the poor of justice in court (verse 12). "It is an evil time," he says in verse 13. The oppression of these leaders will result in their building homes but not dwelling in them and planting vineyards but not drinking the wine from them. He warns them not to look forward to the Day of the Lord for it will be a dreadful day of judgment for them. There will be wailing in the streets, in the farmer's fields, in the vineyards. There will be darkness, not light, and "it will be as though a man fled from a lion, and a bear met him" (verse 19)! This will happen "for I will pass through you, says the Lord" (verse 17). Because of their grave sins, God will despise their feast days, their offerings, and their assemblies- all are unacceptable to Him.

What an utterly bleak and apparently hopeless situation. Yet there are four words found in Amos 5:4 which give the solution for even this dire situation: "Seek Me and live." How simple. Just bend the knee to Me, He says, and I can restore you and bring light to the darkness. Seek Me. That is also the solution to whatever circumstances that bring us down. He longs to be found by us and to bring joy to our sorrow. HE is the joy.

Will you seek Him? Will you let Him be your joy?

Amos 7                                                      June 30

## God Relents

God showed Amos that He would send locust swarms to devour the crops of His people.  Amos prayed for them, and God relented.  "It shall not be," said the Lord.  Then again God called for fire to destroy their territory, and Amos prayed for His forgiveness of His wayward people, and God relented, saying, "It also shall not be."

Amos did what Moses had done on several occasions: He put himself between the holy God and His sinful people.  He did this even though he was spending his life warning them in very vivid ways what the future held for them if they didn't repent of their ways and follow their God.  He had nothing else to give or do so He went to God and begged Him to forgive them.  Twice he interceded and twice God relented, withdrawing His judgment.

"The fervent prayer of a righteous man avails much" (James 5:16).  Amos plainly shows us that we can bring about changes in the lives of people by interceding for them before God.  We can stave off pain in their lives by begging God for them.  Prayer like that must always be tempered with what Jesus said in John 14:36, "nevertheless, Your will, Lord."  Perhaps the pain is what will bring them to Him, so we have to always pray in His sovereign will.  Absence of pain is not the first thing to seek.

God relented, but the remainder of Amos continues to warn of coming mourning, lamentations, and sackcloth in their lives if they continue to go their way.  A particularly chilling prophecy is one of famine, not a famine of food and water, but of hearing God's Word.  Amos 8:12 says, "They shall run to and fro, seeking the Word of the Lord, but shall not find it".  Unimaginable.

Fortunately, Amos ends his book with a hopeful vision of the future, the restoration of Israel.  Repentance will be followed by a rebuilding, a bringing back of the captives, a replanting of them in their land.  This includes "the Gentiles who are called by My name"(9:12).

Isn't it a glorious thought that we can effect changes in the lives of others, even hold back destruction by interceding for them before God?

Obadiah                                                July 01

## Backpacks of Unforgiveness

Obadiah means "Servant of the Lord". This Prophet gave us only 21 verses, but there is much to be learned from his message that pride and arrogance bring destruction. Obadiah wrote about the Edomites who descended from Esau, the brother who contended with his twin, Jacob. Their rivalry continued for centuries, and in the time of Obadiah was still playing out with the Edomites rejoicing over the troubles of the Israelites. These descendants of Esau allowed their self-centered anger to consume their lives and neglect their own purposes.

This reminds me of people today whose lives are centered on anger and revenge against others, and consequently have lost perspective on what they should be about. There are many people going through life wearing "backpacks" filled with memories and unforgiveness. These "backpacks" are weighing them down and affecting every area of their lives, but they will not take them off and hand their contents to God, allowing Him to take charge of them and free the wearer.

God calls this behavior pride. It is pride because it is about us, not God. God knows everything that has happened to us, and His desire is to use it for good and to heal us, but He cannot until we desire to see Him instead of all our hurts. In the case of the Edomites, God says He will bring them down for their insistence on seeking Israel's destruction. Shame will cover them, He says in verse 10. "Your reprisal shall return upon your own head," He says in verse 15. They spent their lives enjoying the misfortunes of others and only brought more grief on themselves.

There is a second lesson in this small book. While the men of Edom did not directly attack the Jews, they stood by and smugly watched as others did. Verse 15 says, "As you have done, it shall be done to you." James 4:17 says, "To him who has the power to do good and does it not, to him it is sin." I think often of Sir Edmund Burke's statement: "Evil prevails when good men do nothing." That is not an option for God's people.

Allow God to show you where the messages in this book may apply to you.

Jonah 1&2                                              July 02

## A Second Chance

Imagine what it would be like to be in the belly of a fish for 3 days and 3 nights. That was the experience of Jonah, and he cried out to the Lord in his "affliction," as he describes it in Jonah 2:2. He further talks about crying out of the belly of Sheol, the floods surrounding him, the waves passing over him, his being cast out of God's sight, the deep closing around him, weeds wrapping around his head, the earth closing off to him, his soul fainting. Unimaginable. It was in this situation, however, that "he remembered the Lord" and prayed to Him (2:7), promising to sacrifice to Him with thanksgiving. God heard, spoke to the fish, and it vomited Jonah onto dry land.

While Jonah's experience was terrifying beyond our ability to understand, it was necessary for God to stop Jonah in his tracks. Jonah had brought this experience on himself by running away from God when told to go to Ninevah and proclaim God's Word. It was the presence of the Lord which he sought to escape. That can never be, as Jonah finally discovered. As terrifying as the fish experience was, to be cast from God's sight would be so far beyond that.

God says He will never leave us and that nothing can separate us from His love, and yet we risk not hearing Him or experiencing His presence when we insist on doing things our way. We put ourselves in great jeopardy and bring unnecessary pain into our lives as a result. Some situations in which people put themselves are not much better than being in the sea in the belly of a fish.

Even in Jonah's gross disobedience, God did not give up on him. He actually protected Jonah with the great fish and gave him a second chance. He does that with us as well. Some of the misery we experience may actually be God's protection, His way of allowing us to see Him so we can have a second chance, or third...

Do you allow difficult circumstances to let you see God, to really see Him?

Do you thank God for them, realizing He is giving you another chance to get it right?

Jonah 1:5,10-16 & Philippians 2:3-4                    July 03

## Our Sin Affects Others

Charles Stanley has said, "You don't sin in a capsule," meaning the sin we allow or choose in our lives affects others.  Nowhere in Scripture is that seen more clearly than in the story of Jonah, where his disobedience brought pain and loss to others.  Not only were the exceedingly wicked people of Nineveh in danger of not knowing what to do about their sin, but Jonah's fellow sailors on the boat in which Jonah fled , were in danger of death due to his actions.  They suffered through great fear and anguish, even feeling guilty about having to throw Jonah overboard.  Jonah was a prophet of God, yet he used all of his energy to thwart God's will by refusing to go to the people God gave him.  Jonah's sin highly affected the people around him, his disobedience causing suffering in them.

Paul warns in Philippians 2:3-4 that nothing should be done through selfishness, but should be done with the best interest of others in mind.  Also in Philippians 4:2 Paul implores two women" to be of the same mind in the Lord," the reason being for the unity of the church and for the testimony they would have before the people around them.  It was in the best interest of others.

When we misbehave before the world, we do great damage to the cause of Christ, preventing people from wanting what we have, ultimately bringing great suffering and sorrow to them if they never receive Him.  Our sin does indeed affect others.

Are you continually aware of how your behavior impacts others, both believers and unbelievers?

Jonah 3 & 4                                                                              July 04

## A Pity Party

Twice we find Jonah at the place where he says, "Please take my life from me, for it is better for me to die than to live!" What brings a person to the place where living is just too painful, and death becomes preferable? In Jonah's case he came to this point because God had called him to prophesy to the people of Nineveh concerning their wickedness, and he feared that if he obeyed, God would relent out of His mercy, and he, Jonah, would not be correct in his prophecy. He preferred that 120,000 people be overthrown than for him to look foolish. Jonah was right about one thing: God indeed is "gracious, merciful, slow to anger, and abundant in lovingkindness, One Who relents from doing harm"(Jonah 4:2). Because the king and the people of Nineveh heard God's Word to them, through the reluctant Jonah, they repented, fasted, put on sackcloth, and sat in ashes. God saw their works and relented from the disaster He had planned for them. Most people with any degree of compassion would rejoice that a people were spared, but not Jonah: He was exceedingly displeased and became angry to the point that he wanted to die. God prepared an object lesson for him, a plant to give him shade as he sat in the sun, having a pity party for himself. Jonah liked the plant, but then God prepared a worm to damage the plant so it withered, and Jonah once again was left with the hot sun beating down on him. Again he was so miserable that he wished for death, saying he had a right to be angry, even unto death! Jonah cared about the plant but not the people of Nineveh, who so badly needed God's Word. It is not clear whether Jonah ever "got" the object lesson God so lovingly gave to him, whether he ever got over his pity party and the misery he brought on himself. I hope so.

Can you think of a time when you brought misery onto yourself by ungodly thinking and behavior, such as wishing destruction on someone and then being angry that God didn't allow it to happen?

Micah 1,3 & 6                                                    July 05

## Who is Like the Lord?

Micah's name means, "Who is like the Lord?" He modeled to his people one who is like the Lord and called them to be the same. While his people's leaders were politically corrupt and greedy, he wept over the punishment the poor would endure. He hurt for them and loved them, even in their sin. He talks about the wailing, mourning and incurable wounds that will come to them (Micah 1:8&9). Because of the leaders' love of evil and hatred of good, he offers a chilling prophecy: "They will cry to the Lord but He will not hear them; He will even hide His face from them…"(3:4). Compared to the other aspects of the coming judgment: the ruins, the captivity, the grief, the absence of God in their lives, this is the one to be most dreaded.

In chapter 6 Micah pleads with Israel, saying in verse 8, "He has shown you, O man, what is good; And what does the Lord require of you but to do justly, to love mercy, and to walk humbly with your God?" This is what God required of His people in Micah's day and still does in this day. God expects us to act justly, to love mercy, to have a love for people as He does, to walk humbly with Him, to know who He is and who we are in relationship to Him.

The Christian life is a progression, a process of attempting, by the work of the Holy Spirit in us, to become like Jesus. Who is like the Lord? None of us, but we are to be moving continually in that direction, allowing Him to get rid of the sin in our lives and to put in the characteristics which are like Him. That happens only as we take in His truth and sit in communion with Him, so we can know Him and know ourselves.

Are you doing justly, loving mercy, and walking humbly with your God?

Is the point of your life to be like Him?

Micah 4,5, & 7                                                          July 06

## A Promise in Affliction

Despite Micah's grief for the state of his people, particularly the evil leaders and the results they will bring, he proclaims the Lord's reign in Zion, what life will be like in the future. Micah 4:3 says, "They shall beat their swords into plowshares and their spears into pruning hooks; Nation shall not lift up sword against nation, neither shall they learn war anymore." He further says the lame will be assembled, the outcast and those whom He had to afflict will be gathered to Him, the outcast made into a strong nation, and the Lord will reign over them. They will stand in the majesty of the name of the Lord. Micah offers a promise of the triumph that is to come, even while showing them the affliction that must result from their sin. He says in 4:12, "They do not know the thoughts of the Lord, nor do they understand His counsel," thus bringing such sorrow to their lives.

Is our affliction sometimes caused by our not knowing the thoughts of the Lord or not attempting to understand His counsel? Surely that is so. In our time people are lazy about knowing God's Word, preferring to take in the little they know in as comfortable a way as possible. Then what they know about His thoughts, they do not follow, thinking it doesn't apply in their case. In Micah's day, not knowing or understanding His counsel brought untold grief, and so it is in our day as well. I see it every day.

Even so, our affliction will not always be.   Our suffering, which WILL be in our lives, from whatever source, will come to an end. Micah paints a glorious picture of God's future reign, and it is good, in the depths of our sorrow, to meditate on what God has planned for us.

Are you seeking to know and understand God's thoughts?

Look forward to what He has planned for you in the day when all sorrow will end.

Nahum 1, 2, 3                                                July 07

## God, An Avenger?

Like Jonah, Nahum was called by God to warn the powerful city of Nineveh of God's coming judgment on them for their wickedness. It was more than a century before Nahum's time that the obstinate Jonah reluctantly obeyed God and told Nineveh of their need to repent, which they surprisingly did. During the century since their repentance, they had returned to their former ways, however, and had fallen morally and spiritually. Nahum was sent to a people who wielded power and were arrogant in their might, not likely to listen to him.

In chapter 1 Nahum shows a picture of God that we would rather not consider, preferring instead to see only His love and grace. He says God is jealous, He avenges, He will not acquit the wicked, and no one can endure the ferocity of His anger. In chapter 2 Nahum describes the destruction of Ninevah: she is empty, desolate, a waste, there is pain on every side, their people's knees shake, their hearts melt , and their faces are drained of color. God says He is against them. In chapter 3 he says they will be scattered with no one to gather them, their injury has no healing, their wound is severe.

How did they come to this place? God had sent Jonah 100 years earlier, and they "got" the message, but they quickly returned to their own ways, enjoying their power, not God's. Now He sent Nahum again with dire warnings. God, in His love, confronts and gives opportunity for change. When people, like the Ninevites, or people like us, are given the truth but refuse to accept it, there will be consequences. He is holy and will not tolerate continual sin in our lives. Like the Ninevites, we invite grievous pain and hardship into our lives by disregarding Him and thinking we have the power to live any way we want. It will not work. He will not acquit the wicked.

Is there any part of your life that God will need to avenge to bring you to the place He desires you to be?

Habakkuk 1, 2:1-4, 3                                        July 08

## Wrestling

The book of Habakkuk is a dialogue between Habakkuk and God. In the beginning Habakkuk had questions for God as he wrestled to understand Who He is. His first question is in the second verse of the first chapter: "O Lord, how long shall I cry, and You will not hear?" Habakkuk is wondering why there is so much violence around him and seemingly, no justice. He doesn't understand why God doesn't do something about Judah's rebellion. When God did offer a reply to Habbakuk, it was that God was going to use an even more unjust nation, the Babylonians, to bring Judah into line, which only prompted a second question from Habakkuk: "Why do You look on those who deal treacherously and hold your tongue when the wicked devours a person more righteous than he?" God's answer is found in 2:4: "The just shall live by faith." He also lets Habakkuk know that He sees and has a plan and that Habakkuk needs to watch and see what God will do.

Habakkuk is in pain about what he sees around him. In his bewilderment and impatience he wants to see God do more, so he expresses it to Him. Nowhere do we detect an arrogance or a wrong motive in his dialogue with God. God replies, showing us that He desires us to be open and intimate with Him. Habakkuk is not disrespectful or doubting God but wants to know Him and His ways better. Out of his pain he cries out, and God accommodates him. By the end of the book He is praying, worshipping and understanding God at a new level.

God can handle our wrestling when it is done from a pure motive, always recognizing Who He is and who we are. I am certain He prefers, in our confusion and weakness, that we seek answers from Him rather than from the world, or that we hide who we are or move away from Him because we don't understand what He is doing. I also think that as we get to know Him better, our questions will become fewer and eventually be close to nonexistent.

Talk to God about what you don't understand.

Make the point of your life to know Him better.

Habakkuk 2:1-4                                              July 09

## The Pain of Silence

We can endure whatever we must because we see HIM. Because we know Him we can wait in those times when we are not experiencing His Presence. It is when there is silence and we take our eyes off of Him that we get into trouble.

Often we are called upon to wait, but most of us don't do it well. When I challenge people as to their lack of devotional time with God, sometimes I hear, "I don't get any answers," or "I'm not feeling His Presence," and so they stop seeking time with Him. Yet, those times of seeming silence are so valuable although I would agree, painful. They are opportunities to rely first on what we know about Him, His character, and then on what we have previously experienced with Him.

While silence can be painful, it really is a valuable time for us to be stretched, to rely on God's Truth rather than on our feelings. Through His Word we can see Him. Even though we are not hearing anything new, we can rely on what we have already seen in Him and know about Him.

How do you do when you are in a period of waiting while God seems to be silent?

Habakkuk 3                                                  July 10

## Rejoicing in the Lord

By chapter 3 Habakkuk has asked his questions, has gotten responses from God, and is now ready to worship, to concentrate on Who God is: The One Who stood and measured the earth; Whose ways are everlasting; the One Who made the sun and moon stand still; the One Who threshed the nations in anger; Who went forth for the salvation of His people. His wrestling brought Habakkuk to the place of seeing God as He is.

In 3:17 Habakkuk says that even when all is negative, when the fig tree does not blossom, when there is no fruit in the vines, when the olive crop fails, when the fields yield no food, when the flock is cut off and when there is no herd, even with all that loss, Habakkuk will rejoice in the Lord and will joy in the God of His salvation. He has learned to rejoice in the Lord, not in circumstances. His love for God is not based on the good things God does for him, but on Who God is. Even when God sends suffering and loss, even then, will he rejoice in the God of his salvation.

Is that your declaration of faith? Can you say that whatever pain God sends or allows in your life, you will rejoice in Him? That is the place where God wants all of us to be, to not only accept what occurs but to rejoice in it. We can only begin to arrive at such a place if we know Who He is.

Will you commit to knowing Him at such a level that you can trust Him in any circumstance and even rejoice, especially rejoice, in it?

Zephaniah 1 & 2                                             July 11

## Zephaniah Mourns

The prophet, Zephaniah, was a contemporary of King Josiah, the young King who made many reforms in Israel. Zephaniah was called by God to show his people that they needed to repent of what was going on in the inside of them, the things that no one saw. Just making outward reforms was not enough. He wanted them to have a new life, which happens by internal transformation. He warned them of coming judgment if they did not attend to and correct their evil ways.

Zephaniah tells his people in 2:1 & 3 to gather themselves together and seek the Lord while there is still an opportunity. In chapter 3 he points out their specific sins of rebellion, disobedience, lack of trust in God, not drawing near to their God, and corrupt leadership.

Like many of the other prophets, Zephaniah mourns for his people, but ends his writing with hope. While in the last day, God's determination is to pour out his anger on the nations, but He will restore a faithful remnant who will call on His name, and they will see disaster no more. He says God will gather those who sorrow and deal with those who afflict them. He will bring back his people.

This is the continual theme through the books of the prophets: God calls His people to Himself, they refuse Him, preferring to suffer all kinds of horrors, including captivity, He warns them of upcoming judgment, yet they continue in their own ways, even while He offers hope to them.

This is not unlike what we see today. People live in immense pain and difficulty while God offers them peace and contentment in Him. I often think of someone eating out of garbage cans while across the street God has a sumptuous banquet prepared for him, if he would only receive it.

Are you accepting all that God stands ready to offer you?

Are you allowing God to work in your heart as well as in what is going on outwardly?

## Striving Without Satisfaction

After God's people returned home from their Babylonian exile, the first prophet that God raised up to serve them was Haggai. His job was to bring them back to their priorities, to remember who they were and why they were brought back. They were to rebuild the temple and focus on their relationship to their God.

Because the people had lost their way as to what they were to focus on first, they were attending to their own houses instead of to rebuilding God's house. The result was that they were spinning their wheels, getting very little accomplished. Haggai tells them to "consider your ways!" in Haggai 1:5. They sowed much but brought in little, they ate but did not have enough, they drank but were not filled, they had clothes but were not warm, the wages they earned were put into a bag with holes. Haggai 1:9 says, "You looked for much, but indeed it came to little; and when you brought it home, I blew it away." There were few results for the effort they were putting forth, and there was no satisfaction in their lives. What a picture of wrong priorities!

Again, isn't that what we see in our society- people striving but never reaching satisfaction, focusing on the wrong things? Disappointment results when we don't focus on the right things. We were created with a need to produce. Even before the fall, Adam was given work to do, satisfying work, given by God. It is He Who makes the work satisfying and worthwhile. Apart from Him, like everything else, it becomes a spinning of our wheels, useless and dissatisfying.

Is your focus such that your work is what God wants it to be?

Zechariah 12                                                    July 13

## Mourning for the One they Pierced

In his writing Zechariah, like the other prophets, calls the people to repent, obey, and seek the Lord.  He uses visions to communicate God's truth to them.  In Zechariah 12 he points to Jesus, the One, he says, Whom they pierced.  "They will mourn for His only Son and grieve for Him as one grieves for a firstborn." There will be great mourning in Jerusalem, and every family and every person will mourn by themselves.

When a person finally comes to the place of seeing Who Jesus is and what He has done for him, grief is a necessary part of the revelation, grief for his own condition and grief that Jesus had to suffer as He did because of his condition.  There is grief amidst the flow of thanksgiving for God's payment and for what he himself could not pay.

The person who refuses Jesus will endure the greatest of grief, knowing what Jesus offered him at such an expense to Himself, yet it was not received.  He will mourn, as Israel will mourn for their part in Jesus' piercing.  They will mourn as one mourns for an only son.  I have a client today who is mourning for her only son, and I believe it is certainly one of the greatest of griefs.  There are times of such intense pain that I can only sit with her.  Other times she sees God's truth and promise for the coming days and is comforted, recognizing that she is God's beloved child.  Israel will mourn but when they will call on His name, He will answer them and say, "This is my people"(13:9).

Do you mourn for the One you helped pierce?

Do you also rejoice that He has made you His through that percing?

Malachi 1                                                    July 14

## "I have No Pleasure in You"

Malachi is the last prophet to speak for God until John the Baptist arrives 400 years later. Malachi calls God's people to be real, authentic, and speaks on such life issues as divorce, infidelity, hypocrisy, tithing, and even arrogance.

In the first chapter, Malachi addresses the offerings God's people bring, saying they show a disdain for His name. They bring defiled food to His alter, and then don't even recognize it as such. They have the audacity to bring the stolen, the lame, and the sick to Him, their God and the Creator of the universe. Now here comes THEIR pain. God says He has no pleasure in them, nor will He accept an offering from their hands (1:10). His name is great, and He will not have it profaned.

We are here to have a deep relationship with God, and if we heard Him say He has no pleasure in us, how devastating that would be. It wouldn't matter what else we had accomplished in our lives if He finds no pleasure in us. He deserves not just our good, but our excellence for Him. What we offer Him shows how we truly think and feel about Him. How I offer Him my time, my money, my gifts, my talents, my abilities, my energy, show Who He is in my life. He must get the first and best of it all. All of it has come from Him, and He deserves it back. Then instead of hearing, "I have no pleasure in you," we will hear, "This is my beloved child, in whom I am well pleased." What better words could we hear?

What is the quality of that which you are offering your Lord?

Can you expect to hear that He is well pleased?

Malachi 2                                                             July 15

## The Pain of Infidelity and Divorce

God established marriage to help meet our need for companionship. That is basically met in our relationship with God but is greatly enhanced by intimacy with a spouse. God told Adam back in Genesis that he would be lonely at times if he did not have a companion like himself, so God gave him Eve. God made them one in a permanent covenant of companionship. It is the only permanent one-flesh relationship established by God.

How much pain and destruction we see around us because this decree from God is treated with such disdain. He meant it for our good, knowing it would bring satisfaction and delight to us, but we have so grossly misused and abandoned it, and the result is untold suffering. I have yet to see a person who has gone through a divorce or infidelity who does not carry both visible and invisible scars. Children, even adult children of divorce, carry "backpacks" of pain that must be sorted through and dealt with in order to avoid being bent over with sorrow. God never meant for it to be so. Malachi 2:16 says God hates divorce. Of course He does. It is as destructive as anything in our society. After my husband died, a not-so-sensitive, divorced person told me categorically that divorce was worse than losing a spouse to death. At the time I didn't think so, seeing that her children still had a Dad, and she continued to be taken care of financially, but over time I have come to see her point. Death just comes, but divorce is intentional. The pain of rejection is ever present. It was never God's intent, and He mourns for the pain it brings.

If you know the pain and rejection of divorce, God waits for you to bring it to Him. Will you?

Malachi 3                                                          July 16

## The Pain of Robbing God

In Malachi 3, God accuses His people of robbing God. "How?" they ask. "In tithes and offerings", He says. The consequence, he says, is being cursed with a curse. They had not thought of what they had as belonging to God, so they kept it for themselves and consequently saw it devoured. Famine, locusts, and wars with enemies were some of the ways they lost God's possessions and brought hardship on themselves.

For the most part we are a blessed people, materially. However, few think of "their" possessions as belonging to God and themselves as stewards of those possessions. Few know of tithing and fewer still of offerings. When that is the case, we invite a "devouring" of what God has given us. We have seen a glimpse of what can happen in the downturn of our economy. We have seen devastation by weather or accident, and so far it has been minor, but God says in Malachi 3:6 that He does not change. What He said from Malachi's mouth to Israel 2,400 years ago, applies to us as His people today.

We are to bring our tithes to His storehouse. If we do, He says He will open the windows of heaven and pour out His blessing that there will not be enough room to receive it. He promises also to keep the devourer at bay so he cannot destroy our work. He promises that Israel will be a delightful land, and He will make them His jewels. We don't give to get, as some suggest, but we simply give back to Him what He has loaned to us for our good. We give Him what He has so lovingly entrusted us with. He deserves that and so much more.

Have you made a decision about tithing and offering with what God has entrusted you?

Recognize that you can't out-give God.

Matthew 2:13-23                                        July 17

## Living in a Dangerous Time

After Mary and Joseph were visited by the wise men, an angel warned Joseph in a dream to take Mary and the Child and flee to Egypt, the reason being that Herod had plans to destroy Jesus. With all the questions and wonders in their minds, to flee from Israel to a foreign country was certainly another sign of the dangers and uncertainties surrounding them. They, however, immediately obeyed.

More danger loomed and became more widespread when we see in Matthew2:16-18 that Herod, when he saw that he was deceived by the wise men, became exceedingly angry and had all the male children who were in and around Bethlehem and were under two, put to death. This event fulfills the prophecy of Jeremiah 31:15:"A voice was heard in Ramah, lamentation, weeping and great mourning, Rachel for her children, refusing to be comforted, because they are no more." What sorrow we see visited on God's people here.

Danger continued, even with the death of the murderer, Herod. Joseph was again warned by God in a dream to turn aside into the region of Galilee since Herod's son, also apparently unsafe, was reigning in Judea. They chose Nazareth, which fulfills the prophecy that Jesus would be a Nazarene.

While there was much stress and uncertainty in their environment, Joseph and Mary were given direction by angels through dreams. They obeyed.

Today we are not spoken to by God in that way. We have the written Word of God and the Holy Spirit communing with our spirit. How blessed we are to have these two sources for guidance and assurance in our dangerous and bewildering world. Let us hear and obey as Joseph and Mary did.

What guidance has God shown you from His Word to get you through a situation you couldn't understand?

Thank Him.

Matthew 4:1-11                                                    July 18

## Being Depleted

After the victory of His baptism and the affirming statement from God, "This is My beloved Son, in Whom I am well pleased", Jesus immediately was led by the Spirit into the wilderness where He was without food for forty days and forty nights.  While He was hungry, weary and alone, Satan came to tempt Him, a common tactic of his to attack when his prey is in a state of vulnerability.  When we are in a weakened state from fatigue, illness, isolation, or emotional pain from sorrow or loss, Satan delights to seek us out.  Hebrews 4:15 describes Jesus as our High Priest Who can sympathize with our weaknesses because He was in all points tempted as we are, yet in His depleted state, He did not yield to sin.

Jesus' defense was the Word of God.  Three times He answered Satan's strategic onslaught with, "It is written".  Satan's response to the Word of God was as expected: He left.  Satan versus God's Word is no contest.

Try as we might to keep ourselves strong and healthy, there will be times when for various reasons, we become depleted, and Satan will take advantage of our weakness.  Our defense needs to be the Word of God, just as it was for Jesus.  When he tells us, for example, that we are all alone, abandoned, and while our emotions may agree with that, we need to quote Hebrews 13:5: "I will never leave you nor forsake you".  No matter what our feelings are, we must call on the truth to refute Satan and his tempting ways.

After Jesus' temptation, the angels came and ministered to Him.  God will minister to us as well.

Talk to God about a recent temptation you have had.  Let Him bring to mind the truth of His Word to refute it.

Matthew 5:1-12                                                July 19

## Discomfort in Jesus' Teachings

Jesus' teachings can be uncomfortable to us. Many examples of this are found in the Sermon on the Mount in Matthew chapters 5-7. In 5:3-10 He says we are blessed if we are poor in spirit, if we mourn, if we are meek, if we hunger and thirst after righteousness, if we are merciful, if we are pure in heart, if we are peacemakers, if we are persecuted for righteousness sake. None of these seem natural to us. He continues by saying we should rejoice and be glad when we are reviled and persecuted or spoken falsely against. In 5:38-42 He tells us not to resist an evil person, but to turn the other cheek or give him our tunic, or go the second mile if he compels us to go on. Then He goes so far as to tell us to love our enemies and to pray for those who persecute us (5:44). Who does that? Who even thinks that way? JESUS. And He wants that way of thinking and living for us, no matter how unnatural and uncomfortable it seems.

We have to be willing to be uncomfortable, if we are to allow the Holy Spirit to transform us into the person who knows he is blessed when he is persecuted for righteousness sake or the person who loves his enemies or who blesses those who curse him. It is uncomfortable to listen and then obey the prodding of the Holy Spirit.

How much discomfort are you experiencing as you take in and live out Jesus' teaching through the direction of the Holy Spirit?

Matthew 5:1-4                                                    July 20

## Our Poverty and Sin

The first words from Jesus as He began His sermon on the mount were "Blessed are the poor in spirit for theirs is the kingdom of heaven". Poor in spirit is the first thing we must be if we are to accept His work on the cross for our sins. No one wants to be poor in spirit, but if we do not see ourselves that way, then we would rely on ourselves for salvation and therefore, never find it. The first step towards salvation is to recognize our need and that we are one-hundred percent incapable of meeting that need. When we admit our dire poverty, only then are we able to see what Jesus has done for us and receive what only He is able to do, reconcile us to God.

Jesus' second statement, "Blessed are those who mourn, for they shall be comforted", again, makes us wonder at first glance how we are to feel blessed when we are mourning. If He is talking about mourning our sin, then there is every reason to feel blessed because He has made the way, the only way, to rid us of our sin. That is indeed a comfort beyond all comforts, to know my sin is not being held against me, and it then puts me in a position to know God intimately.

These two statements are the first two steps in our salvation experience: we recognize that we can do nothing to save ourselves (we are poor) and we are sorry for our sin (we mourn it), so are now ready to look on Jesus and accept the salvation He offers. The pain of seeing ourselves as we are and of recognizing how we can do nothing about it, is painful, but then we are blessed beyond words to have Jesus take us from that sorry state.

Have you seen your poverty?

Have you mourned your sin?

Have you experienced His comfort and blessing?

Matthew 5:38-48 & Luke 6:27-36                           July 21

## Dealing With the Enemy

Jesus' command in Matthew 5:44 to "Love you enemies, bless those who curse you, do good to those who hate you, and pray for those who spitefully use you and persecute you" is one I have not successfully negotiated on many occasions. It is not in my nature (or perhaps anyone's) to turn the other cheek. That is why God had to make it a clear directive to us.

Many of us know the pain of being cursed by someone or being persecuted by someone. Suffering is a natural part of these experiences, and we can acknowledge that suffering, but compared to Jesus' sufferings and how He responded, there is much for us to learn about His amazing love in the way He responded.

God models loving one's enemies. Verses 35 and 36 of Luke 6 present His kindness to the unthankful and evil. His mercy and love is also clearly evident. He instructs us, even in our pain, to love our enemies, do good to those who show hatred, bless those who curse us, pray for those who use us. Do to them, not as they have done to us, but as we would like for them to do to us. Why? So that we may be His sons, be like Him Who shows love to all. Matthew 5:48 concludes the passage with the admonition "To be perfect, just as your Father in heaven is perfect". He knows of our sinful nature and natural responses, but He wants us to be complete in Him, to draw upon His attributes to love as He does in the face of opposition. There is no chance of this on our own, but in Him, He expects it of us. I have some work to do.

What changes do you need to make in your life so that God's love can reach all kinds of people through you?

Matthew 6:25-34                                                July 22

## Worry Brings Suffering

Worry brings all kinds of suffering into every area of life: the physical, mental, emotional, social, and spiritual. It is not uncommon to see people literally making themselves sick from worry. This is a type of suffering about which God warned us and has given us tools to prevent.

First, He tells us in Matthew 6:25 not to worry. When we do, we are being disobedient to Him. We are essentially telling Him that we have no confidence in the many promises He has given us about caring for us so deeply that He even knows the very hairs that are on our heads. If we believed that, really believed that, would we be concerned about so many of the things that plague us? We show no confidence in His promises to provide for us: "I will provide all your need according to My riches in glory".

Then He tells us in verse 27 that we can't change anything by worrying about it. We may need to take some action at some point, when directed by Him, to rectify the situation, but worry itself will only bring on other problems, including distance from Him.

He reminds us of how He cares for His creation, the birds and the flowers. He has set up His creation to provide for every aspect of it. Some time ago I had my grandsons at a zoo, and we were discussing how an animal like a skunk, for example, has neither speed or ferocity to protect itself, but God gave it something else, and we all know what that is, especially if we have ever experienced it. He provides for His creation, especially us, the pinnacle of His creation. We are the ones in Whom He invested everything- His Son. He was willing to watch Jesus' unspeakable suffering and death so that we might be provided for in coming into fellowship with Him. Surely He cares for my wellbeing on a daily basis. Maybe His idea of my wellbeing, however, doesn't match what I think it should be. Who do you think is in a better position to know what is for my good? I'm going to have to keep learning to defer to Him on that and trust Him. Perhaps my worry is not that He won't provide, but He won't provide what I think I should have.

His answer to prevent worry is found in verse 33: Seek first the Kingdom of God and His righteousness and all other things will be added unto you. If I am seeking Him first and foremost in my life, I'll learn to want what He wants-then no need to worry.

Name a worry you are entertaining in your life. Commit yourself and your worry to Him, knowing and believing that if He is first in your life, the worry will take care of itself.

Matthew 10:34-39                                              July 23

## Family Divisions Bring Pain

It is within most of us to desire peace and acceptance with other people. Unfortunately, in this sinful, fallen world in which we live, that cannot always be. In these verses in Matthew 10, Jesus says that sometimes a man's enemies will be found in his own household. How painful that is, especially when a Christian is rejected by his family for his faith in Jesus. I have seen wives ridiculed by husbands for their beliefs and manner of living, occasionally husbands belittled for following the Lord, children prevented from taking part in Christian activities because a parent was opposed, and parents accused of being out of step in their insistence in doing what God commands. Painful situations.

My dad, like most of us had some good parts to his character and others that were not so good. He staunchly opposed anything having to do with God, even though the Lord so lovingly presented Himself to him in so many ways over many years. From the time I was a child I remember his attempting to prevent my mother from taking us to church.

When I was 39, my husband died very suddenly, leaving me with four children, ages 15, 14, 10, and 1. One of the first things I remember my dad saying to me was, "Now you'll see that this (my belief in God) doesn't work." He also told me that if I continued to believe as I did and follow the Lord, he could have nothing to do with me. I still feel the pain of that even as I write this 27 years later. Of course, it had the effect of driving me even closer to my Lord. That is what pain does. I have much pain when I think of my dad, especially since he died never having received Christ as his Savior.

At the feet of Jesus is the only place to receive comfort in a situation like that- and comfort He gives. I don't like rejection and estrangement from others, but if necessary I am willing to carry it for Him and I thankfully embrace what He can teach me about Himself in it.

Is there pain from rejection by another due to your love for Christ? Sit at His feet and receive comfort that only He can give.

Matthew 11:25-30                                            July 24

## Fatigue

At first read it seems like God is talking in these verses about physical tiredness, and how He can provide us restoration from that, but as we look at the context, it would seem that He is referring more to rest for our souls.  He is saying if we are heavily burdened, we can find rest by going to Him.  If we learn from Him Who is gentle and lowly in heart, we will not be heavily laden.  He desires to give us relief from our burdens.

In this context the Jews were laden with many religious responsibilities by the Pharisees and religious leaders.  There was no rest or freedom.  Most of us don't labor under a situation like that today, but we do allow ourselves to be burdened by all kinds of things, like trying to meet others' expectations of us, doing what we mistakenly believe will make God happy with us, taking on tasks that God has not given us to do, serving others in order to feel good about ourselves…It can go on and on.  We spin our wheels doing all kinds of things when what Jesus wants is for us to sit at His feet and learn from Him.  That is where the lifting of our burdens is going to occur.  I find that time in His Presence at the beginning of the day gives me all the strength I need to do what He has for me in that day.  There is rest for my soul.

Sit at His feet and allow Him to ease your burden as only He can.

Matthew 14:1-21                                                July 25

## Jesus' Reaction to John the Baptist's Death

Because John the Baptist had rebuked King Herod for divorcing his wife and marrying his half-brother's wife, the new wife's daughter, prompted by her mother, asked for John the Baptist's head. Herod had no choice but to comply since he had promised to give her whatever she requested.

Verse 13 of Matthew 14 tells of Jesus' reaction to the news of John's death: He departed by boat from where He was and went to a deserted place by Himself. He wanted to be alone to mourn John's death. John had been the forerunner of Jesus, preceding Him in birth, then ministry, and now death. John had baptized His Lord, signaling the beginning of Jesus' ministry. Jesus, even while being God, felt the sting of death of the one with whom He had been so closely linked. John considered himself to be the friend of the bridegroom.

His mourning seems to be interrupted by the needs of the multitudes following Him. When He saw them, even while in the throes of His Own sorrow, He had compassion for them, taught them, healed them, and even fed them, all 5,000 of them. When Jesus saw a need in people, He was moved by it and responded to it. His Own grief, while acknowledging it and attempting to deal with it, did not prevent Him from seeing and meeting the needs of those around Him. We read then, that after feeding the 5,000, He sent them away and once again went up on the mountain by Himself to pray.

I would never counsel someone to ignore his own grief, in fact quite the contrary, but it doesn't have to prevent him from being sensitive to other's needs. His own grief can actually make him even more aware, more compassionate, and provide him with a greater capacity to be used in the life of another. Our grief is not meant to be wasted but to be used, in our own life as well as in the life of others.

Talk to and learn from Jesus as to how He balanced His own sorrow and the meeting of the needs of others.

Matthew 14:22-33                                          July 26

## Peter's Fear

Who among us has not experienced fear? It is part of the human experience. Babies come out of the womb fearful of the lights, the noise, the poking and prodding . Young children fear the absence of their mothers. Teens fear the rejection of their peers. We fear entering into new jobs, taking on a family, having enough money to pay our bills. We fear accidents, medical reports, getting old, being alone, death…The list of fears we are familiar with could fill pages.

In Matthew 14 we are given a picture of Jesus' disciples in a boat in the middle of the sea with wind and waves assailing them. Jesus, Who was not with them in the boat, walks toward them on the water, approaching their boat. Thinking He is a ghost, they understandably cry out in fear. Immediately, Scripture says, Jesus speaks to them, assuring them of His Presence. Peter is so calmed by Jesus' Presence that he asks to be allowed to walk to Him on the water. Jesus agrees. Peter did well until he took his eyes off of Jesus and looked at his circumstances, the howling winds and raucous waves. He became afraid once more and immediately began to sink, crying out to Jesus to save him. Jesus stretched His hand out to Peter and caught him, restoring him to the boat.

It was Jesus' Presence that calmed the disciples and gave Peter the courage to even attempt the "impossible". It was the looking on Jesus that kept him above his circumstances. Having experienced this event, the disciples worshipped Him and recognized Him as the Son of God.

Fears are bound to come, but with our eyes on Jesus we can rise above them and do the "impossible", hopefully bringing us to a deeper understanding of Who He is.

Spend time looking on Jesus today. Watch your fears diminish.

Matthew 16:24-27                                              July 27

## Denying Ourselves

We don't live in a society where denying ourselves is a popular idea. It's more like: "I'll take all I can get. I deserve it. What's in it for me?" It probably wasn't very popular in Jesus' world either when He said, '"If anyone desires to come after Me, let him deny himself and take up his cross and follow me." He was telling His listeners that there would be loss in their lives if they chose to follow Him. There would be a cross to carry, but then in verse 25 He tells them of the gain: "…whoever loses his life for my sake will find it." In the loss of giving up the things of the world, we will find HIM. That is what our souls are hungry for. Only He is going to be able to fill that deep longing we all have within us. It will not come from material possessions, more education, careers, vacations, recreation, even relationships, as good as they might be. Augustine said, "The whole life to the good Christian is a holy longing." For HIM.

Denying oneself doesn't really seem like much of a big deal at all when we consider what we stand to gain. It was Jim Elliot, the martyred missionary, who said, "He is no fool who gives up what he cannot keep to gain what he cannot lose." Let's rejoice in the privilege of denying ourselves and taking up our cross to follow Him. What an opportunity!

Is there something God would have you give up so that you can gain more of Him?

Matthew 18:15-19                                    July 28

## A Sinning Brother

When was the last time you were sinned against by a brother or sister in Christ? Today? Yesterday? That is probably the case since we never lose our penchant for sin, and it is bound to come to the forefront if we do not continually have our needs met by God. People sin against us, and we sin against them on a regular basis. How painful being offended is, especially if it is by a fellow believer. Why does it happen so often? James 4:1 & 2 gives us an answer: We want something and are not getting it. Self-centeredness. We want something because we think we don't have it, but maybe we actually do. In Christ we are given all we need to live a life pleasing to God and satisfying to us. We have an opportunity for intimacy with Him, which is the foundation of our need and God's plan for us. If our innate emptiness is filled by Him, we don't have to go into relationships with others, fighting and clawing for what we think we need and want, since we already have it. There is no need for us to sin against others by competing with them for our own desires.

What if they sin against us? God sets down clear directives in Matthew 18 for dealing with offense. Tell him! We are to go by ourselves and tell the brother (or sister) how we have been offended. Hopefully, verse 15 says, the relationship will be restored. Reconciliation is always God's plan, we with Him, and we with each other. If the person will not hear us, only then do we involve others, but always with the goal of restoration of the relationship. How much pain would be forfeited if we accepted and lived these truths that God has given us?

Think of a recent offense in your life. Were you offended because you thought a need was not being met, when, in fact, Jesus has already met it for you?

Is there someone you need to go to regarding an offense, either yours or theirs?

Matthew 19:1-10                                              July 29

## The Pain of Divorce

There are multiple opportunities to experience gut-wrenching pain when involved in the death of a marriage. Besides the obvious losses of companionship, being loved, financial security, complete access to children, perhaps a home, maybe mutual friends, there are less obvious ones: trust, acceptance (the counterpart being rejection), confidence in making decisions, and probably many more that only a divorced person would know. God knew the pain long before He set down His parameters in His Word. That's why He gave them to us, for our good, always for our good.

The Pharisees asked Jesus the question about divorce in order to trap Him and use what He said against Him, but Jesus used the opportunity to give several reasons why people should work at staying married: In creation God made one male and one female, intending only one spouse for each other. He intends for a husband and wife to be one flesh. It is the only relationship permanently joined together as one flesh. His ideal is for married couples to remain married. That is His hope as He views all weddings as they take place.

One of my counseling sessions today was with a woman who has been divorced for several years, and her husband has since remarried. Even while dealing with other pressing issues in her life today, the pain of the divorce is continual. The worst part of it, she says, is not being loved anymore. Just as a person learns to reinvest after the death of a loved one, but never fully recovers, it seems like the same is even more true of one having gone through a divorce, and God knew that would be the case. Even while He hates divorce, He loves the one going through it and stands ready to walk with them.

If you are or have been in the pain of divorce, Jesus understands the pain and desires to be the One to meet your need.

Matthew 22:11-14                                                    July 30

## Not Being Properly Dressed

In the Parable of the Wedding Feast there was a guest at the wedding who did not have on a wedding garment. He had no excuse when questioned by the king. The king had him bound hand and foot, taken away and cast into outer darkness, saying there would be weeping and gnashing of teeth. The guest, because he was not clothed in correct attire, put himself in a permanent state of suffering.

We are invited to the wedding, to be part of Christ's kingdom, but we can only go if we are in the right garment- Christ's righteousness. His blood needs to cover us if we are to be accepted by God.

I often ask people why they think they should be allowed into the Presence of the holy, perfect God. Sometimes I get these answers: "Because He loves me," or "I've done the best I can," or "I've lived a good life." None of these answers point to the correct garment, Jesus' shed blood for their sin. I've heard a pastor say, "We come to Jesus just as we are but not anyway we want." We come only on the basis of Jesus' righteousness. Our own will never do.

Refusing to accept God's way of salvation results in eternal suffering and separation from Him as well as a life here of struggle and emptiness. He bought us with His blood. We just need to accept His "garment".

Are you wearing the garment Jesus died to give you?

Matthew 22:37-39                                                July 31

## Convenient Christianity

"Convenient Christianity" is a term I think of when I observe how many of us live. We go to church, we may take part in some ministry, we may even put some money in the offering plate, but we don't allow ourselves to be inconvenienced. As long as we can live our lives without feeling guilty or sacrificing too much, we're good. We do just enough to avoid the guilt but not enough to feel the hurt. Then we wonder why we are not fulfilled, not sensing the Presence of God in our lives, not experiencing Him on an intimate level.

The greatest commandment is "To love the Lord your God with all your heart, with all your soul, and with all your mind" (Matthew 22:37) and the second is "To love your neighbor as yourself" (Matthew 22:39). Often that is not at all convenient, but requires great and continual sacrifice on our part. Instead of taking part in the much-anticipated activity you've been looking forward to, God may ask you to sit with a person suffering in a crisis- not convenient. He may require that you give up a lucrative job you enjoy to enter into ministry- not convenient. He may ask you to give up buying something new to support a missionary- not convenient. Even more inconvenient would be if he asked you to BE the missionary. He may ask you to go out on a limb and witness to your friends or to give up the morning newspaper or internet to spend time with Him- definitely not convenient.

Many things Jesus and His followers did were not convenient. Neither should they be for us.

What do you do for Him that is not convenient?

Matthew 23:1-30                                                    August 01

## Whitewashed Tombs

Jesus talks to the multitudes and His disciples about the scribes and Pharisees who tell others how to live but neglect to live that way themselves. They do what they do only to be seen by men. On the outside they look righteous, but on the inside, Jesus says, their hearts are full of pride, selfishness, self -indulgence, and malice. Jesus likens them to a cup that is only cleaned on the outside or to whitewashed tombs which look beautiful on the outside, but inside are full of dead men's bones and all uncleanness. Outside they appear righteous but inside are full of hypocrisy and lawlessness. What an indictment.

Why do I include this passage when dealing with pain and loss? First, in just 16 verses here, Jesus says, "Woe to you" 8 times as He addresses what it is like to be apart from God by refusing to see themselves as He does and Him as He is. They look to themselves rather than to Him for their righteousness. They whitewash their filthy hearts. They will indeed know the deepest of sorrow and regret at some point.

Secondly, people who whitewash their sin will know sorrow even in this life. God created them to know and be known. If we only desire to appear acceptable but have no interest in having our hearts cleansed by Jesus, we cannot know God. We also forfeit knowing and being known by other people, including ourselves. We live a life of hiding, not having intimacy with anyone. That has to bring pain since we are not fulfilling that for which we were created. What a recipe for loneliness.

Are you trusting God and allowing Him to clean you from the inside?

Give to Him any tendency to simply appear acceptable.

Matthew 23:37-39                                      August 02

## Jesus' Lament Over Jerusalem

I have always considered this part of Scripture to be one of the saddest passages. Jesus' repetition of "0 Jerusalem, Jerusalem" shows the depth of His emotion.  Picture a hen in the midst of danger, running to gather her chicks under her wings, but they would not be gathered.  Psalm 91:4 also presents the image of God's covering us with His feathers, and giving us refuge under His wings.  Jesus wanted to gather His people to Himself but instead of seeking His refuge, they killed His prophets and stoned those who were sent to minister to them.  They were not willing.  As a result, Jesus says, their house, probably referring to the Davidic dynasty, was left desolate.  He also said He would see them no more until they were willing to receive Him.  How chilling is that?

Parents sometimes get a tiny glimpse of what it is like to provide everything good for a child, only to have them reject it for something greatly inferior and perhaps even destructive.  How much more does God, Who is altogether holy and loving, mourn when those for whom He sent His Son, reject that salvation and choose everlasting separation from Him, as well as a life of emptiness and misery.  In some cases, the ones for whom He paid such a high price, not only reject Him but forcefully and purposefully attack Him and His people.  I tend toward anger with such people, but I am sure God's emotion has much more to do with intense sorrow and pain, as we see in this passage.  He laments over the lost and over those who choose another way, rather than His way.  Here we are given a picture of God as He mourns.

Ask Him to give you His kind of mourning for the lost and those in rebellion.

Be sure you are willing to be gathered under His wings, like chicks with their mother.

Matthew 25:1-13                                          August 03

## The Sorrow of Not Being Prepared

We have seen sorrow arising from all kinds of situations, but the one that surpasses all others still awaits those who are not ready to meet God. What sorrow there will be for those who have been presented with Jesus as the One Who paid for their sins but have refused Him.

In the parable of the wise and foolish virgins in Matthew 25 there are five virgins who are prepared to meet the bridegroom (Jesus). While they were waiting for Him they readied their lamps with oil so that when He came they could go in with Him to the wedding. The foolish virgins, on the other hand, took their lamps with no oil so that when the bridegroom came, they had to go and buy oil, causing them to miss the wedding. The door was shut, and when they cried for the Lord to open it to them, He said, "I do not know you."

What more shattering words could one hear when they see God? "I do not know you." We are all given opportunities to come to Him and know Him intimately. He has given us His Word, His Church (Christians), and His Spirit Who convicts us of our sin and our need for the Savior. How does it happen that some never come to a knowledge of Him? I think our desire for independence is one reason. We want to come on our terms, not His. To agree with Him that we are desperately wicked sinners who can do nothing to save ourselves doesn't fit with how we would like to see ourselves. To have to completely depend on the death of Another, Jesus, for our salvation, goes against the pride and independence that is the heart of our sin.

Instead of "I do not know you," let us hear, "Come in quickly! I am so waiting to receive you."

Are you prepared?

Matthew 26:36-46                                August 04

## Jesus in the Garden

A painful passage of Scripture to read and meditate on is Matthew 26:36-46, just before Jesus' arrest where He is in the garden of Gethsemane. Gethsemane means "oil press." It is a place where olives were crushed and ground, just as Jesus would be crushed and ground.

Knowing what He was facing, not the physical torture we center on, but the taking on of all of our sins into His holy Being, which would require separation from His Father, prompted Jesus to take His three closest disciples, Peter, James and John, and ask that they be with Him in His grave distress. All He asked of them was that they stay and watch with Him. They fell asleep. They failed Him in His greatest need. He asked them to be with Him because that is what He desired (just as He desires our presence with Him), but it was also for their good. They were about to be tested as well and needed that time with their Savior.

Even though Jesus was left alone to face His greatest trial, He did not fail. He fell on His face and poured His anguish out to the Father to the point of asking Him to take the cup, what He had to endure, from Him. However, that was not the end of His prayer. The end of His prayer was what ours needs to be when we have poured ourselves out to Him: "nevertheless, not as I will, but as You will." He repeated that resolve again, saying, "Your will be done."

After pouring Himself out in agony to the Father, even to the point where Luke's Gospel says "His sweat became like great drops of blood falling down to the ground", He arouses the sleeping disciples, rises and goes to His betrayal, arrest and crucifixion. Jesus, suffering the greatest of pain and sorrow ever known, shows us how to submit to the Father in all things.

Do you say in your pain, "not my will but Yours."

Matthew 26:69-75                                    August 05

## Peter's Pain

At the Lord's Supper Jesus told His disciples that they would be made to stumble because of Him. Peter countered that he would never be made to stumble, but Jesus answered that that very night, Peter would deny Him three times before the rooster crowed. Peter said that would never happen, even if he had to die. All the disciples said likewise. In verse 70 when a servant girl states that Peter was with Jesus, Peter says he does not know what she is talking about. When confronted by another girl he says, "I do not know the Man!" He repeated that same statement a second time when others accused him of being a follower of Jesus. After the third denial, a rooster crowed immediately, and Peter remembered Jesus' prediction. He went out and wept bitterly, indicating his sorrow and repentance. This is all we are told about Peter's reaction to his colossal failure. Since we also fail our Lord in so many ways, we have some idea of how he must have condemned himself, how he must have revisited the encounters, how he must have longed to have an opportunity to go back and do them differently. I am sure he was totally engulfed in what he had done. I am sure the rooster's crow was a sound that rang in his ears over and over.

After His resurrection, Jesus appeared to His followers at various times. One encounter, recorded in John 21:1-17, was with His disciples at the sea of Tiberias, when He helped them catch 153 fish. He asked Peter three times if he loved Him and then gave him great responsibility in feeding and tending His people, indicating His forgiveness and trust in Peter. Peter's pain most assuredly turned to joy as he experienced Jesus' restoration of Him.

Do you weep over your failures? It is then, as we feel the sorrow and seek forgiveness, that God can restore.

Matthew 27:45-46                                    August 06

## The Sorrow of Jesus

Of all the seven statements that Jesus spoke on the cross, this, "My God, My God, why have You forsaken Me?" is the most painful to hear. It shows us the depth of His sorrow as He was separated from the Father. God made Him Who knew no sin, to be sin for us, that we might become the righteousness of God in Him, as seen in II Corinthians 5:21. We do not have the ability to fully take in the significance of that cry, of what it cost both the Father and the Son. For the holy, perfect Son to take on all that sin is such an anathema to the Father that it defies our understanding. What we can understand, however, is that Jesus did it for us, so that we could be reconciled to the Father. His sacrificial death is the only way that could be possible. The Father allowed it and orchestrated it, knowing that many for whom He did it, would reject the work of His Son.

Jesus cried out this prayer between noon and 3:00 pm when Matthew tells us there was darkness over all the land, further adding to the agony Jesus was enduring. How ashamed I am when I remember complaints I have made to God about being lonely or not hearing Him when I think I should. Jesus endured the ultimate in aloneness, and He did it so I would never be truly alone. Thank You, Jesus, for taking on the ultimate in sorrow for me.

Sit with Jesus, meditating on what He did for you. Thank Him- in words, attitudes and actions.

Matthew 27:55-65 & 28:1-10                    August 07

## From Pain to Joy

Mary Magdalene, Salome, and Mary, the mother of James and Joses, and many other women were present as Jesus suffered on the cross. Mary Magdalene and James' and Joses' mother sat together opposite the tomb after Joseph of Arimathea had buried Jesus and left. We see the two Marys again on the first day of the week at the tomb when an angel of the Lord rolled back the stone and sat on it, telling the two not to be afraid, that He is risen. He also told them to go quickly and tell the disciples that He is risen and that they can see Him in Galilee. "So they went out quickly from the tomb with fear and great joy, and ran to bring His disciples word."

What a gamut of emotions these two women experienced: Fear for what was happening and abject sorrow in losing the One Whom they loved and Who had loved them so deeply. Is there a more mournful picture than the two sitting alone opposite the tomb, waiting and watching while everyone else had gone? Then imagine going to the tomb at dawn, experiencing an earthquake, seeing an angel whose countenance was like lightning and whose clothing was as white as snow, and seeing the guards, out of fear, becoming like dead men. The confusion and concern they endured in those moments must have been paralyzing. Then they were told by the angel not to be afraid! But then imagine the joy that came when they were shown the empty tomb and told that He was risen and that they would be seeing Him soon. That would not compare with the joy that came when Jesus met them on their way to tell the disciples what they knew. They held Him by His feet and worshipped Him. From the worst of pain to the greatest of joy- only Jesus can do that for us.

Worship the One Who turns our sorrows to joy.

Mark 11:25 & 26                                    August 08

## The Sorrow of Unforgiveness

God in His grace and mercy forgives us our sins.  He was even willing to allow His Son to die for them, to take them on His perfect Self so we could know forgiveness.  How, then, can we, sinful, fallen creatures, refuse to forgive others when they sin against us.?  They are simply doing what we do on a regular basis, offending.  The holy, sinless God reached down into the dirt of this world to free us from sin, but we so often refuse to forgive another who is on the same level as we are.  That is unthinkable, yet we do it regularly, and along with the unforgiveness, bring great pain into our lives as well as into the lives of those around us.

I have seen people suffering in every area of their lives due to the unwillingness to forgive.  They may have been sinned against as children, causing great pain, but lack of forgiveness continues to allow the sin to affect them decades later.  The perpetrator of the sin may be oblivious to the sorrow he has caused, but the offended one continues to be affected, often physically, emotionally, socially, and spiritually.  He continues to allow himself to be bound by the offense of another.

Not only do we allow the sin of another to continue to affect us, but we also risk being forgiven by God for our own sins.  We cannot be in close, intimate relationship with Him if we have something against another.  Some offenses against us have caused so much damage that it seems impossible or unnatural to forgive, but God does not ask us to do what we cannot do.  He stands ready to enable us to forgive, not for the benefit of the offender, but for our own benefit.  He wants to free us.  It is a decision we make because of our relationship to the One Who has forgiven us.

Does lack of forgiveness against another interfere with your intimacy with God?

Mark 12:28-31                                                    August 09

## The Greatest Commandment

Jesus presents the greatest commandment in Mark 12:28: to love the Lord our God with all our heart, soul, mind and strength. The second, given in verse 32, is to love our neighbor as ourselves.

How much pain we cause ourselves and how unfulfilled we are because we don't obey these commands. How many women I see who think their husbands can fulfill in them what only God can fulfill. Only He can meet the longing of their souls. God made most of us to desire a husband or wife, but we don't really need them in the sense of true need. We need God. We desire a mate. When we get those two confused, not only are we disobeying the two greatest commands given by God, but our horizontal relationships do not work out well either. HE has to be enough. When that is true in our lives, we are also on our way to good, healthy relationships. Getting our needs met from God opens the way for freedom to have a great spousal relationship.

I see others who love careers or jobs more than they love God or others. They show it by how much time and attention they devote to them. They forfeit so much peace, joy and fulfillment in their lives by making this illegitimate substitute. At the end of their working years I have seen much regret because they see the emptiness of looking to their work to meet their need. Work is a good thing, and we are created to produce. We can get some enjoyment and fulfillment from it, but it is not enough- HE is. Nothing we look toward to give us complete fulfillment will ever work apart from the Lord. We were created with a need for Him and secondarily, a desire for relationships with others. God, our Creator, knew that when He gave us these two commands in Mark 12.

Can you say to the Lord that you love Him with all your heart, soul, mind and strength?

Luke 1:26, 38, 47-55 &2:19,33 &50-51                    August 10

## Handling What We Don't Understand

In the joy of the story of Christ's birth, recorded in Matthew and Luke, there is also bewilderment, pain and sorrow. In Luke 1:26 we see Mary, a virgin, betrothed to Joseph and encountering the Angel Gabriel, who tells Mary she is highly favored and blessed. The following verse tells us Mary is troubled at his saying. When Gabriel goes on to tell her that she will be conceiving a Son, Jesus, Who will be the Son of God, and there will be no end to His Kingdom, there is immediate acceptance but also a measure of bewilderment. "How can this be, since I do not know a man?," she says. This news presented Mary with some difficult problems, particularly in that society. How was she to explain her pregnancy to Joseph? To her family and friends? How could she understand such a thing, even for herself? After Jesus' birth and the visit of the shepherds, we read in Luke 2:19 that "Mary kept all these things and pondered them in her heart." How could she not? Again, when Jesus is presented in the temple and Simeon blessed God for Him, Scripture says "And Joseph and His Mother marveled at those things which were spoken of Him." (Luke 2:33). In Luke 2:50 it tells us that Mary and Joseph did not understand Jesus' question when He stayed behind to teach in the Temple: "Did you not know that I must be about My Father's business?" No, they didn't. The following verse says, "His Mother kept all these things in her heart". Lots of questions, not so many answers. Nevertheless, Mary's response in Luke 1:38 shows us who she is: "Let it be to me according to Your Word". Her magnificat in Luke 2:46-55 shows us even more about why God chose her. She didn't have to know all the answers, maybe not any of them, to respond to her God.

Let God bring to mind how you respond when you don't understand what He is doing.

Read Mary's song in Luke 1:47-55 again.

Luke 4:16-30                                                      August 11

## Jesus' Rejection

Today I read the passage in Luke 4 of Jesus teaching from Isaiah in the Synagogue and being soundly rejected to the point that His listeners thrust Him out of the city and sought to throw Him over a cliff. He Himself refers to rejection as He speaks in verse 24, saying, "No prophet is accepted in his own country." He responded to His rejection simply by passing through their midst and going away. He was to suffer many more rejections throughout His life, culminating with many for whom He died, not believing and receiving Him. He willingly went to the cross knowing that would be true, even asking God to forgive His tormentors for they didn't know what they were doing.

It so happens also on this day that I read a passage from Elisabeth Elliot's book, Keep A Quiet Heart. In those few pages, God spoke to me about meekness being a quality needed for dealing with rejection and how Jesus was the epitome of that. "He was despised, rejected, reviled, pierced, crushed, oppressed, afflicted, yet He did not open His mouth," she writes. That so spoke to me about how to deal with rejection.

Who am I to think I need to react when feeling hurt and rejected? What right do I have to demand acceptance? Jesus, the Son of God, did not. When rejected I can take the hurt to Him. He knows all about it- and more, much more. He says to come to Him, take His yoke, learn of Him for He is meek, humble, lowly. He will give us rest. How much suffering I would save myself if I learned of His meekness.

Talk to Jesus about your feelings of rejection.

Ask Him to show you His meekness.

Luke 6:46-49 August 12

## A Ruined House

Jesus has given us His Word. When we hear it and don't act on it we are like a house built on the earth without a foundation. When water beats against it, it will fall, He says, and the ruin will be great. On the other hand, a man who digs deep and lays a foundation on the rock as he builds a house, will find that it is not shaken when the waters come. That is a picture of one who hears God's Word and follows it.

When we take in God's truths and allow Him to apply them to our lives, we can handle whatever comes our way. The circumstances may be dire but He will walk with us through them. Our "house" will not fall even though it is assailed at every turn. II Corinthians 4:8 &9 says "we are hard-pressed on every side, yet not crushed, we are perplexed, but not in despair; persecuted but not forsaken; struck down, but not destroyed". If God and His Word are our foundation, we cannot be moved, only strengthened as we stand firm.

I see people who call God Lord, but they do not obey His Word. When difficult circumstances arise, they are overwhelmed by them because they have no foundation of truth. Because they have not taken His Word in, they do not understand that the problems and sufferings in their lives are opportunities to trust Him, to hold onto Him and know Him better. They have nothing with which to counteract the storm, so they are swept away with it. Their troubles overtake them, and they miss the opportunity with which they are presented.

What kind of foundation do you have to rest on when the storms come- because they surely will.

Luke 10:38-41                                            August 13

## Worried and Troubled

Being a Martha by nature, in my mind I have often defended the Martha of Luke 10. She welcomed Jesus into her home and was intent on serving Him. She became irritated that her sister, Mary, was not helping her but was sitting at Jesus' feet, listening to Him. Didn't someone have to make all the preparations for caring for guests? Yes, Jesus needed sustenance, but verse 40 says that Martha was distracted by much serving. She seemed to be majoring on a minor. She was anxious in her tasks, revealing to us that she was not centering on the Person of Jesus. Sitting with Him, listening to Him first, would have enabled her to go about her preparations without anxiety. He came to bring us peace. Sitting with Him enables us to take care of all the tasks that are before us. People tell me they don't have time to sit with the Lord at the beginning of their day- they have too much to do. I say they have too much to do NOT to sit with Him.

Jesus' response to Martha was a tender one, calling her by name twice, "Martha, Martha". He understood her plight, but He was also quick to let her know that she was missing "that good part", the one thing that is needed, intimacy with Him, the reason for which we were created. How much trouble and anxiety we would save ourselves by being in His Presence and giving our day (actually HIS) over to Him.

Are you missing the good part, the part that is needed?

Luke 13:22-30                                              August 14

## I Do Not Know You

If we think we know pain now, it cannot begin to compare to the sorrow and abject suffering that awaits those who hear the Lord say when they come face to face with Him at the end of their lives, "I do not know you, where you are from.  Depart from Me, all you workers of iniquity." This will apply to those who seek entrance to God's Kingdom by their own terms, not on the basis of Jesus' shed blood for them.  How could there be more painful words to hear than those from Jesus than "I do not know you.  Depart from Me." However, many will indeed hear those very words.

We live in a generation of independence.  "I'll do it my way."  There is even a song with that title.  It may work in some areas but not in our relationship to God.  He is God.  I am not.  I am His creation, and it is in His domain to decide what my life will be.  He is the Creator while I am but His created.  I submit to Him.  That is His plan, and that is what works.  Any other way of living brings pain and eventual death.

Our country thrives on independence, but it doesn't work in our relationship to God.  To see ourselves as needing God goes against our very nature.  Our sin programs us to want to be independent of Him, to be our own god.  If you have tried that for any length of time (and who hasn't?) you will conclude, if you are honest, that it does not work.  It never will.  He is God.  I am not.  I am made to submit to Him, to know Him intimately.  That is what works.

Are there areas of your life that you need to turn over to Him, to submit to Who He is and who you are?  Talk to Him about them.

Luke 15:11-24                                              August 15

## The Lost Son

In the parable of the Lost Son (often referred to as the Prodigal Son), the younger son in the family asks for his inheritance and upon receiving it, leaves home for a far country where he squanders it. So, the son began to be in need since there was a famine in the land. Actually we can assume that he was in need before he even left home. He was aware of a dissatisfaction and was looking for something to fill the emptiness. Now, in addition to that, he has real physical needs and in order to take care of them, he takes a job feeding pigs, a shameful task for a Jewish young man.

The father, of course, is a picture of God. While the son was a great way off, the father saw him coming. Apparently he had been watching for him, hoping he would return. The father had been feeling the pain of his son's sin and his separation from him, as well. Having compassion, the father ran to meet him, fell on his neck and kissed him. He then prepared clothes and a meal to celebrate his home-coming, again a picture of how God receives us back to Himself when we go to Him, confessing our sin.

The son was lost and was found. While he was lost he suffered much. Yet, all that while he was suffering, the father was looking for him to return. The father stood ready to put an end to his suffering, as does our Father.

Picture God waiting for us to return to Him after we have sinned.

Luke 15:25-31                                            August 16

## The Pain of the Prodigal's Brother

The prodigal son had an older brother who chose to stay home with his Father while his brother elected to go off and waste his entire inheritance on riotous living. While the lost son was being received by the father, this older brother was working in the field. When he came home and saw the celebration going on for his brother, he was angry and would not join the party, even when his father pleaded with him. In refusing to join them, he brought a great deal of pain on himself. He was not able to participate in the joy of one who was dead and is now alive. How sad that his own self-righteousness prevented him from enjoying the good fortune of another. The younger brother knew he was unworthy, but this older one knew nothing of grace but instead demanded justice.

Just because the prodigal was offered grace did not detract from the blessing the older brother could receive if he chose it. He could have had a fatted calf to celebrate his blessings at any time had he chosen to do so. Apparently he did not.

This older brother is a picture of the Pharisees of Jesus' day, who thought of themselves as righteous and did not want sinners to be accepted by God. They missed it, as did the older brother, having no concept of who they were and Who God is. They missed the freedom of being forgiven of their sin and being accepted by God. Unfortunately, that left them in the pain of trying to make themselves acceptable, which is impossible. Only suffering can be the result.

Do you celebrate being found? Do you truly celebrate when others are found?

Luke 16:19-31                                          August 17

## The Contrast of the Rich Man and Lazarus

In this parable Jesus presents the story of a rich man who lived a sumptuous life style and when he died, found himself in the torments of Hades. In his suffering he saw Abraham at a far distance with a former beggar named Lazarus, who in his lifetime was full of sores which the dogs licked while he lay at the rich man's gate, hoping for some crumbs to eat. What a contrast in life styles. What a contrast in death styles. The rich man cried for mercy from Father Abraham, asking that the former beggar be sent to cool his tongue with a drop of water from his finger. Abraham reminded the rich man of all the advantages he had in life while Lazarus had none, but now in eternity the opposite is true, based on what each had done in their lives. The rich man is suffering while Lazarus enjoys peace and comfort.

Abraham talked about the great gulf between where he was and where the rich man was. The gulf is our sin. Until we accept Jesus as payment for that sin, the great gulf between God and us will continue. That gulf will remain if we die without our sins being taken care of.

Jesus further teaches here that if a person is not persuaded by the written Word, neither will he respond to seeing one raised from the dead. "For by grace you have been saved through faith, and that not of yourselves, it is the gift of God" (Ephesians 2:8). What torment awaits those who refuse the gift.

Allow yourself to think of the torment of the rich man, despite how distressing it is to contemplate. Determine to present the truth to others so they avoid this fate.

John 5:1-15                                      August 18

## Do You Want to be Made Well?

It seems strange to think that there are people who do not want to be made well, but that is what Jesus seems to be suggesting in John 5:6. The infirmed man had been beside the Pool of Bethesda for 38 years, waiting for someone to put him into the water. Thirty-eight years! Jesus asked him if he wanted to be made well, a fair question after all those years. He then told him to take up his bed and walk, which he immediately did. He also told him to sin no more, lest worse things befall him.

It would seem like a miserable existence to lie by a pool for 38 years, waiting to be put into the water, but perhaps there was something about it that the man actually liked. It was certainly familiar to him. It kept him from taking any responsibility for himself. Jesus' statement about his sin may suggest that he had not been willing to give it up in all those years. Only the encounter with Jesus was able to put him in a position to be healed.

I see people who live miserable existences. Sometimes they think it is what they deserve. Maybe it is what they have always known. Maybe they enjoy their sin too much to give it up and accept a different way of life. I look at people sometimes and think, "God offers them a banquet, but they are choosing to eat out of a garbage can." He can make them well, but they refuse, choosing to live a life of a sick beggar when they could be the children of the King.

If you are suffering, do you want to be made well? Jesus stands ready to do it. Let Him.

John 5:6-15                                              August 19

## Can Suffering Be Enjoyable?

We are comfortable with the familiar, even when the familiar does not serve us well. It has been my experience that when I am going through pain, I seek the Lord on a deeper level, the more intense the pain, the more I go to Him. That is, of course a good thing, and, in my thinking, the beauty of pain. Does that mean then, that I should seek to keep myself in a constant state of pain and unease, so that I can be assured of seeking Him more deeply? Other Scripture does not suggest this. In John 5:6, once again consider the paralyzed man by the pool of Bethesda, the one who had lain there for 38 years. When Jesus asked him if he wanted to be made well, Jesus seems to be suggesting that there is a time to accept His healing and move on. He told the paralytic to "Rise, take up your bed and walk." Later, Jesus told him to "sin no more." The man was then able to testify to the Jews that it was Jesus who made him well. He would not have had that testimony if he had remained in his former state.

Even though my greatest times of growth have been during loss and pain, Jesus doesn't want me in that constant state. He teaches me so much in it, but He wants me to take His comfort and truths and "walk" with them, to testify to others that it is HE who makes me well. While painful, our times of loss and suffering can become familiar, and the comfort and closeness Jesus provides can become an end in itself, but it must not be. I believe His desire is for us to testify of His making us well, if not physically, then spiritually and emotionally. He desires that we seek Him with the same intensity when all is well.

Do you seek wellness, so you can testify of God's healing?

Seek Him in every circumstance of your life.

John 8:32                                                                    August 20

## Some Lies About Suffering

To say something is a lie is rather a strong statement, but not too strong when it opposes what God says in His Word. Some examples of lies about our suffering are: It shouldn't be happening; they must have deserved it; God must be abandoning me; He doesn't care about me... Technically, because of our sin, we all deserve what befalls us, but God in His great mercy, chose to intervene for us and allow His Son to take the punishment, so to assign blame to others for the pain that comes into their lives takes the focus away from where it should be, as do the other examples of wrong thinking. The question, "Why?" is typically asked when difficulty arises. While it is in our human nature to ask that, the mourning process is designed to get us past that to another question, "What now?" Incorrect thinking will not help us get through the denial, anger, bargaining, and depression to the "What now?" We will stay in the "Why?" and miss the opportunity God wants to bring out of our pain. I may feel abandoned, I may feel unloved, I may feel that God only has punishment in mind for me, but I need to meditate on the truths of His Word: "I will never leave you nor forsake you"; "Nothing can separate you from my love"...

His truth shall indeed set us free from needless and prolonged suffering. Then we can ask, "Lord, what do you have for me now?"

Do you sense your relationship with God being hindered by prolonged suffering? Check your thinking about Him and see if it is consistent with His written Word.

John 11:1-44                                      August 21

## That You May Believe

John 11:5 tells us that Jesus loved Martha, her sister Mary, and her brother, Lazarus. When Jesus heard that Lazarus was sick, He stayed two more days where He was. During that time Jesus told His disciples that Lazarus had died and that He was glad He was not there for their sakes, because now they had the opportunity to believe. It was for their good that He tarried. They would grow through this trial.

When Jesus arrived at Lazarus's home in Bethany, He found Mary and Martha being comforted in the loss of their brother. Martha reacted like many of us do when unexpected tragedy occurs, "Why, Lord?" "If you had been here my brother would not have died." Is there an accusation against God here? I hear that often from people in the throes of grief. It seems to go with the territory.

When Jesus found Mary, she expressed the same idea to Jesus, that if He had been there, Lazarus would not have died. She also fell at His feet and worshipped Him. "Jesus groaned in the Spirit and was troubled," verse 33 tells us. The Jews saw Jesus weep, causing them to wonder also why He could not have prevented Lazarus from dying. Why, Lord?

Verse 40 gives the answer to the why- that they would see the glory of the Lord, and that they would believe that Jesus was sent by God. Many of the Jews did believe, and those who were already believers grew in their faith as they saw Lazarus raised from the dead. Jesus didn't do what everyone expected because He had a greater good in mind.

Do you trust God, even when what He does or doesn't do makes no sense to you?

John 12:27-28                                    August 22

## Glorifying God in Our Sorrows

A week before Gethsemane Jesus expressed His agony over His impending death, when He said in John 12:27: "Now My soul is troubled, and what shall I say? Father, save Me from this hour? But for this purpose I came to this hour." Then in verse 28 He said, "Father, glorify Your Name," meaning through what Jesus was about to do. Jesus was indeed "A Man of sorrows and acquainted with grief," as Isaiah said, and in His sorrows and grief, His main concern was to glorify the Father.

Instead of thinking that difficulty should not come, or when it inexplicably does come, thinking how quickly I can get through it, my attitude must be how can I allow God to bring out the person He intends for me to be. How can the person He created me to be come out of this pain? That person usually will not come out when all is well. Often only a prideful pull towards an ungodly independence comes out of times when we are not challenged. Sorrow takes care of that prideful independence because we see that we can't manage apart from God. We NEED HIM to walk with us through our pain and to make sense of it for us. Pain takes care of a shallowness and a superficiality that is naturally in our lives. It reorients our priorities and puts our Lord in His proper place. His plan is for us to glorify Him in it.

Think with God about a major time of suffering in your life. How did you change as a result of it?

John 15:18-25                                      August 23

## The World's Hatred

Being disliked is not pleasant, but being hated dramatically affects how we feel and causes us great pain. This passage of Scripture, John 15:18-19, says the world hates us because we are not of the world, and it hated Jesus before it hated us. The Pharisees, the religious leaders of Jesus' day, hated Him so much that they planned for His death. We who know Him wonder how it is possible that anyone could hate Him to that degree. It was because they saw themselves in contrast to Him. Even though the leaders were careful to project righteousness, on the inside they had to know who they were, sinful to the core. Because they hated Jesus, they also hated the Father, and those like them hate us.

In our world a person can stand up for almost anything he chooses, even things that God has condemned in His Word. However, when someone speaks out about Jesus, God, or the Bible, that person will often be soundly ridiculed and vilified. With all the evil around us, how can that be? People don't want to hear the truth, God's standard, since it condemns their behavior. They want to go on and be allowed to live as they choose without being confronted with God's truth. They want to be their own gods, again the very basis of our sin. Because Jesus told the Pharisees He was the only Way to God and eternal life, they were so offended that they planned to kill Him.

Being hated by the world is not something we aim for or something we enjoy, but it will happen. "If they persecute Me, they will also persecute you." They do it because they do not know Him and do not want to bow to Him.

How do you feel when someone rejects you for being a follower of Jesus? Are you willing to bear it for Him? It should actually be our honor to do so.

John 16:5-24                                          August 24

## The Advantage of Being Left Alone

Leaving someone we love and depend upon or being left by that one is a painful experience, often not only bringing sorrow but also fear, anxiety, and feelings of abandonment.

Jesus' followers in John 16 were about to experience the pain of separation from Him. Jesus recognized that sorrow was filling their hearts (verse 6), but He also knew that it was "to their advantage that He go away for if He does not go, the Helper will not come, but if He departs, He will send the Helper to them." How could it be an advantage to be left alone? They were surrounded by people who hated them; only Jesus loved them, and now He was leaving them. This Helper, the Holy Spirit, was going to be sent to them, but how could He be better for them than the physical Presence of Jesus? He could dwell in all believers at the same time; He would convict people of their sin and need for Jesus as the disciples witnessed; He would show them the righteousness of Jesus and the coming judgment for sin; He would guide them into all truth; He would tell them of the future and help them to glorify Christ.

Even though the coming of the Holy Spirit would ultimately be a blessed thing for the followers of Jesus, weeping, lament, and sorrow would precede it. They would go through great pain, much like a woman in labor, but also like her, when the child is born, they will experience great joy. "Your sorrow will be turned into joy", Jesus tells them. "I will see you again and your heart will rejoice, and your joy no one will take from you." In God, great joy often follows great pain. Sometimes we have to suffer loss in order to have great joy.

Think how blessed you are to be one who experiences the joy of having the Holy Spirit forever within you. Jesus sent Him to you.

John 16:33 August 25

## He Enters Our Sorrows

Today one of my counseling sessions was with a woman whose 27-year-old married son is dying of cancer. Another was with a recently widowed woman left with four children. Another was with a woman whose daughter is out of control and barreling at breakneck speed down the wrong path. It seems that the only solution is to have her leave their home. Another was with a beautiful, young adult woman who was never loved by her own dad. Another was with a woman whose life was moving along well after many previous struggles, when a car drove into her path and left her with a myriad of physical problems, many operations, financial uncertainties, the end of independent living, and an end of the dream of a career she was working toward. Today is only Monday.

I cannot possibly enter that counseling office on my own. It is only He Who can make sense of all of this and bring comfort to these dear people as they go through so much pain. It is only He Who can bring courage for them to even enter into a new day. It is only He Who can offer His presence as they enter yet another dark, lonely night. It is only He Who can give them direction for their very next step. He offers Himself to them, and that is what they need before anyone or anything else. They need Him. Thank You, Lord, for entering into our sorrows with us, for never leaving us alone. Thank You, Lord, for having a plan to redeem these sorrows. He Himself knows sorrow beyond our understanding and has indeed overcome.

Are you giving your sorrows to Him, expecting Him to redeem them?

John 16:33                                                  August 26

## There Will Be Tribulation

Because Jesus has overcome the world, we can "be of good cheer" while we are in the midst of tribulation. He is not surprised that we are experiencing trouble, nor should we be. He has told us to expect it, and in the midst of it His plan is that we draw upon Him, not for deliverance from it, but for deliverance IN it. That deliverance from the power of the trouble comes when we put it in its proper place. It is temporary, and even if it were to take our physical life, it can never separate us from our deep intimacy with God. In fact, it can serve to drive us even closer to Him. Even if Satan or the world means our suffering for evil, He Who overcomes has other plans which will not be thwarted, if we keep our focus on Him and His ultimate purpose.

As we progress in our relationship with Him, eventually we will find ourselves asking less often why a certain thing, which causes us such pain, had to happen. Instead our questions will, at some point be: what do you have for me in this? What purpose of Yours can I accomplish in it? Am I being whom you desire in this? Am I pleasing and glorifying You? We begin to look at our painful circumstances as a privilege to be called to by Him, as an honor to be trusted by Him to carry. He Who has overcome the world, has called us to our circumstances, and we are privileged to walk with Him through them.

If not exactly feeling of "good cheer", do you accept your trials as a privilege and an opportunity to walk with Him?

Acts 9:1-19                                              August 27

## Poured Out Wine

Elisabeth Elliot in her book, 'Keep a Quiet Heart,' cites Ugo Bassi, an Italian preacher who said, "We are to measure our lives by loss and not by gain, not by the wine drunk but by the wine poured forth, for Love's strength standeth in Love's sacrifice, and he who suffereth most hath most to give."

It is in loss that we grow, since in the loss we see our need for the Savior. We may praise Him for the gain, but we don't seek Him and recognize our need for Him as we do in loss. When we have entered and then grown through the dark nights of suffering, we have something to give to another soul in his pain. We can't give what we don't have.

Paul, the former persecutor of Christians, whom God so dramatically converted in Acts 9, the writer of many of the New Testament letters, is said in 9:15 to be a chosen vessel of God's to bear His name before all kinds of people. Verse 16 says he would suffer much for Jesus' name. His life would be poured out in the form of beatings, stonings, imprisonments, shipwrecks, and attacks by Satan as he preached Jesus as the Son of God. Paul knew adversity beyond our ability to comprehend, yet he continued to pour himself out as a sacrifice for God. His sufferings resulted in the giving of the Gospel throughout the world of his day. In the adversity Paul faced, he was able to write to the various churches of his time, teaching and instructing them, encouraging them, correcting doctrine, establishing them in the faith, pastoring them. God changed him and used him through everything that occurred in his life. We have much of the New Testament because Paul allowed his sufferings to be used by God.

Are you pouring yourself out as a sacrifice to God and for the good of His people?

Acts 12:1-19                                                    August 28

## The Pain of Persecution

Compared to the days of the early church, our country knows little of persecution for the cause of Christ. Acts 12 records how King Herod, seeking to please the Jews, violently went after the church, first beheading James, the first of the disciples to die, and then imprisoning Peter with the intent of execution. This was Peter's third arrest so he was placed, with his wrists chained, under the watch of four squads of soldiers. None of this was enough to prevent an angel from rescuing him. Imagine his thoughts as he sat in that cell, knowing James had already been killed. This was Peter who, out of his fear, had denied his Lord three times. After the angel led him out of the prison and departed, Scripture says, "When Peter had come to himself, he said, 'Now I know for certain that the Lord has sent his angel, and has delivered me from the hand of Herod and from all the expectation of the Jewish people". His experience, as miserable as it was, enabled him to "know for certain" who God is.

Peter's experience had another purpose as well, in that his fellow believers saw their God as One Who heard their prayers. Peter's escape from prison was not something they were expecting. In fact Acts 12:16 says they were astonished. They even accused Rhoda, the girl who answered the door to Peter, of being "beside herself." Even though they were praying for the answer, they didn't expect one at that point. They had a lot of learning to do about Who God is. Now they knew for sure what He was able and willing to do for them.

They saw that nothing was going to thwart the will of God. Herod and the other powerful men of their day were not in charge, as it appeared. God was. Peter's time of painful turmoil was an opportunity for him and the other believers to see God.

Think of your most recent time of painful adversity. Did you view it as an opportunity to see God at a deeper level, to understand Him more? Will you now?

Acts 16:16-34                                                    August 29

## Imprisonment Joy

Again we read in Acts of imprisonment. This time it is Paul and Silas who suffer this fate. They were imprisoned for commanding a spirit to come out of a fortune-teller. In excising the evil spirit, the masters of the fortune-teller were deprived of the money she was earning for them. In their anger, they took Paul and Silas to the magistrates and made false claims against them, accusing them of teaching against the Roman law. Their garments were removed, they were beaten with rods, thrown in prison and had their feet fastened in stocks as they were held under tight security.

Under these conditions, what do we find Paul and Silas doing at midnight? They were praying and singing hymns to God while the other prisoners listened. What a testimony! Their fellow prisoners saw two men in the most painful of circumstances, unjustly accused, praising God, but there was to be even more for them to witness. God sent an earthquake so that the doors were opened and everyone's chains loosened. The keeper of the prison, thinking the prisoners had all escaped, was preparing to kill himself, knowing death would be his fate anyway if prisoners escaped on his watch. When Paul informed him that they all remained, he immediately wanted what they had. He said, "Sirs, what must I do to be saved?" They told him, "Believe on the Lord Jesus Christ and you will be saved, you and your household." They presented God's truth to the jailer and those in his house, and they were all baptized. The jailer took them into his house

Paul and Silas suffered much pain and hardship, but consider the outcome. Knowing what we know about them, we can be sure that they would be willing to take on that pain every day to have the outcome they saw here. Their pain was so unbelievably redeemed by God, and resulted in the saving of many souls.

How much suffering and discomfort are you willing to undergo to see souls come to the Savior?

Acts 20:17-38                                                    August 30

## Seeing a Loved One's Face No More

In Acts 20 Paul is meeting with the elders of the Ephesian church to say goodbye to them. In verses 17 to 21 he reminds them of their time together, times of living together, serving together, enduring trials together with many tears, proclaiming God's Word to them, teaching from house to house, and testifying to the Jews and Greeks about Jesus. Those times were not going to be happening with them again because Paul was going to Jerusalem where he knew he would have tribulation and probably more chains, as well as other things that he did not know.

Paul was being a wonderful testimony to these leaders of the Ephesian church, telling them that it wasn't his own life that was important but the furtherance of the Kingdom of God. He challenges them, as overseers, to shepherd the church, even while there will be attacks both from outside and within. He wants them to be careful in these trials and to remember what he has told them in their three years together. He commends them to God. What a glorious time of intimacy and sharing they had.

However, the closer the bonds, the more difficult the parting, and that is what the Ephesians experience here, much pain and sorrow at the prospect of seeing Paul's face no more. As Paul knelt and prayed with them, they wept freely, fell on their knees and kissed him, full of sorrow at the parting. They literally had to tear themselves away from him.

Many of us have had the experience of knowing we would see a loved one's face no more. There is nothing else to do in that kind of pain than to allow God's comfort and assurances to wash over us. HE will never leave us, HE will take over our sorrows of that moment, and He will redeem them for His glory, if we allow Him to.

When we are in the midst of any kind of sorrow, even the parting of one we hold dear, we get comfort in beholding the Face of Jesus. It can never be said that we will see HIS Face no more.

Acts 26:1-23                                    August 31

## Dealing With Background Pain

As I begin a counseling relationship, I often discover early in our sessions that a client has some long-standing issues that go back to childhood. This is something that at first glance, Scripture does not address. Or does it?

We are privileged to read of Paul's early life in Acts 26 as he gives his defense to King Agrippa. He, from his youth, was a Pharisee, one who observed strict religion and the letter of the law. He did everything he could to oppose Jesus, imprisoning His followers and orchestrating their deaths. He even attempted to force Christians to blaspheme, and he persecuted them even as they tried to escape.

Paul is an example of one who we would not consider, in our own lack of wisdom and understanding, to be a good candidate for salvation. Yet God had other plans as we see in verses 12-23. His plans involved knocking Paul to the ground by a bright light and having Jesus speak directly to him, commissioning him to minister and witness for Him. He was to be an instrument to open the eyes of those who had been blind, those just like himself.

Based on his background, we would consider Paul a poor choice for this call, yet God chose him, changed his mind and heart, and used him to bring salvation to many. God wasn't concerned with the issues in his background, but He was concerned about how He would use him in the present and future.

It doesn't matter what wrong thinking we may have carried from childhood, nor does it matter what we have done or what was done to us. God is bigger than all of that. Whatever has made us who we are, He can make us into who He wants us to be, just as He did with Paul. Our part is simply to hear, to submit, to repent, to let Him direct us. He has plans for us, plans that can't be thwarted by who we used to be.

Talk with God about the "stuff" from your background that is holding you back. Let Him show you who He intends for you to be.

Romans 1:18-28                                    September 01

## God's Wrath

God's wrath was seen on multiple occasions in the Old Testament: in the flood, Babel, Sodom and Gomorrah, etc. Now here in the New Testament Paul presents it in his letter to the Romans. According to Romans 1:18 & 19, God is exceedingly angry when people suppress the truth about Him. He is full of wrath because He was so careful to show Himself to them through creation, and so they are without excuse. Even those who perceived God did not glorify Him as God and were not thankful, so- He gave them up. He gave them over to their sin, allowing them to revel in it. He let them see how truly evil they could be apart from Him, how a debased mind could result in all kinds of horrors: homosexuality, sexual immorality, wickedness, covetousness, maliciousness, envy, murder, strife, deceit, rebellion against parents, violence, unforgiveness... Any evening news program or daily newspaper is filled with example after example of what life brings to those who have been given over to themselves. Not only do they embrace their own sins, but they encourage, and often even insist, that others do likewise. They oppose with vehemence anyone who does not agree with them. Their arrogance and disdain for the truths of God result in great suffering on earth as well as suffering beyond imagination in eternity. To be given over to one's desire for a life without God is the epitome of pain. When I see a heart hardened to the things of God so that the person is unable to hear God or see Him, it is a frightful condition to witness. That condition comes about when a person refuses to respond as God reveals Himself. Man is without excuse.

How do you feel when you recognize one who has been given over to his sin? Bring that person before the Lord that He may be given another opportunity.

Romans 5:1-5                                                    September 02

## To Glory in Tribulation

It is rare to see someone glorying while in the midst of trouble. Those who do are ones who have been in trouble before and have seen what God can do in it, so they have learned to look on those times as opportunities.

Here in Romans 5 Paul, having been in much tribulation himself, writes that it produces perseverance, and the pressing on. It builds muscle in us, spiritual muscle, as we exercise in the disciplines God has given us- the continuing in His Word, the connecting with Him in prayer, the acknowledging of His truths, even as we endure difficulties. Perseverance, he says, builds character, which is who we are when no one is looking. Perseverance in trouble makes us into who God wants us to be. Character, then, produces hope, which never disappoints because it is from the Holy Spirit Who dwells within.

Enduring trials gives us an opportunity to exercise our faith, to prove what we really believe. We can be confident in our trials because the love of God has been poured out in us through the Holy Spirit Who dwells within us. Until we hit a valley, we are not sure how we will act. Once we are there, and see that He is enough, then we have confidence for the next, even deeper valley, confidence in Him to sustain us through it and even cause us to soar.

We rejoice in hope of the glory of God. No matter what situation we are in, we can glory in it because of Who He is and what He will do.

Have you had the experience of glorying in trouble? If not, what about Him are you not seeing?

Romans 7:2&3                                         September 03

## Lifelong Marriage

I Corinthians was written by Paul to the Church at Corinth, an immature, troubled church in need of direction and correction in how to live. In Romans 7, for example, He lays down God's intentions concerning marriage, even while teaching a larger principle of law and grace. Verses 2 and 3 teach that marriage is planned by God to be a lifelong union, only to be broken by the death of one of the spouses.

What pain all of us see around us on a daily basis because so many consider this principle not necessary in our culture. I have adult clients who are continuing to suffer from their parents' divorce which occurred 20 or 30 years ago. I see clients themselves who are still angry and hurt from a long ago divorce. The feelings of rejection remain. God never intended for us to suffer that kind of pain.

His intention has always been that we get our innate needs for love and significance met in Him and then our desire for companionship and oneness with another, met mainly through the marriage relationship. People get in trouble and cause themselves and others considerable pain when, instead of getting their needs met by God, they insist that others, often a spouse, meet them. It is impossible. Only God can give us the love and significance we need. We can expect and hope that a spouse meets our desires, but when we demand from a spouse what he cannot give, we put our marriage in jeopardy. God surely mourns when we don't seek Him first, mainly since He longs, and is able, to give us what we need, but also because we invite heartache into our lives and into the lives of others when we refuse His way. Everything in our lives, including our marriages, springs from our relationship with Him. "Put Me first and everything else will be added unto you," the Word of God says.

Are you getting your needs met in the Lord, freeing your spouse to meet only your desires?

Romans 7:15 & 24-25                                    September 04
Romans 8:1-6

## O Wretched Man

Paul is mystified (and so are we) by the fact that he so often does not do what he wants to do but instead does what he hates to do. He says in Romans 7:15 that he doesn't understand this about himself. He recognizes the evil, the sin that is within him, and that is what makes him declare himself " a wretched man". We do feel wretched when we will to do a good thing but don't carry it out, yet we practice the thing that is not good, even when we will not to do it. We are defeated by sin, no matter how we desire not to be, causing us much suffering and despair. Blessedly, in Romans 7:25, Paul presents us with a Deliverer from this wretched state: Jesus Christ our Lord!

It is He Who enables us to walk not in the sinful flesh, which always entices us, but according to His Spirit Who dwells within every believer. Instead of being bound by sin, the believer has the freedom and power to live in the Spirit. Romans 8:1 says there is no condemnation to those who are in Christ Jesus. We are not under the law which judges sin, but could not do anything about it as Jesus did, putting sin to death when we surrender to His Spirit.

The Christian has a choice: to live in our flesh, that which comes so naturally, or to live in the power of God's Holy Spirit Who lives within us. It is He Who continually offers us all we need to stop doing the things we don't want to do and to start doing the things we want to do. In ourselves we are incapable, wretched indeed, but in Him we can do all things. We can avoid the "wretched life" that brings so much misery.

Are there things that make you wretched, things that you need to give over to the power of the Holy Spirit Who dwells within you?

Will you?

Romans 8:16- 17                                         September 05

## Co-heirs With Christ

If we received the Spirit of adoption we can cry "Abba, Father".  We know we are children of God, and since Jesus is God's Son, we are co-heirs with Him, standing to receive all that He receives, including being glorified together with Him.  We also stand to suffer with Him, and Who has suffered more than Jesus, having laid down His life in the taking on of all our sin.  We appreciate the anticipation of being glorified with him and reigning with Him in eternity, but we often rail against the sufferings of the present day.  We can't have one without the other, nor should we desire to.  Through our sufferings there is the opportunity to identify more closely with Him, to know Him more deeply.  Consider it a privilege to be a co-heir in that respect with Him.  When God adopted us into His family, He adopted us whole -heartedly and gave us all the privileges that entails.  We are not distant relatives, neighbors, or friends who are treated as guests.  We are IN the family, meaning we get to wash the toilet bowls, clean the messy dishes, sweep the dirty floors, take care of a sick child, work together to lift a heavy burden, all the while knowing we belong and are deeply loved and valued, which is the need of all men.  The neighbors don't do these things in our homes but neither do they completely belong, nor will they receive the inheritance of the family.  Yes, we suffer, but we do not suffer alone, and one day we will receive our inheritance.  We will reign with the One Who knows so much more about suffering than we can ever imagine.  What a privilege to belong to HIM.

Do you see yourself as a co-heir with Jesus- in every respect?  Believe Him.

Romans 8:18- 25                                      September 06

## Groaning Within

"The sufferings of this present time are not worthy to be compared with the glory which shall be revealed to us", says Romans 8:18. The tears that I see on a regular basis, and the many tears that I have shed myself, cannot be compared to the glory that awaits us.

Our entire creation groans and labors with birth pangs. That cannot be surprising to us since we know the fall corrupted all of God's perfect creation. As a result, adversity and suffering have to be the rule, not the exception. Yet, how we fight that. Even we who have the Holy Spirit within us, groan within ourselves (8:23), as we wait for the day when we will be with Christ, and all will be made right. We groan within ourselves, we suffer, but not forever. We look to the day when the groanings, the unmet needs, the pain within that we can barely articulate, are no more. Romans 8:25 says we are to wait for that day with perseverance. Even in our pain we go on, knowing Jesus awaits our being with Him, knowing He will end the groanings within. Having that hope gives us the courage and ability to take the next step God shows us, no matter what heartache lies within.

Take your groaning within to Jesus. He will sustain you in it until that day when you see HIM.

Romans 8:18-30                                    September 07

## From Suffering to Glory

Paul is saying in these verses that the present sufferings we are familiar with cannot be compared with the glory we shall see in the future. We know all about our present pain, but we don't have the capability to know the glory that awaits us in Him. We simply have to trust in what He says about it. In comparison, our present sufferings are "light affliction" when we consider the joy that awaits us.

Paul also says that all of creation "groans and labors" because of the fall. God's perfect creation was thrown into turmoil; nothing is as it was, and so we need to expect hardship. Work requires the sweat of our brow, new life requires birth pangs, nature is beautiful but also results in destruction, life eventually ends in death and with it much sorrow, our nature is one of sin and constant temptation to think and act apart from God, bringing with it untold grief- none of this being at all what God intended when He embarked upon creation.

In our fall, though, He had a plan, a plan which while it brought great grief to Him, freed us. We have the assurance of one day being with Jesus, rescued from the heaviness of our sin, from the present sufferings we endure. The knowledge of Christ's return and all the glory that entails, gives us the hope we need to endure today. We will indeed be going from suffering to glory. What a day to imagine and anticipate with excitement.

We also see in this portion of Scripture how when we don't even know how to pray, the Holy Spirit intercedes for us and presents to God what we can't express. What comfort comes from that truth as well as the truth in verse 28, that we can be assured that all that comes into our lives will work together for good when we love God. We will be conformed to Jesus and will reign with Him.

As you read this Scripture, talk with the Lord about the insignificance of your present sufferings in comparison to what He has planned for you.

Romans 8:26-27                                                    September 08

## Groanings Which Cannot Be Uttered

The whole creation groans, we groan within ourselves, and now we read in Romans 8:26 that the Holy Spirit intercedes for us with groanings which cannot be uttered. We don't know what we should pray for as we should, so He goes before God for us. He helps in our weakness for we don't see as God sees, so we don't even know what to pray for. Even if we knew what to pray for, we would have difficulty expressing it in our weakness. It is necessary for us to put ourselves under the control of the Holy Spirit so He can and will intercede for us. What a relief, in my weakness of not fully seeing or knowing, to realize that He takes over what I cannot do, and He does it for me. He stands between God and me and presents to Him what I don't know and what I cannot express of what I do know. He knows the perfect will of God and when I submit to Him, goes about seeking it for me.

In the depths of our pain, sometimes we don't know how to express what we feel. That is when we simply present our broken hearts to the Lord. We just sit with Him with the tears flowing and minds confused, our strength gone, and our hearts numb. He receives us in that condition, especially in that condition, because it is then, when we have come to the end of ourselves, that He can really do a work in us. That is why the most painful times, the times when we have groanings that cannot be uttered, are the most valuable times in our lives. Submit those times to the Holy Spirit and let Him do His work.

Do you have groanings that cannot be uttered. pain that you cannot put into words to others or even to God?

Let the Holy Spirit do it for you.

Romans 8:31-37                                                    September 09

## If He Is For Us

No matter what we face, God calls us "more than conquerors "(Romans 8:37). Not only can we manage tribulation, distress, persecution, famine, nakedness, peril, or sword, but we can conquer them, excel in them, because HE is for us. Paul begins this passage by asking the rhetorical question, "If God is for us, who can be against us?" HE will be with us in all things, HE Who was willing to give His Son for us. It is His Son, Who at the right hand of God, is going to bat for us, interceding. Nothing can keep Him from offering that love to us, not "death nor life, nor angels, nor principalities not powers, nor things present nor things to come, nor height nor depth, nor any other created thing, shall be able to separate us from the love of God, which is in Christ Jesus our Lord."

As we go through the troubling experiences that life brings, the tribulations, the distresses, the pain, we can never think that we have been abandoned by God, that He has withdrawn His love and cast us aside. This passage soundly refutes what we may be tempted to feel and believe as truth. In fact, it may actually be true that we, like Paul, the writer of these verses, are enduring what we are because He trusts us with it, and intends it for our good and the good of others, as well as His glory. Our security in Him is absolute.

Have you ever been tempted to doubt His love when you are in the depths of despair? Memorize these verses and apply their truth.

Romans 8:38, 39                                    September 10

## The Pain of Feeling Unloved

Probably the most invasive pain in our lives comes from a feeling of not being loved. When couples come into my office and complain about the way their mate squeezes the toothpaste or who is not doing what chore, I begin to think and search for the real problem. Often it is a doubt that the other really loves him or her. We have been created by God with a deep need for a relationship with Him and then for a relationship with other people. We can work eighty hours a week, exercise until our muscles scream, shop 'til we drop, try all the addictions known to man, but nothing will satisfy until we recognize that our deep hunger is to be loved. Much of the pain in our lives is caused by our failure to recognize this truth and go to the source of the One Who can fully meet the need.

Our text today, Romans 8:38 & 39, tells us that NOTHING can separate us from the love of God- not death nor life, neither angels nor demons, neither the present nor the future, nor any powers, neither height nor depth- not ANYTHING. His love is shown to us through Christ Jesus, our Lord, Who gave Himself for us that we might live.

People around us will fail to make us feel loved at times, just as we will fail them. But God's love will never fail. It is the one thing that is always there for us. The tremendous pain that comes from not feeling loved has a remedy. We just need to claim it.

Do you see that some of your pain may be from not feeling loved?

Meditate on Romans 8. Accept the love He offers you. Let it sustain you when others fail to show you their love.

Deuteronomy 8:1-3                                    September 11

## Reflections on the Years Since September 11<sup>th</sup>

Every year I dread the coming of September 11<sup>th</sup>, with all the feelings and anguish rushing back to remind me of what we and 3,000 other families have lost, of what our entire country lost.  I am writing this just after the ninth anniversary, and I found this year to be particularly painful, not only because of my own sorrowful reflections on the loss, but because of the state of my country.

I went to a small town gathering and was disheartened with the remarks of several local officials who spoke briefly.  There was little if any reference to what our nation suffered that day, how we were attacked by evil forces, bent on our destruction- and I believe, still are.  The messages were about hope, love, moving forward, all that good stuff we want to hear and hope for, but simply cannot believe in the world in which we live.  The national news coverage of September 11<sup>th</sup> this year and for the past several years were similar.

After that experience, I got in my car, and heard on the radio someone singing a song about how heaven needed the 3,000 who perished on September 11<sup>th</sup> more than we do.  Again a wave of discouragement momentarily engulfed me.  It simply is not true.  God indeed took those who had received His Son to Himself but not because He needed them, but because in His grace and love He had made a way for them to be with Him.  How He must mourn at our distorted thinking, when we refuse His truth and replace it with what we would like to be true.  How He must mourn when we interpret what we see going on in our world on the basis of our penchant for peace at all costs and refuse to see things in the light of His Word, when we refuse to remember the truth.  When we refuse to remember what has happened and refuse to see it from God's perspective we are often condemned to repeat it.  Remember the Israelites' 40 years in the wilderness?  They refused to learn and remember.

Do you see world events in light of what you would like it to be, or in light of God's truth as seen in His Word?

# John 10:27-29 & Proverbs 16:4, 7, 9, 33; 21:30,31     September 12

## Nothing Surprises God

The Scripture in John 10 tells us that, if Jesus is in our lives, no one can snatch us out of His hand. Psalms 73:23 &24 says He is always with us. He holds us by His right hand. He guides us with His counsel and afterwards takes us to glory. He knew on September 10th that the events of September 11th would unfold just as they did in our country. He knew on that day that His children, including my son-in-law, were coming to be with Him. Certainly He didn't want the terrorists to have the hatred in their hearts that they displayed that day, but He lets all of us be who we choose to be. How He must grieve over the sin that brings so much pain to His world.

Nothing comes into our lives that does not pass by Him beforehand. I Chronicles 29:11 &12 tells us that everything in heaven and earth is His. Everything. Every morning when I have my time with Him, I try to offer to Him whatever is going to enter my life in that day, accepting it beforehand and giving it to Him as a willing sacrifice, knowing that He has already allowed it and stands ready to use it for my good, whether the thing itself is good or evil. He is in control. A September 11th shows us that our security has to be in Him. Proverbs says "Many are the plans in a man's heart, but it is the Lord's purpose that prevails. When I woke up on September 11th, 2001, I had plans for that day and the days ahead, but they were not to be. God had other plans, plans for my good and the good of others, who would work through the process of seeing Him in all the chaos and pain. I remember one day in the throes of grief, shaking my fist at Satan and saying, "You will not win." And indeed he will not. Proverbs 20:24 says a man's steps are directed by the Lord.

God's plan is to bring His glory and our good out of the most heinous circumstances. I have seen Him do it.

Talk with Him about Who He is- His sovereignty.

Is there some control you are hanging onto that you need to give up to Him, trusting Him to bring good, not temporary good, but ultimate good, out of it?

Psalms 68:5                                              September 13

## A Father of the Fatherless

Who does not remember where you were on the morning when the planes hit the towers at the World Trade Center, the Pentagon, and the field in Pennsylvania? For 3,000 families life would never be the same again. My family is one of those. Daily I am reminded of the pain as a husband, dad, son, brother-in-law, son-in-law was so cruelly taken from us. I weep as I see my grandchildren without their dad, my daughter without her husband. Even now as I write this, over nine years later, tears are once again escaping. My Granddaughter, who was born four months after September 11th is the most outspoken to me about her loss. A day full of fun and activity can quickly turn to one of heartache for me as she shows me something she has written about the absence of her dad in her life. She grieves, even though she has never actually seen what she has lost. This most delightful of children feels her loss as she sees others with their dads. I see her and her two brothers taking part on their various sports teams, concerts at school, church programs, and I think: How I wish their dad could be here to see them. How proud he would be and how he would delight in them. I think that also for my own four children as their dad has been gone from them for the past 25 years.

My pain is only eased when I remember that their heavenly Father is here, as He has promised to be. He has His hand on my grandchildren. He calls them the apple of His eye. He has already brought all of them to a place where they have received Him as their Savior. He is never going to leave them or forsake them. The same is true for my children who were 15, 14, 10 and 1 when their dad died.

I personally know the Lord at a much deeper level than I did on September 10, 2001. It is the reason I am able to write what I am writing today. Whatever our loss is, He stands ready to comfort us and lift us above it, so we can be used for His glory. September 11th happened because men can be evil. They meant it for our destruction but God means it for our good. He redeems even the perpetual sorrow of a September 11th in our lives.

Is there a September 11th experience in your life that you need to trust Him with, so He can redeem it for good?

Psalm 73:23,24                                                    September 14

## Real Security Comes Only from God

While we all recognize the unspeakable pain of the loss of life of
September 11th, every day my family feels the loss as do the other 3,000
families who lost loved ones. There are countless residual losses also, one
of them being the loss of security for all of us in our country. We came
face to face with our vulnerability that day. Is it safe to go out our doors
and walk into our workplaces, dare we get on airplanes again, can we trust
the person behind us in the grocery store line, are our children safe in their
classrooms, should we drive across that bridge, is that food safe to eat….
The questions remain to this day. Just this week as I write this, I had a new
client come into my office. No one in her family had been lost on that day,
but her husband worked in the area of the towers. The issues she brought
to our session that day, eight years later, were directly related to
September 11th. They have invaded so many areas of her family life. One
could become paralyzed with fear if he were only looking at the world
around him and all that was lost on that day.

Psalms 73:23 and 24 says, "Yet I am always with you; you hold me by my
right hand. You guide me with your counsel, and afterward you will take
me to glory." If that doesn't bring us perspective, nothing will. The
terrorists' purpose was to saturate us with fear and chaos, while God's
purpose is to take us by our hand and give us the truth that He will always
be with us, even to the taking of us with Him into glory. That has to
assuage the fear and bring us security like nothing else can.

One of my thoughts after September 11th was, "The terrorists have already
taken so much from me, I will not allow them to take more in the days
ahead. I will mourn, but I will not fear. I will look to Jesus for my security
and peace. I will hold onto His hand."

As you sit in God's Presence today, picture yourself holding His right hand
and He, holding yours. Rest in that security. Praise Him for it.

Isaiah 43:1-3                                          September 15

## Getting Through Before Seeing the Good

God is a Master at bringing good out of evil, but what truths do we hang onto while we are getting through the evil, before we can see the good? There are situations where we may never see the good before we enter eternity with Him. In some of my dark days of grief, people would say, "You'll understand this when you get to heaven" or "You can ask God "Why?" when you get there". I don't think so. When I get there, the whys will not be necessary, nor will the reasons why something occurred. When I see Him that will be enough. Until then, though, what does He reveal to us that enables us to face another day?

Isaiah 43:1-3 tells us that He calls us by name; for we are His. Isaiah 41:10 tells us not to fear; He will uphold us. Psalms 50:15 says if we call upon Him in the day of trouble, He will deliver us, and we will honor Him. In Deuteronomy 32:10-12 is Moses' description of how He is with us: "He shielded him and cared for him, he guarded him as the apple of his eye, like an eagle that stirs up its nest and hovers over its young, that spreads its wings to catch them and carries them on its pinions. The Lord alone led him, no foreign god was with him." The idea that I am the apple of His eye is monumental to me, and that He hovers over me. The Creator, the Savior, cares for me in that way. That is what gets me through the dark days.

One could write an entire book just on the promises God gives to sustain us before we see the good. They are all about HIM, Who HE is and how HE views us- the apples of His eye. I will trust Him in those valleys of darkness and let Him be my refuge and strength.

Think about some of the promises God has given you to sustain you in the tough times.

Claim them.

Psalms 57:1,2 & Psalms 50:15                    September 16

## What Good?

It is not easy in the midst of a September 11th to see the good. We know the pain very well, but at the time of a calamity, the good may be elusive. In the days following September 11th, however, while the grief and confusion in our country were seen at every turn, there was also a coming together of our people. The support to those who had lost loved ones was remarkable. The heroic actions of the first responders to the Trade Center showed what many of our people were made of. The resolve to never let this kind of thing happen again widely prevailed among us, and it was inspiring. Of course, the climate that we experienced then has strongly faded. Life went on, and most people returned to their familiar ways, albeit with more vigilance and caution. However, in the lives of those who sought God, He was able to show Himself. As He promised in Psalms 50:15, He delivered them, and He was honored. Many came to know Him for the first time, and others rededicated themselves to Him as they saw that life without Him didn't work very well. As Psalms 57:1 &2 says, they took refuge in the shadow of His wings until the disaster passed. They saw HIM. I know I did. Our family received many accounts of these things occurring in the lives of people. God WAS honored.

In those days there was an openness for sharing the things of the Lord. It was an opportunity to see the big picture: this is not all there is. Eternity awaits us, and we need to be prepared for it. In the now, however, God desires relationship with the ones He created. At the time of September 11th there was a renewed sense among Christians to tell others what we know of Christ. We were forced into a position of appreciating what we had left, one another, while continuing to mourn what we had lost. Yes, God brought much good from September 11th. The main thing is what is always THE THING: We were given the opportunity to see Him as He is and ourselves as we are. We saw our need for HIM.

Think about how September 11th changed you.

Sit with Jesus and ask Him if you need to return to some of the truths you learned in those days.

Romans 9                                         September 17

## Paul's Great Grief

The apostle Paul suffered much in his life: stonings, imprisonments, shipwrecks, physical weakness, persecution...but he describes his great sorrow and grief as coming from Israel's rejection of the Gospel. While enduring his own suffering, the main source of his mourning was over his peoples' spiritual state. So it should be with us, but instead we mourn over much that affects our loved ones, particularly our children: a friend rejects them, they don't make the team, they don't get in the college they desired, they lose a boyfriend or girlfriend, they don't get the job they wanted... What we need to mourn is their eternity if they have not received Jesus as their Savior, and their relationship with God if they are not living for Him. This is what leaves them wide open to devastation in their lives, both now and in the future.

In Romans 9:2 Paul says that he has "great sorrow and continual grief in his heart" for those of Israel who are really not His people because they have pursued righteousness on their own, but not through Jesus, Who is the only way to righteousness. They did not receive Him by faith but attempted to come to God by the works of the law. They stumbled at the Stumbling Stone, Jesus.

When we see people doing that today, seeking to be accepted by God through their works, through the church, or through any other means other than through Jesus as the payment for their sins, it should bring real sorrow to us, just as it did to Paul in his day.

Do you mourn when people reject Jesus and seek their own way to God, knowing they are destined to an eternity apart from Him?

Romans 10:20& 21; 11:                                        September 18

## A Spirit of Stupor

Romans 10:20 & 21 says, "I was found by those who did not seek me; I was made manifest to those who did not ask for Me", meaning the Gentiles, but to Israel He says, "All day long I have stretched out My hands to a disobedient and contrary people". Because of Israel's continued resistance, God then gave them "a spirit of stupor", eyes that cannot see and ears that cannot hear (Romans 11:9).

God will not always strive with men. He gives everyone an opportunity to know Him, but most refuse. When we do know Him, He wants to grow us, but again, many refuse. It is a frightful thing to have Him stop striving with us, particularly with salvation, but also how sad to miss the growth He has for us because we do not choose to listen. His Spirit convicts and illuminates, but if we refuse Him, He may cease striving. If we are saved, His Spirit does not leave us, but He is not manifested in us if we quench Him, resulting in a spirit of stupor in us. Lord, may it never be.

There is nothing more joyous than to sense the Spirit being active in our lives, giving us direction in even the most minute things, giving us new understanding of a Scripture that we have read many times before, even convicting us of something that offends God and does not belong in our lives, using us in the lives of other people in giving out His Word, introducing others to Him, connecting deeply with Him in prayer. Lord, let our eyes see and our ears always hear from your Spirit.

What are you doing to avoid "a spirit of stupor"? Are your eyes seeing and your ears hearing what He has for you?

Romans 12:1&2                                    September 19

## The Need to Belong

To sacrifice means to offer or give up something that is important to you for the sake of another. Paul tells his brethren in Rome to give their bodies as living sacrifices, meaning to live a new kind of life, to willingly give up the old. Verse 1 says it is a reasonable thing to do in light of what God has done for them (and us). We are comprised of body, mind, and will, and all are to be holy, pleasing to God as we offer them. We are to be different from the world. The difference begins with a transformed mind, a new way of thinking. If we insist in fitting in with our culture, we are going to be the most unhappy of creatures, finding ourselves not fitting anywhere, alone.

One of the basic needs of man is the need to belong. A person, who knows God and is sold out for Him, fits with God's people. He is a member of the body of Christ and instantly feels a connection when he meets another believer. He belongs. A person who has not received the Lord is a member of the world and usually has no problem fitting into the values and activities that go on in it. He belongs. A carnal Christian, one who has received Christ but has not made Him Lord, one who has not made himself a living sacrifice, however, fits in neither place. He is not at home with God's people, nor is he totally at home in the world. He goes through life trying to walk on both sides of the fence, finding satisfaction in neither, not belonging in either. He is, of all people, the most unhappy and often the most burdened with unnecessary trouble. His life is turmoil, both on the inside and the outside. Receiving Christ as Savior is the beginning to being part of God's family. The next step is to offer ourselves as living sacrifices, to live our lives for Him.

Talk with God as you sit with Him today about where you belong.

Romans 12:1-2                                    September 20

## A Living Sacrifice

Paul beseeches the Romans (and us) to present our bodies as living sacrifices, holy, acceptable to God. He also says not to be conformed to this world but to be different, to be transformed by the renewing of our minds.

Both of these things are going to cause some degree of pain. They require a giving up of what we might naturally choose for ourselves. A sacrifice is surrendering or offering up to God something that we have and could keep, so there is some tension as to whether we will give it or not, even though we only have it because He has allowed us to have it. Our bodies, Paul says, are to be living sacrifices. We are to lay them down daily, to offer all aspects of them to Him for His will. Our bodies when we offer them are to be holy, acceptable to God. Presenting our bodies to Him that way requires that we not live any way we choose. We are to live as His Word directs, which can sometimes cause us discomfort.

To not conform to all that is going on around us also causes us discomfort. Like the Israelites, we want to fit in, to be like everyone else. God says "no". There is the tension again concerning which way we will choose. We are to be transformed by the renewing of our minds. How are our minds renewed? By taking in His Word. That requires our time and focus, time and focus that has to come from other things that we might enjoy doing. There is tension again, but what a reward, to conform to God, not the world.

Will you make your body a living sacrifice?

Will you allow God to transform your mind through His Word?

Romans 12:9-13                                    September 21

## Patience in Affliction

Paul says to be joyful in hope, patient in affliction, faithful in prayer, and to share with God's people who are in need.

Who is patient in affliction? We just want it to go away as quickly as possible, that is if we look at it as the world does. We think affliction is something to be avoided, something that should not be happening. Even some Christian preachers tell us that lie. If God tells us to be patient in it, He is saying for us to sit with it and let it surround us until we get from it what He intends. Wait. See what God has to show us in it. Receive from Him. Never thrust affliction aside like an unwanted encumbrance. Hold it, examine it, question it, and let it do its work.

No matter how difficult the affliction, be joyful in hope. Lord, what are You going to do with this? How are you going to change me? How does this fit into Your eternal plan? Look forward to His work. Draw near to Him in prayer, knowing this is an opportunity first and foremost to know Him at a more intimate level.

In this Scripture in Romans 12 Paul also says to share with God's people who are in need. We shouldn't do that in order to escape our pain but to use it for good. We can minister more effectively in the lives of others because of our pain. The idea of looking to the needs of others to forget our pain is not a good one, I believe, since we would miss what God wants to do in our lives with Him. Acknowledge and be patient in the pain, seeking Him, then we are fit and ready to minister to others.

Talk to Jesus about being patient in your affliction.

Romans 12:9-21                                        September 22

## Weep with Those Who Weep

Paul continues to give admonitions for the Christians in Romans 12. Give preference to one another, be patient in tribulation, continue steadfastly in prayer, bless those who persecute you, as well as, "Rejoice with those who rejoice, and weep with those who weep, found in verse 15.

Since we are all members of one body, when one rejoices, that is an opportunity for all to rejoice. Coincidently, when one weeps, we also should weep, to feel the pain of that one. Paul also wrote in I Corinthians 12:26: "If one member suffers, all the members suffer with him; or if one member is honored, all the members rejoice with him".

Paul does not just tell those who have a natural affinity for compassion to weep with those who weep. It is a directive given to all the believers as he tries to establish in them their oneness in Christ. Sometimes it is difficult for us to understand why another believer is so overcome with grief, but we are not called to understand it, simply called upon to weep with them, to be with them as they mourn. Having owned a number of pets, for example, I "get it" when someone is inconsolable over the loss of one. Non-animal lovers often struggle to understand or even worse, brush aside the loss as if it were of no consequence, leaving the person to cry alone. We may not feel the need to weep, but if another person does, we are admonished to be with them in it. We can weep for their sorrow, if not for the cause of it. It is my opinion that Christians need some work in this area. Certainly we have a hope that the world does not, but that does not mean we don't feel the deep sense of loss when it occurs in the here and now. We are to rejoice with one another and weep with one another, acknowledging and being present with one another in pain and sorrow.

How are you at joining with another person in his pain?

Romans 12:14-15                                      September 23

## Joining Others in Their Emotions

How can we get to the place where we rejoice with those who rejoice and weep with those who weep? Our sinful nature is such that, if we are honest, we can be jealous of those who are rejoicing when we are not, and we can be thankful and maybe even self-righteous that we are not the ones who are weeping. Those are indeed ugly parts of ourselves but nevertheless, sometimes present. We also are so caught up and concentrated on our own lives that we often are unaware when someone is mourning or rejoicing. In our self-centeredness, we miss it, also a sign of our sinful nature.

Yet here, Paul is telling us to join others in their emotions- to be present with them, to recognize where they are and to come alongside them. We are to be happy with them and to be sad with them, to make an attempt to feel what they are feeling. To do that requires a giving up of where we are emotionally for that moment and being willing, for that time, to put the other person before ourselves. It does not mean that we disregard how we are feeling and never deal with ourselves, but on the contrary, because we have dealt with our own emotions with God, we are free to be with another in his. It also does not mean getting down in the pit with someone so we are rendered ineffective in our attempt to help. Jesus ministered to us, and we are told for a time to let go of ourselves and truly be with another.

Paul writes here that we can even get to the place where we bless those who persecute us. How? Because we have been with Jesus, and He met our needs so we are free to deal in a loving way to others.

How are you doing with the rejoicing and mourning with others?

Romans 13:7-8                                    September 24

## Debt

Another area that at first look would seem to be new to our society and therefore, not addressed in Scripture, is credit card debt. I see many individuals and couples who are suffering anxiety and depression because they have been tempted and have succumbed in this area. There was no Master Card, nor stores in which to use them, when Scripture was written, so how can God give us direction about it? He does- quite often.

Malachi 3 presents the truth that we are stewards of what God Himself owns and that He has entrusted us with it. We manage it for Him. If that is true, do we need to build up debt and have large interest payments hanging over our heads? He owns the cattle on a thousand hills, and He is our Father. Does He want His children living under the stress of owing large sums of money?  Luke 19:11-26 gives us the parable of the talents, showing us that we are expected to take what is given to us and use it wisely. In II Corinthians 9:6-11 God presents the idea of resources being like a farmer sowing seed liberally and reaping the benefit. That's a much different picture than being under the load of debt. We can't invest our resources wisely if we are continually running to pay interest on debt. Romans 13:7-8 also speaks about our heart being where our treasure is and that we cannot serve both God and money.

God gives us many admonitions in Scripture about how to handle our money, yet there are so many Christians in trouble with it. It is often one of the first issues that surfaces in marital counseling. I am always amazed at that. If we were in that abiding relationship that God so desires with us, that would never be. "Put me first and all these other things will be added unto you."

Do you need to do some work with God to become more pleasing to Him in the area of handling finances?

Romans 14:13-21 & 15:1-5                               September 25

## Edifying Another

Romans 14:19 says, "Pursue the things which make for peace and the things by which one may edify another". That may mean having to give up something that I want. Verse 15 says, "If your brother is distressed because of what you eat, you are no longer acting in love". I may be perfectly at ease doing a thing, but if my brother finds it offensive, or it causes him to stumble, for his sake I should be willing to give it up. It is not about doing or not doing but being pleasing to God. He desires that I seek peace with His people and build them up, rather than cause them to stumble.

To give up pleasing myself for the sake of another requires sacrifice. How can that be a problem for me when Jesus gave His all for me, sacrificing Himself? Fortunately for me, He did not look to please Himself, but to look to the will of the Father and to what was crucial for me. Romans 15:1 says I am not to be about pleasing myself but about pleasing my neighbor for his good, which then leads to his being lifted up. We are to be like - minded toward one another, that we together may glorify God.

The idea of glorifying God and edifying others before considering ourselves is so foreign in our society, where everything points to looking after ourselves first. We have to give that up, and sometimes it is uncomfortable and may even cause us pain, but the rewards are so great, mainly the satisfaction and fulfillment of who God always intended us to be and how he intended for us to function. Jesus' redemption brings us back into the relationship God always intended. We need to desire that for others and act toward them in a way that it can be made possible.

Are you willing to give up your desires and comfort for the edification of another and for the glory of God?

Romans 15:22-33                                      September 26

## Hindered

Paul writes that he was hindered in going to the believers in Rome (Romans 15:22). He desired to go and felt the need of their help and companionship. He coveted their prayers and sought refreshment with them. Yet up to this point he was hindered from going, hindered because God had other things for him to do, like preaching the gospel to those who had not heard and ministering to those who needed to grow in the Lord. He wanted to be with them, even listing many of them individually in chapter 16 with whom he had close relationships, but he only wanted to go "with joy by the will of God" (verse 32). He wanted to go "in the fullness of the blessing of the gospel of Christ" (verse 29).

Paul felt the need for fellowship and rest among the people he had grown to love, but he was willing to put that aside for a time to do the will of God. He acknowledged and expressed his feelings but did not allow them to determine his actions. He did not live on them but instead lived and made decisions based on God's truth and directives, laying down his own desires to fulfill God's plan. His plans are not our plans. When we are hindered, and it is clear the hindrance is from God, we need to lay aside our desires and submit to Him, sometimes causing us temporary discomfort and pain. Being hindered requires that we give up our independence and put ourselves where we belong, in His hands.

Think how you respond when you are hindered from doing what you want and think you need.

Do you readily submit to Him?

I Corinthians 2:1-5                                    September 27

## Paul's Fear and Trembling

As Paul goes to the Corinthians, his desire is to give them direction and equip them to serve the Lord. He also had to confront sin in their lives, which because of his love for them, caused him a great deal of sorrow. He goes to them in weakness and fear (I Corinthians 2:3). It is difficult to think of Paul feeling fear and weakness as he ministers, but that is indeed how he describes himself, and it is a good thing since it causes him to seek God's strength and wisdom, knowing his own will not suffice.

At the beginning of my work week, I often pause at the door to my counseling office and say to God, "If You don't go in there before me, I'm not going". I know in myself that I have nothing to offer. Anything of value that happens in the life of a counselee is from God, and if He doesn't do the work, good change will not occur. That is not always a comfortable feeling, having to depend on Someone other than ourselves. It is painful to say, "There is nothing in me that fits me for this work". Often when I hear the entanglements of a person's life story, I can so identify with Paul's feelings of "weakness, fear, and much trembling". "I can't do this", I say to God, but then in my weakness, He begins to do the work. In that pain of knowing I, myself, am ineffective, His Spirit takes over and brings power and wisdom.

Many of us experience similar fear and trembling as we attempt to witness to those around us or when we step out into ministry for God. The feelings are not pleasant, but they are good, because we learn to trust God in them, and we give the results over to Him. Paul accomplished much even in his fear and trembling, ESPECIALLY in his fear and trembling.

Don't let your fear and trembling keep you from doing what God directs. Let Him use it for you to trust Him to do the work.

I Corinthians 2:13- 16                    September 28

## Foolishness

A great sadness in my life is that my Dad died without coming to the Lord. He saw my Mother, my brother, and all of our families come to know Jesus as our Savior, but he would not. We had a Christian neighbor who witnessed to him. One time we were on vacation in Vermont, and my Dad wanted to visit an attraction with steam trains. They had a film, which he insisted that we see. He thought it was only about trains, but it turned out to be mainly about the owner of the trains and his testimony of knowing Jesus. The owner himself came and spoke to my Dad about his need for the Savior. Just as when we in our family, even the grandchildren, witnessed to him, he became angry and refused. There are many other examples of how God sent people to my Dad to tell him the truth about Himself. He died at the age of 74, walking off the field at one of my son's baseball games, never having received the One Who died for his sins. There were so many opportunities.

"But the natural man does not receive the things of the Spirit of God, for they are foolishness to him, nor can he know them because they are spiritually discerned" (I Corinthians 2:14). At times when I am dealing with an unsaved person, it is plain that they are not receiving God's truth- they cannot, until they receive the mind of Christ. To my Dad, things of the Lord were foolishness to him- He could not know them. He told me shortly after my husband died that now I would see that "this Christian thing" did not work. Of course, it "worked" more than it ever had before because I needed Jesus even more. He could not know that.

It is painful to see souls who refuse the redemption that Jesus so lovingly offers. They remain closed off to the things of the Spirit of God, those things that bring life.

It is right to mourn for those who have not received what Christ offers. Pray for those you know who are in that condition. Continue to pray.

I Corinthians 3:1-8                                         September 29

## Envy, Strife, and Divisions

Paul writes how he had to feed the Corinthians milk, not solid food, because they were unable to receive it. They were carnal Christians, saved, but grossly immature. One of the examples he uses to show their carnality is in the strife and divisions going on among them. They were behaving, he says, like mere men, not like men who have been transformed by the power of the Spirit.

When we are not allowing God's Spirit to control us, we so easily fall into difficulties with our brothers and sisters, bringing much pain to ourselves, sorrow to our God, and dysfunction and powerlessness to our community of believers. This is an example of pain that does not have to be. We bring it on ourselves by not putting ourselves in a place to receive "solid food". God's Word and the power of His Spirit give us all we need to walk the life that He desires, a life where we are so focused on Jesus that we have no time to spend on envy, strife, and divisions. When our focus is on being whom He desires and bringing others to a saving knowledge of Him, we won't be a party to envy, strife, and divisions. Our time and energy will go into working together with other believers to accomplish His will, and there we will find real fulfillment. How sad God must be when He witnesses our immature behavior to one another. He has so much more for us, but often because of our immature state, we are unable to receive it. I tell clients who are living in carnality that they are in the worst possible position. They know Jesus but are not living for Him, yet are held accountable to Him. This puts them in a constant state of guilt. Unbelievers, meanwhile, are freely living in their sin, usually having no guilt, not knowing any better.

Do you grieve God by the behavior you demonstrate with other believers?

Will you allow Him to begin to feed you solid food?

I Corinthians 4:10-13                                    September 30

## Paul's Experience

Many of us experience the discomfort that comes from not fitting into our society. Listen to Paul's experience found in I Corinthians 4:11-13: He hungers and thirsts, he is poorly clothed, he is beaten, he is homeless. He also describes himself as being reviled, persecuted, defamed, made as the filth of the world, and made a spectacle to them. He calls himself a fool for Christ, weak and dishonored. Even in all of this he continues to labor, to bless others, and to entreat them. In verse 16 he then urges the Corinthians to imitate him, essentially to live like he does, and to suffer as he does in order to follow Christ.

Who would sign up to have an experience like Paul's? Who would purposely choose a lifestyle that would cause the world to call him a fool and that would deprive him of all that brings comfort? Paul did. Then he calls on the Corinthian church to do likewise. He calls on us to do likewise. He did, and we can, because he looked past the present suffering and saw a much bigger picture, a broader view of God's intent, not just for now, but for eternity.

The world will not understand, and may even consider us fools, when we give up its pleasures for those things that matter for eternity, when we choose work that changes lives rather than increases our bank account, when we spend time, money, and energy on what God directs, rather than what we might desire. We can, like Paul, be considered fools when we consider the reward of being in His will, both now and in eternity.

Can you withstand being considered a fool for Him?

I Corinthians 8:13; 9:12 & 19-23                    October 01

## Giving Up Our Rights

Paul describes himself as a servant to all, serving all men so that they will come to the Lord. In I Corinthians 8 he says that while he was free to eat meat he was willing to give it up if it caused a brother to stumble, showing his willingness to put another before himself. In chapter 9 he lists various things to which he surrendered his right for the good of others: a wife, wages, grapes from his vineyard, milk from his animals... He had rights, just like anyone else, but did not claim his rights but instead, endured all things rather than hinder God's work.

In our country our rights are important to us, and they should be. In our history many have died so that we have the right to life, liberty, and the pursuit of happiness. We have the right to free speech, to pursue work that we desire, to get an education, to live where we choose and with whom, to be protected from those who disobey the law... We are blessed to live in a land where we have so many human rights, and we should appreciate them, but God asks something of us that goes beyond these rights. He asks that we be willing, like Paul did, to give them up at times so His gospel can impact others. We have freedom, but we may need to sacrifice it for the good of another. We may have to hand God our freedom to use in a way that will promote His work.

Paul calls himself a servant to all. A servant gives up his rights- to serve, to serve God and others.

How do you behave when called to give up what is your right?

When we accepted Jesus as our Savior and Lord we gave up our rights to HIM.

I Corinthians 11:27-32                                    October 02

## Examine Yourself

In I Corinthians 11 Paul gives instructions regarding the remembrance of the Lord's supper. It is to be an opportunity to examine ourselves and make anything that is not in line with God, right- before partaking of the bread and cup. It is a painful thing to examine oneself. If we are honest, we see much that needs correction. Our behavior may be reasonable, but when we turn to our thoughts, attitudes and motives, the things that no one else sees, there will surely be things with which we are ashamed. God knows us intimately, and He describes human nature as being deceitful and desperately wicked. That time before communion can be quite painful as we contemplate who we are, until we see our Father Who is waiting to forgive us our sin. The joy that comes from knowing He receives us with open arms, just like the prodigal father did his son, when we confess who we are, is worth any amount of pain we feel when viewing ourselves.

The alternative to not seeing ourselves and dealing with our sin is to eat and drink in an unworthy manner. Paul writes to the Corinthians that this is the reason many are weak and sick and even sleep- they eat and drink the Lord's supper without examining themselves.

The next opportunity you have to partake of the Lord's supper, use it to bring those things before Him that do not please Him.

Then eat and drink in a worthy manner.

I Corinthians 12:12-31                                    October 03

## Belonging in the Body

Rugged individualism is a trait which Americans treasure and in which we take pride. We enjoy independence, and yet we also have a basic need to belong, to be part of something beyond ourselves. We were not created to be an island off by ourselves, relying only on ourselves, but in our way of life that seems to be the reality for many. Since God did not create us that way, it does not work. Isolation, not belonging, brings distress to our being.

Paul writes how we are individuals but at the same time, we are part of the body of Christ. We are God's children, co-heirs with His Son, and brothers or sisters with every other believer. We belong to the family of God from the moment we receive Christ into our lives. God even fitted us specifically to function in that body, giving us gifts to make the whole body work, just like the organs and other parts of our physical bodies work together.

I have seen clients who, for various reasons, have no sense of belonging to a family. They suffer with the pain of that, but God, knowing their need, provides them with His family. How blessed we are to have one another. We belong.

Thank God for meeting your most basic of needs by placing you in His family.

I Corinthians 13:4-13                                             October 04

## Love Hurts

No one knows better how much love hurts than God.  Paul says in I Corinthians 13:4 that love suffers long, which immediately brings to mind the 40 years God loved, but was continually rejected, by the Israelites in the wilderness.  He suffered long- because of His great love.  He continues to suffer, having given His Son to die the cruelest of deaths so that men might know Him and live, and yet they refuse and choose to live lives of pain and emptiness, resulting ultimately in an eternity of separation from Him.  How He must grieve as He looks on such lives.  His love cost Him so much and yet it is so often rejected.

Paul tells us what love looks like in I Corinthians 13: "It suffers long, is kind, does not envy, does not parade itself, is not puffed up, does not behave rudely, does not seek its own, is not provoked, thinks no evil, does not rejoice in iniquity but rejoices in truth, bears all things, believes all things, hopes all things, endures all things.  It NEVER fails."  To love like this requires a giving up of ourselves.  We will have to be willing to suffer long, to not seek our own, to not be provoked, to be willing to bear all things, to endure all things.  We will have to sacrifice our own self to serve others in love, to serve our Lord in love.  As we sit with Him and take in these truths, we have to suffer the pain of knowing how we fail in loving the way He does.  We have to be willing to want to give up ourselves and want to allow Him to help us love the way He desires.

One of the main reasons a person has difficulty loving is that he may not feel loved himself.   If this is the case with you, know that your Father stands ready and is longing to love you to the depth of your being.  Only He can rectify your love deficit. Let Him.

Sit with Him and let Him show you what you need to do to begin to love in the way He describes in I Corinthians 13.

I Corinthians 15:50-57                                    October 05

## The Sting of Death

We grieve over many things from the trivial to the truly devastating. We rebel against even the minor losses: when the weather doesn't cooperate and we can't do what we planned; when one of our treasured electronic gadgets inexplicably ceases to work; when a much anticipated event is cancelled. We also experience a sense of loss when a child goes off to school for the first time, when we say goodbye to a friend who is moving away or when we experience the effects of an aging body. Then there is the grief that comes from something that sends our entire world reeling, a loss that is final, one which cannot be rectified or made right. The death of one we love is such a loss. I have experienced several of these myself, and I have sat with many others as they seek to find their way through the pain and emptiness that ensue in such a loss.

Death stings us like no other loss. I have vivid memories of seeing a loved one's face for the last time, of watching a coffin being lowered into the ground, of walking away from a cemetery and leaving a loved one's body there, never to enjoy their presence again in this life- pain like no other.

Paul offers us a verse, I Corinthians 15:52, which brings not only comfort, but joy, to us in such a time: "In the twinkling of an eye, the trumpet will sound, and the dead will be raised incorruptible, and we shall be changed." "Death is swallowed up in victory "(I Corinthians 15:55). We have the victory over death through the death and resurrection of our Lord and Savior Jesus Christ. He will redeem our pain of losing loved ones to death.

What seems so very final is not final at all. There is still another chapter to come as we walk from those grave sites.

Even while mourning the loss of someone dear, know that Jesus will have the final victory.

II Corinthians 1:3-4                                    October 06

## Helping Others Through Loss

Not only does God intend to redeem our losses for ultimate good, but He wants others to benefit by our comforting them with the same comfort with which He has comforted us.  We cannot give what we ourselves have not received.  In other words, we are to pass on the comfort to them that He has given us.  We first must remember the truths and then pass them on: It is good to mourn; mourning is an opportunity.  If we believe these truths, what will we do with the grieving person?  We will allow him to mourn, even if it is uncomfortable for us, and often it will be.  We will support them as they cry and protest.  We will be there with them as they go from the Why? to the What?  And the How?  We will listen and be present without trying to fix them.  They may mourn differently than we would or about something that we might not, but it is their pain, and we need to respect it and be obedient to God's Word while offering our comfort as God offers us His comfort.  They need someone to hear how they are feeling, so we do that first, and later, sometimes much later, when they are able to hear, perhaps deal with the incorrect thinking they may be exhibiting.  Of course, we pray for them..  Offer practical help by taking the initiative in it since they may not be able.  Admit to them that we don't have all the answers.  In fact, we may have no answers, BUT...and this is a big BUT... we know the One Who does.  Carefully point them to Him, the Real Comforter.  There is that intimacy again which sustains in everything, every day.

Think about how God has taught you and comforted you in your sorrows.

Is there someone to whom He wants you to offer that same comfort?

II Corinthians 1:3-7                                    October 07

## Comforting Others

As Paul writes his second letter to the Corinthians, he begins by presenting God as "the God of all comfort, Who comforts us in all our tribulations." This young church was subjected to false teachers, they had personality difficulties, and they had problems staying the course on basic behavioral issues, so Paul was called upon to correct and plead with them as well as offer comfort and hope, which he does in II Corinthians 1:3-7. He tells them that while they suffer tribulation, it also opens the door for them to experience God's comfort. As sufferings abound, so do consolations, which lead to a deeper knowledge of Jesus. They will not know the comfort that Jesus can bring if they do not first know the sufferings.

Paul writes about another purpose for suffering and the ultimate comforting that comes: "that we may be able to comfort those who are in any trouble, with the comfort with which we ourselves are comforted by God." We can offer others what God has given to us. We cannot give what we do not have. Our afflictions, Paul says, are partly for the consolation and salvation of others.

I know what it is, when in affliction, to be instinctively drawn to another who has gone through a similar circumstance. They "get it" and have something to offer. Support groups work on this principle and can be highly effective, especially if the members offer that which God has given them.

The greater the suffering, the greater the comfort God gives. There is nothing sweeter than sitting with Him and being surrounded by His comfort. HE, knowing pain like no other, offers exactly what we need.

Will you receive the comfort that God longs to give you in your sufferings? Then will you allow Him to use it in the lives of others?

II Corinthians 1:8-11                                      October 08

## Burdens Beyond Measure

Paul does not hide the trouble he has endured. He writes that they were "burdened beyond measure, above strength, so that they despaired even of life" while in Asia. He was willing to share the depths of his feelings, something that I fear is absent in many Christian circles. Is it because we think that we are doing something wrong if all is not going well in our lives, and therefore, should not share it with others? Surely that was not the case with Paul. He WAS where God wanted him to be, doing exactly what God had ordained, yet there were troubles that took him close to death.

Paul's assessment of the troubles he endured is that he saw that he could not trust in himself, but in God. It is such a simple principle, but one with which we continually struggle. Apparently Paul did also. In himself the sentence of death was upon him, but it was God Who delivered him from it. Only God.

His near death experience and his "burdens beyond measure" also drove him to include others in his work. He needed their help in the form of prayer. He needed them to thank and praise God on his behalf. We are here to have intimacy with God and then with others. Both are accomplished here as Paul suffers "burdens beyond measure."

Do you see the importance of sharing your "burdens beyond all measure" with others, even as Paul did?

II Corinthians 2:3-11                                      October 09

## Paul's Affliction, Anguish, and Many Tears

In both I and II Corinthians, Paul saw the need to confront the behavior and immaturity of the believers in Corinth, but he did it with much love and compassion. II Corinthians 2:4 says he wrote to them with many tears, tears that flowed from his desire that they live rightly before God, knowing only that kind of living would meet their needs. When I feel the need to weep for people, it is not only for the situations they are in, but often it is for what could be, for what God desires for them, but they have refused. It is a recipe for deep grief in us to consider how God feels when He offers us so much, and yet we insist on going our own way, ending with much anguish.

Paul expresses his own grief as he writes to the church at Corinth, but he also has a message for them in how to relate to an erring brother. When a brother has fallen in sin, he needs to be disciplined, but with forgiveness and comfort, lest, Paul says, he be "swallowed up with too much sorrow." There is a time to confront and set down consequences, but there is also a time to reach out and reaffirm love. While Paul can emphatically confront when necessary, he also presents us a model of one who offers compassion, so the one in error has an opportunity to return to the place God wants him to be. As he writes with "much affliction and anguish of heart" and "with many tears," we catch an insight into Paul's heart and have a model as to how we should approach one another.

Do you look on fellow believers with affliction, anguish and many tears when they have succumbed to sin?

II Corinthians 4:10-11                                    October 10

## Manifesting Christ

"Always carrying about in the body the dying of the Lord Jesus, that the life of Jesus also may be manifested in the body.  For we who live are always delivered to death for Jesus' sake, that the life of Jesus also may be manifested in our mortal flesh," says Paul in II Corinthians 4:10-11.  In his own suffering Paul participated in Jesus' suffering, constantly manifesting Jesus' life, not considering himself.  He was willing to face death for the sake of Jesus.

So, in the center of adversity, our questions must not be the natural one of, "How do I get out of this as quickly as possible?" or "How do I make the pain go away?", but instead must be, "How do I manifest Christ in this?"  He knows about the pain, has even allowed it, maybe even orchestrated it at times, so that we have the opportunity to manifest His Son.  When we center on our hurt, turn to self-pity, or look for a quick fix, we are short circuiting the opportunity to show Him to people around us.  Not only can others see Him, but we can also see Him and marvel once again at what He does when we fully give ourselves over to Him.

In your pain do you quickly come to the place of desiring that He will shine through, so others and yourself can see Him?

II Corinthians 4:16-18                                    October 11

## Eternal Weight of Glory

If there is a verse in Scripture which captures the idea of the place of suffering in our lives it is II Corinthians 4:17: "For our light affliction, which is but for a moment, is working for us a far more exceeding and eternal weight of glory." Our pain, as far as eternity is concerned, is but for a moment. It is "light" in comparison to the glory that awaits. Our pain is working for us. God is redeeming it so that our eternity will be so much more glorious. My pain causes me to seek Jesus and know Him better. He is the One with Whom I am spending eternity, so how can my suffering not contribute to a more glorious eternity? To see this we have to look at the things which are not seen and not rely only on what is seen. In other words, believe God rather than only what our limited and flawed views shows us. "The things which are seen are temporary, but the things which are not seen are eternal" (verse 18).

When we are going through the mourning process, due to a loss in our lives, our tendency is to look only on our pain, but Paul tells us not to lose heart. Our bodies are deteriorating, but "the inward man is being renewed day by day." It is being renewed as we allow God into our suffering, depending on Him to make sense of it and show us Himself as we look to the glory of eternity with Him.

Do you consider it a privilege and honor to go through any amount of suffering for Him?

Lorraine Brosious

II Corinthians 4:7-15                                    October 12

## Hard- Pressed but not Crushed

Some of the people I meet with are hard-pressed on every side: They lose jobs, have insurmountable debts, have health challenges, have little family support, grieve the loss of a loved one, have sole responsibility for an aging parent... Yes, they are hard-pressed, but Paul says, not crushed (II Corinthians 4:8). Sometimes they are perplexed, without understanding, but Paul says not in despair. Some are persecuted, reviled for their faith, but not forsaken. Some are struck down, having the very wind knocked out of them, but, Paul says, not destroyed (verse 9). Why? Because the life of Jesus is manifested in them. II Corinthians 4:14 says, "knowing that He Who raised up the Lord Jesus will also raise us up with Jesus." Because of HIM we can be hard-pressed but not crushed.

I am amazed at some of the stories I hear from my adult clients concerning their childhoods. Several have been on their own from twelve years of age, living on the street, one even living in a cardboard box for a time. I have heard heart-wrenching stories of both physical and sexual abuse, and yes, there are ramifications from these horrors, but I am always struck when I hear one of these accounts of how God had His hand on them, even years before they were in a position to know and receive Him. They were not crushed, nor forsaken, nor destroyed. Because of Jesus they survived, and in many cases, triumphed, and were used greatly in their witness to others.

If you are feeling hard-pressed on every side, remember, you are not crushed because Jesus is in you, and He will raise you up if you let Him.

II Corinthians 5:1-11                                    October 13

## Burdened By Our Bodies

Yesterday, amongst my work and other responsibilities, I swam, rode my bike, and did some weight exercises, all in an attempt to maintain the body God gave me (quite a long time ago!).   I also struggle, as do many others, to eat good foods, even sometimes counting the number of fruits and vegetables I have consumed.  I have had a life-long struggle with weight, and while I tire of it some days, I know it will always be that way in this life.  Paul says in II Corinthians 5:4 that in these earthly bodies, we groan, being burdened, not just because some of us have to devote our attention to exercise and right eating, but because we know that there is more for us.  There is always the knowledge that something is not quite right, even when all appears to be going well.  That something is sin, always lurking, always ready to gain our affection.  Just like having to exercise to keep our bodies healthy, we have to be constantly vigilant to maintain our spiritual health, to be in close relationship with God.

Paul says in II Corinthians 4:19 that "our outward man is perishing, yet the inward man is being renewed day by day." We work to maintain ourselves to fend off the aging process, but we know we will lose that battle, and for many, that is a distressing thought- unless we agree with Paul when he says in verse 4 that "mortality may be swallowed up by life"- real life.  Real life is being home with the Lord.  There will always be somewhat of a dissatisfaction as long as we are in our bodies.  We like them for the most part, some may even love them, but they burden us and cause us to groan because we desire more.  That more is to be with HIM.

While seeking to be well pleasing to God while in your body (II Corinthians 5:9), do you look forward to the day when you will no longer be burdened but will be complete in Him?

II Corinthians 5:12-21                                    October 14

## Living for Him

Jesus died so that we could be reconciled to God, so now we can no longer live for ourselves, but for Him Who died and rose again (II Corinthians 5:15). He bought us and so we belong to Him, no longer owned by ourselves. Verse 17 calls us new creatures- the old is gone, the new has come. The old was that we did what we wanted, when we wanted, with no thought of anyone but ourselves. The new is that we submit every aspect of ourselves to Him. Verse 18 says, "Now all things are of God." It is not about us now, but about Him. We are ambassadors for Christ, giving ourselves in pleading with others to reconcile themselves to Him.

What might that mean for us? Because Christ lives within us, it is no longer we who live but HE Who lives within us, so we give Him permission to do whatever He wants in our lives. That "whatever" may be highly inconvenient for us, even bringing suffering and pain, for the purpose of others coming to reconciliation with the Father. It may mean sacrificing time we have set aside for ourselves and instead using it for the good of another. It may mean having to accept offense in order to have the opportunity to present Jesus to an unbeliever. It may mean putting our own needs and desires aside for a time so that another can come in contact with God's truth. It may mean being willing to carry pain so that Jesus can show Himself to those who so desperately need Him. It WILL mean a giving up of ourselves to HIM, for HIS glory and other's good.

Are you willing to give up living for yourself and to begin living for Him?

II Corinthians 6:1-13                                   October 15

## Pouring Out

In II Corinthians 6 Paul describes his life: in much distress, in tribulations, in needs, in distresses, in stripes, in imprisonments, in tumults, in labors, in sleeplessness, in fastings. These are experiences that he himself has had. He also talks about long sufferings, dishonor, evil report, and deceivers, again things with which he is quite familiar. I have been surprised as I have looked into Paul's writings at how much there is for us to see about adversity and suffering. He can write about it because it has been so much a part of his life. He knows whereof he speaks. He has experienced being chastened, and yet not killed, being sorrowful, yet always rejoicing, being poor, yet making others rich, having nothing, yet possessing all things (verses 9 and 10). He has earned the right to tell us what suffering is about, and God has called him to that. Open his heart he does, pouring out God's truth about pain.

Recently I was part of a discussion about the meaning of ministry. Paul exemplifies it here, pouring out on others what God has given him. Then he calls on the Corinthians to be open themselves, to pour out on others what God has given them. The more He gives us, the more we have to pour out. I remember hearing a man in my church, a dear friend, say that at the end of his life he wants to be completely spent for God. He doesn't want anything to be left behind, unused. He wants it all poured out for the glory of God and the good of others.

Are you ministering to others in the sense that you are pouring yourself out, ministering in the lives of others with what God has given you?

II Corinthians 6:14-18                                    October 16

## Unequally Yoked

Sorrow comes upon us for various reasons, one being our own disobedience of God's Word.  This particular passage in II Corinthians 6:14 presents a command that, when not obeyed, often results in untold pain.  When we choose, as believers, to make close alliances, such as marriage or a business partnership with unbelievers, we have no commonality to make the arrangement work.  We will not have the same foundation, values, or goals.  We will be at odds, and strife can be the only result.

I have seen many women, particularly, who did not heed this truth and have suffered a life-time for it, never knowing what it is to have a spouse who shares their love for the Lord and His work.  Their children pay a price also while growing up in a home of conflicting values and beliefs.  I grew up in such a home.  Fortunately, God's grace prevailed, and my brother and I, and subsequently our families, all found the Lord (or more correctly, He found us), but I still have painful memories of a dad who attempted to undermine anything concerning God.

God has called us to come out and be separate unto Him, to let Him be our God and for us to be His people.  In marriage we are called to become one.  How do we become one with another who is not separate from the world?  To be separate we need our closest relationships to be like-minded, to encourage and support us as we follow Him.

Do you seek out like-minded people in your closest associations?  If not, you are inviting unnecessary pain.

II Corinthians 7:1-12 October 17

## Sorrowing in a Godly Manner

In his first letter to the church at Corinth, Paul was confrontational in an attempt to bring change into their lives, and it worked, even though it caused sorrow in them. In one respect, Paul says, he was sorry for their sorrow, but in another respect, he is no longer sorry (II Corinthians 7:8). He rejoices now because their sorrow, though only for a while, led to repentance. "For Godly sorrow produces repentance leading to salvation, not to be regretted" (verse 10). The Corinthians sorrowed over their sin in a Godly manner, and it served to bring much needed change into their lives. It was a good, productive sorrow, temporary, based on the will of God, and leading to repentance and new life.

What Christian of any maturity has not known the sorrow of Godly confrontation concerning sin. How painful it is! Recently in my personal time with the Lord, He showed me how badly I was failing Him in a certain area. It was crushing for a time, until the joy of repentance and restoration eventually came. It is never pleasant to see ourselves as we are.

These same people whom Paul had to "hit" hard, became great sources of comfort to him as they comforted Titus, who then comforted him, when he was exhausted, troubled on every side, fearful, enduring conflicts. These same people mourned as they heard of Paul's circumstance. He rejoiced, hearing of their care for him. Their Godly sorrow produced in them diligence, a clearing of themselves and zeal. Paul ends by telling us that he said the hard truths to them because he not only wanted them to change, but he wanted them to know his care for them.

Do you confront to produce Godly sorrow and because you care for him who needs to change?

II Corinthians 8:1-15                                        October 18

## Giving in Affliction

Paul continues to instruct the Corinthians, this time by citing the poverty-stricken churches of Macedonia, who were under much affliction.  He used the Macedonians as a worthy example to the Corinthians of a people who had little, yet gave liberally, beyond their ability.  Not only were they willing to give but they actually implored Paul "with much urgency" that he would receive their gifts.  How did they arrive at a place where they, in their deep poverty, begged to be allowed to give?  Verse 5 of II Corinthians holds the answer: "They first gave of themselves to the Lord, and then to us (other believers) by the will of God."  They first gave themselves to God.

Paul goes on to say that Jesus, even though He was rich, became poor for their sakes, giving up all that He had, even to his very life, so that they through His poverty, might become rich.

He also says that he does not expect them to be burdened so that others should live in ease, but when one has a need, the other should meet it, and when the other is lacking, the one, out of his abundance should supply what is needed.  "He who gathered much had nothing left over, and he who gathered little had no lack."

In your affliction do you continue to give yourself to the Lord and then to others with an interest to meeting their needs?

II Corinthians 11:22-33                                    October 19

## Paul's Experiences in Adversity

Paul felt the need, somewhat reluctantly, it seems, to remind the Corinthians of who he is and of his commitment to them.  In verses 23-27 of II Corinthians 11 he gives them an account of what he has gone through: Labors more abundant, stripes above measure, prisons more frequently, deaths often; He received 39 stripes three times, was stoned three times, shipwrecked, in the deep, in journeys, in perils of waters, attacked by robbers, and with his own countrymen and the Gentiles, in perils in the city, wilderness, sea and among false brethren, in weariness in toil, in sleeplessness, in hunger and thirst, fasting often, in cold and nakedness.... He notes a time when he was close to being arrested and was let down in a basket through a window in the wall but was able to escape.  That should cover anything we could even imagine going through.  Besides all that, Paul has the added burden of his deep concern for all the churches (verse 28).  Because of these experiences, his many sufferings for Jesus, he can defend himself against criticism and reestablish his credibility with the people he is trying so desperately to influence for the Lord.  His burden for them alone was a heavy weight to bear, affecting him daily, but then he had all the other adversities he mentions.  Surely they were burdensome for him, but they also proved to the Corinthians what he was willing to suffer for his God- and for them.  The sorrows he endured gave him the right to be heard.

Do you carry adversities willingly so God can use them and you in the lives of others?

II Corinthians 12:7-10                                    October 20

## Paul's Thorn

Imagine taking pleasure in an infirmity, something that constantly affects your very being, something that Satan uses in your life to buffet you, to toss you around. To put up with it or endure it is one thing, but to say you appreciate it and even take pleasure in it is quite another, and yet Paul did just that. He was given some sort of thorn in the flesh (verse 7). There has been much speculation about what the exact nature of the thorn was, but it would appear that God purposely did not tell us- perhaps so that we could better identify with Paul in it, thinking maybe it was similar to ours. Anyway, Paul asks not once, but three times, that the Lord might take it away, but He did not, saying that "My grace is sufficient for you" and "My strength is made perfect in weakness" (verse 9). Paul learned in the face of infirmity that God's grace and strength would help him deal with it. Had it been removed, that would have been a one-time miracle, but God's constant sufficiency in it was a continual miracle. I have often thought when prayer is given for one's healing, that the greater miracle would not be the healing, but that it would be one's gracious acceptance of carrying the infirmity. I have been privileged to witness this on several occasions. That is what happened in Paul's life, even to the point of taking pleasure in it.

Talk with God about your willingness to carry some adversity in your life-for the opportunity of His showing His sufficiency and strength.

II Corinthians 12:14-21                                    October 21

## Spending and Being Spent

Paul's great love for the Corinthians causes him to have concerns that when he visits them he will not find them as he wishes. He is concerned that there will be contentions, wrath, selfish ambitions, back-biting, whisperings, conceits, tumults, besides lack of repentance for sins of uncleanness, fornication, and lewdness, which would produce great mourning in him. If he did not love them so, he would not be filled with mourning for their sin.

Paul is out for the edification of these people he so deeply loves, even though the more he loves them, the less he is loved by them. He says he will gladly spend and be spent for their souls (II Corinthians 12:15). He gives of himself even though the return is sometimes negative. The more he gives of himself, the less they love him, yet he is determined to continue- because he loves. In I Corinthians he wrote that love suffers long, does not seek its own, is not easily provoked, bears all things, endures all things... Here in Paul's life we see that kind of love being modeled.

How difficult it is to continue to spend and be spent when, not only are we not loved in return, but get negative results. Our only chance of succeeding in continuing to spend and be spent, is to keep our focus on HIM, as we allow HIM to do HIS work through us. We should mourn as Paul did, when other believers are not living as His Word commands, but we need to focus, not on how we feel, but on their continued edification.

Can you stand to continue to spend and be spent, even though the results you see are not what you would wish?

II Corinthians 13                                    October 22

## Being Complete

In II Corinthians 13 Paul twice mentions the goal of completeness for the believers of the church of Corinth. That is a good goal in counseling- for the Lord to bring counselees to a place of wholeness, or being complete. I think that for myself, Lord, that You would show me what part of me needs Your work to move me toward completeness. He does, on a regular basis.

Paul finds it easier to write to the Corinthians, fearing that if he were present with them, he may use sharpness in attempting to get them to live as God desires. Paul desires to edify and not to be destructive as he moves them to edification.

Paul also feels the necessity to ask them to examine themselves to see if they truly know God and if He is in them. It can be a difficult question to ask someone, even causing discomfort, both his and ours, but it is a necessary question if we care about his eternal destination. Paul felt the need to ask the question because of what he saw going on in their lives. Their behavior was not matching what God had set down for a believer. He ends his letter by telling them to "Become complete". That completeness begins with Jesus' forgiveness of their sins through His shed blood and continues with their obedience to His Word, which then puts them in a position to know Him more deeply.

Examine yourself. Have you started the process of being complete in Him? Are you continuing in it by taking in and living out His truths?

Galatians 4:8-20                                             October 23

## Fear and Doubt

Fear and doubt, both considered negative words, are the two words Paul uses to describe how he feels about the Galatians, who have departed from God's truth, particularly in the area of justification by faith, rather than by the works of the law. While he loves them, he uses the word "foolish" to get their attention in his quest to bring them back to faith in Jesus. He wants them to see that they are no longer slaves of the law, but sons, heirs of God through Christ.

Paul is afraid for them (Galatians 4:11) and has doubts about them (verse 20), feeling that all his labors for them have been in vain. Many times I have sat with people who are afraid for their children, fearing, like Paul, that all they have poured into them has been in vain. They came to this conclusion because their children are not living out what the parents have given them and what they know to be true. The suffering the parents endure in this situation is painful because they love their children and want the best for them. Paul's writing in Galatians reveals his suffering for those he loves. Because he loves so deeply, just like a parent of an erring child, he suffers deeply. His love, however, does not allow him to enable "his children" to continue in the wrong way. On the contrary, it causes him to confront and to continue to present the truth in love, in hopes that they will eventually respond and change their behavior to align with God's truth.

Do you become afraid for others when they err in following God's truth, or is anger a more likely response in you? If we love, we fear for those outside God's will.

Galatians 5:1-10                                    October 24

## Estranged From Christ

Estrangement carries with it the idea of being alienated, particularly as regarding affections. It means being apart, separated by choice. Paul tells the Galatians in his letter to them in 5:4 that they have become estranged from Christ by their insistence on attempting to be justified by the law instead of by faith. It is a choice they made by refusing to believe God's truth, and the result brings the greatest pain known- separation from God. God did not bring them to this place. Instead they got wrong ideas by listening to others and then allowing those lies to grow in them. "A little leaven leavens the whole lump" (verse 8). Once they began to entertain the lies, their estrangement from God began. Paul describes them as having "fallen from grace" (verse 4).

When someone tells me they are estranged from a loved one, it brings up a picture of loneliness, pain and anger. There is a great gulf separating the two. One of the two has to be willing to move towards the other, and the other has to be willing to receive. God has done everything He could to put an end to the estrangement between Him and us, even allowing His Son to die. He waits for us to return, just as we are, but only on His terms, meaning as professed sinners with no hope beyond His grace. Jesus died, rose and lives so there is no need for estrangement between the Father and us.

Have you allowed Jesus to take care of the estrangement between you and God?

How about between you and others?

Galatians 6:1-10                                        October 25

## Carrying Our Own Load

In just 10 short verses Paul packs the end of his letter to the Galatians full of admonitions for a responsible and fulfilling life. First, he writes that we need to restore with gentleness one who has been overtaken with sin, but at the same time, not putting ourselves in a position where we also may be tempted and fall. It would not be wise, for example, for a recovering alcoholic to go into a bar to retrieve an erring brother, lest he himself also fall into temptation. I have seen people find a great deal of trouble for themselves by attempting to help another while deceiving themselves about their own ability to resist.

While Paul writes that we should bear one another's burdens, he also says that we should bear our own load. When we don't, it affects how we view ourselves. God has declared us conquerors through His Son, but if we don't take responsibility for our own burden, we feel weak and of little value. Sharing ourselves with others is one of God's chief intents for us, but we share in a healthy way only when we maintain our own load. Trouble ensues and relationships break when we expect others to carry what God has given to us.

Finally, Paul says a man will reap what he sows. If a farmer sows bad seeds, he will reap a bad crop, of course. If we sow from our flesh, the works of the flesh listed in Galatians 5 will most assuredly come to pass. Sowing from the Spirit will reap the fruit, also listed in Galatians 5. I see the sowing and reaping principle lived out on a daily basis.

Do you expect someone else to carry the load God has given you?

What kind of seed are you sowing?

Ephesians 1                                    October 26

## Remembering Who You Are

One of the reasons we can be overcome with the pain of life is because we forget who we are.  We can't succumb to trouble and at the same time know we have been chosen in Christ before the foundation of the world to be holy and blameless before Him, and to know that we were predestined to adoption as sons by Jesus (Ephesians 1; 4-5).  We are redeemed, bought through the blood of Jesus and forgiven for our sins.  We have an inheritance: "He works all things according to the counsel of His will" (verse 11).  We have been sealed by the Holy Spirit, Who lives within us, and does His work of direction, conviction, and illumination.  When trouble comes, as it surely will, how can we separate these truths and not live them out?  How can we forget that we are called, redeemed, made heirs, sealed?  Does God, the One Who accomplished all these things in your life, not know that you are without a job, that you are suffering from an illness, that you are bitterly disappointed in how your child is living, that your husband has been unfaithful, that you are in desperate pain from the loss of a loved one, that....  Whatever the suffering, your identity, who you are, enables you to not just get through it but to triumph in it with power and confidence.  He Who called you to Himself will be with you in your suffering and will use it in your life for good.

Are you remembering who you are- Whose you are?

Ephesians 2                                                    October 27

## Made Alive

Being dead in trespasses and sins is the epitome of pain and suffering, and yet that is what we all were, and some still are, walking according to the ways of Satan and fulfilling the desires of their flesh and mind. I shudder to think what my life and the life of my family would be like today had I continued on the path of my pre-salvation days. To have no hope and to be without God, as it says in Ephesians 2:12, is unimaginable. I would not want to live apart from Him, and the reason is given in verse 14: "For He Himself is our peace, Who has made both one, and has broken down the middle wall of separation." Verses 17 and 18 say: "And He came and preached peace to you who were afar off and to those who were near. For through Him we both have access by one Spirit to the Father." Before salvation at age 18, I had no idea how dead in trespasses and sins I was. I knew something was wrong but I didn't know that ever-present, nagging feeling was due to separation from the Father. I knew ABOUT Jesus, but I didn't KNOW HIM. I remember all those years ago (47!) how amazed I was that up until that point I had missed it, had not known that Jesus died for ME, so that I could finally be in fellowship with God. Not only was I made alive in Christ, but I now had direction for every step of my life- there was now a purpose. Verse 7 also tells us "that in the ages to come He might show the exceeding riches of His grace in His kindness toward us in Christ Jesus." I am loved by Him, and I belong to His family, "no longer a stranger and foreigner, but a fellow citizen with the saints and members of the household of God" (verse 19).

Being loved and belonging are two of our deepest needs, and cause great pain when they go unmet. Are they met for you through Jesus?

Ephesians 3:20                                                    October 28

## Immeasurably More

"God is able to do immeasurably more than we can ask or imagine, according to His power that is at work within us" (Ephesians 3:20). Some versions say, "exceedingly abundantly above all that we can ask or think." I have claimed that verse over and over for myself, not only in the midst of suffering but when I know He has asked me to do something in which I feel totally incapable. Whatever it is that I must get through or do, I have this promise that I can't even comprehend what HE is able to do in it. I am correct that in myself it can't happen, but with HIS power within me it most assuredly CAN.

I remember on several occasions after my husband's death feeling totally overwhelmed with the reality of bringing up four children on my own with limited resources. I can even remember all those years ago (26), exactly where I was when I momentarily thought, "I can't do this." I was right, I couldn't, but HE quickly gave me the assurance that HE could, and He did and has.

When God let me know I was to go into counseling, my thoughts were similar. Every time I am asked to speak publically, my first thought is, "not me!" When He gave me this writing to do... and on it goes. I CAN'T, but HE CAN- not only can He do it, but He can do immeasurably more than I can even imagine through me because of His power that is in me. It is painful when we have those thoughts and feelings of inability, but how exhilarating it is to experience HIS ability to a degree that we can't even fathom.

Talk to Him about His ability to do through you what you can't even think, because of His power in you.

Ephesians 4:7-16                                          October 29

## Tossed To and Fro

As Paul writes to the Ephesians, he tells them that they should "no longer be children, tossed to and fro and carried about with every wind of doctrine." Sometimes I am amazed at the thinking I see in people who seemingly desire to follow God. Their thinking bears no resemblance to what God clearly says in His Word, and, of course, results in pain and chaos. How can that be? Paul says it can happen "by the trickery of men, in the cunning craftiness of deceitful plotting." So, some men are out to deceive, and we, if not vigilant, can be easily misled, especially if the deceivers are telling us what we want to hear. "Life is short, enjoy it," "Look out for yourself, no one else will," "God just wants you to be happy"... These ideas sound good to us but lead to destruction because they are in direct opposition to what God, in His love for us, tells us in His Word. We need to "grow up" in His Word. A child does not have the maturity to sacrifice the now and wait for something better. He is by nature immature, and is tossed to and fro, running to his immediate desires, often ending in disaster. We expect that of children but it must not happen with adults who have the privilege of knowing what God says.

The truth of the Word of God is what prevents us from being childish and being "tossed to and fro" by those who would deceive. We need to be in the Word on a daily basis, there being no substitute for it. What a gift God has given, and yet so often it is neglected. We need to handle His gift with great intensity and purposefulness.

Are you in danger of being deceived, or are you diligently taking in God's Word so you can live without being tossed to and fro?

Ephesians 4:17-24                                        October 30

## The Old Man

What could be worse than being alienated from the life of God because of the ignorance that lies within? That is how Paul encapsulates the condition of an unbeliever. He also says they walk in the futility of their mind, their hearts are blinded, they are past feeling, and they have given themselves over to lewdness to work all uncleanness with greediness. What indeed could bring more pain into a person's life than to be so ignorant within that one cannot think, see, or feel and so then, lives out the ignorance, resulting in gross sin?

This conduct can "be put off" by being renewed in the spirit of his mind, by "putting on" the new man, meaning receiving Jesus into his heart. At that point he begins to see, to have a new way of thinking, to feel the moving of the Spirit within him. His thoughts, behavior, and feelings will be completely new. He begins to live, really live, for the first time. The old man is death, the new man is life.

The ultimate in pain is being alienated from God. We were created first and foremost to have an intimate relationship with Him. If we miss that, nothing else in our life can be right. Even "good" things we do will not fulfill us, and that is not even the worst outcome. The worst outcome is the pain that comes from never knowing Him, from spending all of eternity apart from Him.

Talk to God about being renewed in the spirit of your mind. Have you put on the new man?

Ephesians 5:21-33                                    October 31

## A Recipe for Fulfillment

The idea of mutual submission, given in Ephesians 5:21 is a recipe for living a peaceful, fulfilling, joyful life. Paul gives more information in the verses that follow that, if adhered to, brings into existence the kind of life that God intends. It does not mean that we will know no sufferings. In fact, quite the contrary may be true, but we will have a foundation on which to deal with the suffering and will even triumph in it, first, because God will be with us as we follow His instructions. Secondly, His Word works because He created our inner beings and knows what we need.

Ephesians 5:22 is a section of Scripture where society, and even some Christians, balk: "Wives, submit to your own husbands." It does not mean that women are to lose who they are, have no opinions and march in formation, but instead means they become even more of who they are. They are free to follow God in every way, as they take on, with joy, the role for which they were intended. They have a natural inner desire to yield to another, to a husband, and to God, even though they may not recognize it. Life works best when they glory in this role, rather than fight for supremacy, which comes naturally to their sinful nature, but goes against the nature God gave them.

Then verse 25 says husbands are to love their wives JUST as Christ loved the church and gave Himself for her, to love their wives as their own bodies. What a challenge to a man, much more difficult than submitting, I think. Yet, what a fulfilling life ensues and what pain is averted when we obey God and love and respect as He says.

Do you seek to be who God has called you to be in this important area of life?

Ephesians 6:1-4                                        November 01

## The Value of a Dad

There is very little said in Scripture about the parent-child relationship. It seems that if we are following God's truths in other areas of our life, particularly in the husband-wife relationship, the parent-child relationship will take care of itself. Yet, I have far too many young people coming into my office in pain so deep that they resort to self-destructive activity. I also see adults who still carry deep wounds from their childhood relationships with their parents.

Ephesians 6:4 gives one of the few direct admonitions to a father regarding his children. He is not to provoke them to wrath, but instead, he is to train them up in following the Lord. He is also to be diligent, as it says in the preceding verses, in loving his wife. So, a father is to be involved with his child, teaching her God's truth. He is not to live with her in such a way that anger is the result. Anger comes when a dad is not active in his child's life or when his involvement is one of discipline without love, or when his own issues negatively impact his family. When I see self-destructive behavior in teens: cutting, anorexia, school failures, drinking, problems with the law, rebellion, disrespect for authority... I think "anger" and "hurt". This kid is suffering. Her behavior is abhorrent but when I look at her brief history, it makes sense. Of course, the entire load cannot be dumped on the dad, as there are many factors leading to a teen's pain, but having an involved, loving father will do much to ensure that none of this need-to-act-out will occur in a young person's life. Kids need a dad whose heart and behavior will belong to God.

As a parent, are you training up your child, or are you opening the way for anger in her life?

Ephesians 6:10-20                                    November 02

## Protective Armor

If anyone doubts that we are going to face trouble in this world, he should read Ephesians 6:10-13. There is so much to stand against that God has provided armor. What we have to stand against is not just what we can see and touch but that which comes from the devil: "principalities, powers, rulers of the darkness, spiritual hosts of wickedness in the heavenly places." We are up against Satan himself, whose plan is the same as it was when he deceived Eve: to destroy us. We cannot stop his onslaughts on our own. God is the One Who will defend and deliver us, and He gives us everything we need not just to survive, but to triumph, not just to withstand, but to stand.

The armor He provides for us includes His truth and His righteousness, His Gospel of peace, His shield of faith, His helmet of salvation, and His sword of the Spirit, His Word. Besides all this armor, we have the continual resource of prayer and supplication in the Spirit. While we must be aware of, and be prepared for, the devil's wiles, we need not fear because we have the very power of God within us. We have His presence as we wrestle against the very active powers of darkness. I remember in the days following September 11th, literally shaking my fist at Satan and saying, "You will not win", and he did not, nor will he, because of the power of God.

Are you aware of how God has fitted you for warfare against the enemy? Resolve to use His armor.

Philippians 1:1-26                                       November 03

## That Christ Be Magnified

Paul writes the book of Philippians while in a jail cell in Rome, awaiting his trial with the possibility of death ensuing. He writes that he greatly longs for the people of the church at Philippi. Even while in this extreme adversity, Paul recognizes that this imprisonment and other difficult things that have happened to him "turned out for the furtherance of the Gospel so that it has become evident to the whole palace guard, and to the rest, that my chains are in Christ" (Philippians 1:13). He also knows that his confidence, even while in chains, encourages other brethren to be bold and not fearful (verse 14). He doesn't care about his circumstances but only about preaching Christ, knowing he has been appointed to do that. Therefore, he rejoices, he says, and will continue to rejoice. Paul is one hundred percent satisfied with where he is- no, delighted, with where he is- knowing with great confidence that this is God's plan for showing Christ to all those around him. He does not even mention the harsh conditions in which he is living and his concern for what lies ahead of him, but instead, focuses on the big picture, that which really matters - that Christ be magnified (verse 20), whether it means life or death for him. Either is fine with him, knowing to die means being with the Lord while living means an opportunity to minister to others in their needs.

In adversity is your main thought that Christ be magnified?

Philippians 1:27-30                                    November 04

## Suffering for His Sake

Paul tells the Philippians to look on their adversaries as proof of their salvation and not to be terrified by them. I know people who do the opposite: when adversity comes or someone comes against them, they doubt God and wonder where He is and why He is allowing it to happen to them. "Doesn't He love me", they wonder. Yes, and that is why He is trusting them with these particular adversities and allowing them throughout their lives. At the very least He has allowed them, if not orchestrated them. Of course, He knew they would happen, and come, they will. They are opportunities for us to see what He will do and also for us to build spiritual muscle. Did Paul not say that he was so much the better for having to endure hardships? Did he not rejoice in the Lord, even in his prison cell, while looking at the distinct possibility of death?

Paul writes in Philippians 1:29, "For to you it has been granted on behalf of Christ, not only to believe in Him, but also to suffer for His sake..." We want to be a co-heir with Christ in His glory but we prefer to forego the suffering part. "Why me?" we ask. Why Him? Because He loves you and saw your great need long before you were even born. That night in the garden, before the day of the cross and His separation from the Father, when He wrestled with what He had to face, He thought of you and chose to go. Can we not suffer, for His sake, in ways that are so comparatively small to what He endured? It is granted to us to suffer for Him- it is given to us, and should be considered such a privilege. Our conduct in our sufferings is to be worthy of Him.

Do you consider your sufferings as being granted to you, a privilege to bear for Him?

Philippians 2:1-17                                    November 05

## Sacrificing Our Own Interests

The attitude of our culture is "Take care of number one", meaning yourself. Demand your rights, look out for yourself- no one else will. If need be, step on others to get to the top. This is how the world would teach us to think and behave. Yet, in Philippians 2:4, Paul writes that we should look out not only for our own interests, but also for the interests of others. Verse 3 says, "In lowliness of mind let each esteem others better than himself." Is he telling us we need to sacrifice, to lay down what we want for the good of another? It would seem so. I am glad he wrote this in such a way that he is not telling us to make no consideration of ourselves at all, because I know that God values us and does not want us to lose ourselves, but to be more ourselves, and that involves living like Christ, who took the form of a bondservant, humbling Himself, even to the point of death. Look to your own interests but also to the interest of others.

Paul writes in verse 17 that he is "being poured out as a drink offering" in sacrifice and service for the good of the Philippians, and he rejoices while doing it. He considers himself, but considers them and their needs even more. He is willing to give up his own desires for their good.

Talk to the Lord about your attitude concerning the pouring out of yourself in sacrifice for the good of another.

Philippians 2:19-30                                    November 06

## Comfort in Sorrow

Even though Paul is the one offering direction and encouragement to the church at Philippi, he also demonstrates his own need for encouragement when he writes in Philippians 2:19 that he is sending Timothy to them so he can be encouraged when he knows their state.  He needs to know how they are doing.  He also writes about Epaphroditus, one who had ministered to him and whom he had sent to them and would send yet again, showing his own need for care.  He writes how Epaphroditus, even while sick and close to death himself, provided for Paul in his need.  Caregivers also need care- even Jesus did.

Epaphroditus was near death, but Paul writes that God had mercy on him and on Paul by allowing him to live.  If he died, Paul says, he would have had sorrow upon sorrow.  Instead, God gave him life, and Paul then eagerly sent him to the Philippians, knowing they would rejoice in his presence and also knowing that that in itself would make Paul, in his difficult situation, less sorrowful.  He could be happy for them.

This is the only place in Scripture that we read about Epaphroditus, but what a minister of comfort and encouragement he was.  He went from Philippi to Rome to visit Paul in prison, then carried Paul's letter back to the Philippians.  He worried, when he was gravely ill, that the Philippians would worry about HIM!  He disregarded his own well-being to meet the needs of Paul and his brethren.

Do you have the kind of concern that Paul and Epaphroditus show here?  Do you consider that caregivers also need comfort and encouragement at times?

Philippians 3                                           November 07

## Counting All things Loss

Paul was willing to give up everything about himself for one thing: To know Christ, to have intimacy with Him.  He had at one time been so very proud of his heritage, "A Hebrew of the Hebrews," "a strict keeper of the law".  That was what gave him his very identity, but he had to give it all up, count it as loss, because in that state, he could not know Jesus.  "That I may know Him and the power of His resurrection, and the fellowship of His sufferings, being conformed to His death" became his only focus, considering everything else of no account.  He wanted only to know Jesus, live in His power, share in His sufferings, and eventually be conformed to His death.  Can we honestly say that of ourselves?  Are we willing to let go of things we cherish, our very identity, even "good" things, for the sake of knowing Jesus?

How about the part of knowing the fellowship of His sufferings?  Why would we want that?  Like Paul, we desire it to know Him more deeply.  For me, I see I have a way to go to have the attitude and focus of Paul, but I desire it.  Lord, help me to focus on You and count anything that hinders that, as loss.

Are you willing to give up everything to have that deep intimacy with Jesus for which you were created?

Philippians 3:7, 8                                              November 08

## Personal Remembrance of Dealing with Loss

Like many people, pain began for me in early childhood with a parent, my dad, who was the son of an alcoholic. The alcoholic, my grandfather, lived next door. I loved them both, but the impact that ensued from the alcoholism traveled with me for many years, and even today, rears its ugly head from time to time. The other devastating losses [ there were plenty of lesser ones along the way also] occurred when my husband, Paul, died suddenly on October 26, 1984, leaving me with four children, ages 15,14,10, and 1, and on September 11, 2001, when my son-in-law, Todd Beamer, died on the plane that crashed in the Pennsylvania field during the terrorist attacks.   Even now as I write this, some of the pain of these events rushes back, and probably always will. I feel the tears forming, the lump in the throat, the emptiness of their not being here, but I have more perspective now. Even though the deaths were not good, God has brought good from them, just as He said He would. I know people who have come to the Lord as a result, especially after September 11th. Personally I know the Lord at a much different level than before 1984. My counseling ministry of nearly 20 years and this writing are outcomes of what God has brought me through.

In my losses I instinctively turned to people who knew pain. One of the writers I often read when dealing with my own loss or in working with others in grief is Norman Wright. Why is he so effective in communicating about loss? He has experienced it himself, having a profoundly disabled son whom he cared for and eventually lost. He has comfort and wisdom to offer others because he, himself, received it from God in his need.

Think of people who have been through difficulty and have allowed God to use it in their lives.

Do you see the difference between them and someone who has remained stuck in their grief? Ask God how he wants you to use the difficulties in your life.

Philippians 4:1-9                                        November 09

## Giving Up

Philippians 4 is a chapter I refer to often in counseling. I think of it as a chapter full of "giving up" to Him. It begins with two women in conflict. Paul urges them to give up their differences and come to the same mind in the Lord.

Then in Philippians 4:6 Paul urges the Philippians (and us) to give up their anxiety and replace it with supplication and trust in God. In verse 8 he asks them to give up wrong thinking and replace it with thinking that is true, noble, just, pure, lovely, of good report.

Our old nature often enjoys holding resentments against another with whom we disagree. In a sense that old nature also enjoys worrying, giving us a false sense that we can do something about the situation. It enjoys meditating on imaginary things, things that are not pure, noble, just, lovely, of good report, and certainly, not true. How much pain and suffering people bring on themselves simply by thinking things that are not even true. I often ask clients what they are getting from having a continual contentious spirit, from anxiety, or from wrong thinking. Their immediate answer is "nothing except pain". But we DO get something from these things that God condemns or we couldn't keep them in our lives. They serve us in some way, speaking to our sinful nature, perhaps giving us a false sense of power, feeding our penchant for independence from God, or preventing us from really selling ourselves out to Him...

Think about how these things, contentions, worry, or wrong thinking, serve you. Covenant with God to begin to obey Philippians 4 and give up that which he condemns.

Philippians 4:10-23                                        November 10

## Contentment in Suffering

Lack of contentment brings dissatisfaction and pain into our lives.  What is the root?  For we who claim Christ, isn't it, "You, Jesus, are not enough?" I need other things to make me content, and when I can't have them, I am going to complain.  How must Jesus feel when we believe like that?

Paul, who we remember, is sitting in a prison with his life hanging in the balance, says, "I have learned in whatever state I am, to be content" (Philippians 4:11), so he was content where he was, even when bound.  After all, God knew he was there and had plans for him there.  Paul goes on to say he has learned both to have nothing and to be full, he can abound, and he can suffer need, both in a contented state.  Why?  Because God knows and has allowed it.

Having nine wonderful grandchildren, I have the privilege and fun of seeing lots of childish behavior.  It is appropriate for a four-year -old, while in the midst of a well- planned, fun activity to say, "What are we going to do next," or while eating a bag of candy, to say, "When are we going to get ice cream"? At Christmas, after opening a stack of presents, what child will not look for more?  We laugh at such childish behavior, even while having to address some of it, but that same behavior is not funny in adults.  It shows a blatant disregard for God's place in our lives and a lack of appreciation for all that He has given us.  It shows an ugly self-centeredness, again, expected in young children, but not at all acceptable for a follower of Christ.

Can you say with Paul, "I have learned in whatever state I am to be content"? He IS enough.

Philippians 4:19                                      November 11

## God Uses the Mourning Process to Show Us Our Need

As we have noted, the work of the mourning process gets us from denial, anger, bargaining and depression to acceptance. As Christians, its purpose is not just to make us feel better. Hopefully, it will show us our need for Jesus, that our need and desire for Him surpasses all other desires. Hopefully it will cause us to pursue Him, to seek Him.

Larry Crabb in his book Shattered Dreams, paints the picture of Satan's masterpiece as being "the self-sufficient person who has made life comfortable, who is adjusting well to the world and truly likes living here, a person who dreams of no better place to live, who longs only to be a little better- and a little better off- than he already is." On the other hand, he says "the Spirit's masterpiece is the man or woman who much prefers to live elsewhere, who finds no deep joy in the good things of this life, who looks closely in the mirror and yearns to see something different, whose highest dream is to be in the Presence of the grace-filled Father. It is the person whose life here is consumed with preparing to meet Him there." So, what looks to the world like responding well to sorrow may not be responding well at all. It may be simply adjusting and finding something new in which to invest, something that brings him back to a degree of comfort. What looks like prolonged mourning from the world's viewpoint may actually be a desire to get to a place where he has never been before, a place where he finds what he has always been searching for, a place where he realizes it is God, and only God, Who can meet his deepest needs. Through the pain, we have the opportunity to desire Him more deeply. We have the opportunity to see that what life offers us cannot begin to compare to knowing HIM.

Do you recognize cheap substitutes that entice you as you work through mourning?

Sit with Him and see that He wants to give you Himself.

Colossians 1:19-29                                    November 12

## Presenting Every Man Complete

Paul's goal is found in Colossians 1:28: "Him we preach, warning every man and teaching every man in all wisdom, that we may present every man perfect in Christ Jesus." He labors and strives, even while in prison, to present every man to Jesus. He is not sitting in prison thinking about himself, but is thinking about how he can make Christ known to others. He is expending himself in that purpose, knowing God and making Him known. He suffers doing that but says he also rejoices in it (verse 24).

His example in making his life about presenting others to God comes from Jesus Himself, Who went to His very death to present us, who were once alienated from God, holy and blameless and above reproach to Him. Without Jesus' willingness to suffer and die for us, there would be no way for us to be reconciled to God. We would be dead in our sins, without hope.

Paul, seeing Christ's great sacrifice, claims as his own work, the sacrifice of himself in bringing others to a full knowledge of Christ- to present every man complete to God. He was willing to give up much concerning himself for that goal.

On my desk in my counseling office, I have had those very words written for twenty years- "To present every man complete." They serve as a constant reminder of what the work is about that God has given me.

Are you willing to give of yourself in whatever way God directs to bring every man complete in Jesus?

Colossians 2:10 & II Corinthians 3:5                    November 13

## God Desires to be Enough for Us

I have noticed in my own life that there are times that something has become too big, too important to me.  Often it is even a good thing that I am treasuring, but God wants me on my own to give it up to Him- because it stands in the way of His being Number One in my life.  He doesn't take it away, but He asks me to give it up to Him.  Even though it is not taken from me, pain is still involved in giving it to Him, but what peace and freedom ensues when I do that.  Something very interesting has happened, at times, when I give something dear to me over to Him, something that I have been holding too tightly.  He gives it back.  That doesn't always occur, and it only occurs when He is restored to His proper place in my life.  HE is enough.  HE is sufficient.  He desires to give us good things.  We are, after all, His beloved children, and like all good parents, He wants the best for us.  The best for us is knowing He is Who we need.

This restoration of something we were willing to give up occurred in Abraham's life.  God asked for his only son, Isaac.  When Abraham was poised to obey, God gave Isaac back to Abraham and provided another sacrifice for them.  Abraham proved God's sufficiency in his life.

Today as you spend time with God, ask Him if there is someone or something that you are holding above Him.  If so, will you begin the process, with His help, of giving it over to Him?  Enjoy the freedom of that.

Colossians 3                                    November 14

## Putting Off Old Things

Before salvation, we were friends with anger, wrath, malice, blasphemy, lying, filthy language. We knew them well, but after salvation, knowing Jesus, God says we have to put them off (Colossians 3:8). Not only do we have to put off old things, but we have to put on the new man, he who is renewed in knowledge, according to the image of Jesus. We can no longer behave as we once did, even though most people around us are. We, being the elect of God, must constantly decide to put off the old nature and put on the new, meaning to show "tender mercies, kindness, humility, meekness, longsuffering, the bearing with one another, the forgiving of one another, the loving of one another, and allowing peace to reign within, while being thankful (verses 12-15). We have no chance of doing these things if we keep on "the old man". We must put on "the new man," provided to us by God's Spirit. It is there for us but we must make a choice to put it on and put off the old, like taking off old, dirty clothes and putting on new ones. It is a continual choice we have to make, and we can, as we seek to do all in the name of the Lord Jesus, giving thanks to God the Father through Him" (verse 17).

Are you continually making the choice to put off the old, the things that come so naturally, and put on the new?

Colossians 4                                      November 15

## Remember My Chains

There are moments in life when all is well with us, when there is no conscious pain or suffering going on, when we are at peace. I am thankful for those times and enjoy them, as Paul says, being content in whatever state I am. Towards the end of his letter to the Philippians, Paul also tells Jesus' followers to be earnest in prayer and to be vigilant in it. He also says that he is sending to them two beloved brothers, Tychicus and Onesimus, so they can tell them news about Paul and also comfort them. Just before he closes his letter he asks them to "Remember my chains". It is evident that the believers in Philippi were not enjoying a time free from adversity, but even if they were, Paul is calling them to remember that he is not. He wants their prayers and their vigilance for him.

In our times free from adversity, we need to remember that that is not the case for other believers, those around us, and those far from us in other parts of the world, where suffering is so beyond our comprehension. "Continue earnestly in prayer, being vigilant in it with thanksgiving, meanwhile praying also for us, that God would open to us a door for the Word, to speak the mystery of Christ, for which I am also in chains"...(Colossians 4:2&3). Remember the chains of others.

Talk with God about your part in remembering the chains of others.

I Thessalonians 2                                              November 16

## The Sacrifice of Parenting

Paul had planted the church of Thessalonica and, having been driven out by the Jewish leaders, wrote to the church to establish them in God's truth, much as a parent would. He writes in I Thessalonians 2:8 of longing for them, being willing to impart not only God's Word, but his very own life to them. In verse 10 he says he and his co-workers behaved in devout, just, and blameless ways among them, working hard to be examples to them. They also exhorted, comforted, and challenged them "as a father does his own children" to bring them to a place worthy of the one Who called them to Himself (verse 13). Paul and his fellow workers gave themselves to the Thessalonians as a parent gives himself to his child, requiring great sacrifice, energy, and selflessness. The church at Thessalonica was so much a part of him that they became his glory and joy.

Paul not only gave of himself in becoming a parent to them, but at the same time suffered great opposition while doing it, so much so that he had to go away from them for a while, physically, but not in his heart, he says. He writes of his great desire to come to them but was hindered by Satan. All is more than worth it as he considers the hope and joy of their presence with the Lord Jesus at His coming.

Are you willing to give of yourself and take on the parental role and all it entails so that others can be established in the faith?

I Thessalonians 3                                      November 17

## Appointed for Affliction

Paul writes that his afflictions were so great that he could no longer endure it, so was staying where he was and was sending Timothy to the Thessalonians to establish and encourage them. The afflictions he speaks of have to do with the harassment of the Jewish religious leaders against him, and even the possibility of his death at their hands.

Paul is saying in these Scriptures that affliction is part of the territory of being a follower of Christ. He prepared his followers for it from the very beginning so they would not be surprised and thrown from their faith.

Yes, there is affliction in the Christian life, but there is also the potential for joy and comfort beyond our understanding, as Paul says in verses 6 and 7. He received good news of the faith and love of his brethren in Thessalonica- they were doing well in their faith. There was also the deep bond he had with them, even while at a distance, a bond that was unknown in other circles, but one in which Paul found comfort and joy. He loved hearing about them, thanking God for them. He felt such a connection to them that he says he prayed exceedingly night and day to see their faces and to continue ministering to them. His goal was to "establish their hearts blameless in holiness before our God and Father at the coming of our Lord Jesus Christ with all His saints," even while enduring the affliction in which he was appointed. Consider that. Paul felt appointed to affliction.

Do you feel "appointed to " whatever God has brought or allowed in your life?

I Thessalonians 4                                    November 18

## To Not Sorrow as Others

What greater comfort is there for a follower of Jesus who has lost a loved one to death than I Thessalonians 4:13-18? Paul wrote these verses, he says, so we will not sorrow as others who have no hope. Standing by the grave of a loved one, we have hope because of the truth written here: Jesus died and rose again, so when He returns He will bring with Him those who have died in Him. Then those who are still alive when Jesus descends from heaven with a shout and the voice of an archangel, and with the trumpet of God "will be caught up with them in the clouds to meet the Lord in the air" (verse 7). Then that verse continues with a truth that makes our heart sing: "And thus we shall always be with the Lord". What a day that will be- to meet together, first with Jesus, and then with our loved ones and begin an eternity with them. Paul says to comfort one another with these words (verse 18).

No, we cannot sorrow as the world does. We sorrow when our loved ones are torn from us, but not without hope. When we see HIM, Who gave His life for us, we will also see them, and it will be in a place where there will be no more sorrow or partings.

Do you sorrow- but with hope?

I Thessalonians 5:23-24 & II Timothy 2:21          November 19

## Sanctification- A Loss?

Paul writes in I Thessalonians 5:23-24 for God to sanctify us holy and that our whole being, spirit, soul, and body be blameless when He comes.  He again writes in II Timothy 2:21 that if we get rid of the things in our lives which dishonor God we will be fit for the Master's use and ready for every good work.

Do you see the need to go through loss in these verses before we can get to the place of being set apart for God's work?  If we are to be blameless when He comes we are going to have to let go of the things of this world that hinder us from being one with Jesus.  We cannot tolerate anything in our lives which brings dishonor to God.  That sounds like a giving up of many things- things we see others doing, things which seem quite normal in our society, things we enjoy.

Oswald Chambers says sanctification will cost an intense narrowing of all our interests on earth, and an immense broadening of all our interests in God.  He says it means intense concentration on God's point of view.  So, I need to stop lazily looking at things the way the world does and work hard to hold God's point of view.  He says sanctification will cost everything that is not of God in us.

Yes, that requires losses for us.  However, think of the freedom and joy of being one with Jesus, of being set apart by Him to do works that we can't even imagine.  The losses, the giving up, quickly become gains beyond description.

Sit with God and let Him show you what you need to give up to be set apart for Him to good works.

I Timothy 3:1- 13                                     November 20

## Sacrifices of Church Leaders

In I Timothy Paul mentors the young Timothy as he is pastoring the young church, which Paul had established at Ephesus. In chapter 3 Paul tells Timothy what the qualifications are for those who desire to be church leaders. They must be blameless, above reproach, reverent. They also must take care of their own families well, having reverent wives and obedient children. They should be able to teach, be hospitable, not given to wine, not greedy for money, gentle, not quarrelsome, not covetous. Their behavior must be such that no one can find fault with them. To fulfill these things requires sacrifice, a constant monitoring of one's behavior to test if it is Christ-like. A church leader cannot be satisfied with mediocrity, with living like everyone else. He will have to keep himself in such a place that he will hear the conviction of the Holy Spirit so at the first sign of any deviation from Christ-like behavior, he can allow God to correct it, and correct it He will, desiring that all who serve Him be different, above reproach. Following the Lord means sacrificing what comes naturally to us and embarking on that which requires vigilance and effort. We do not have the luxury of living anyway we like, as the world does.

Are you willing to constantly examine your behavior to see if it measures up to what God requires of you?

I Timothy 4:12-16                                      November 21

## Feelings of Inadequacy

As Paul mentors Timothy in his letter to him, he encourages him not to be concerned about his youth and inexperience. It is possible, maybe even probable, that the young Timothy had doubts about his ability to pastor the church at Ephesus. It would be daunting, quite uncomfortable, for a young person to take over a church from an experienced and well-established pastor, especially if that pastor happened to be the apostle Paul. It is not surprising that Timothy would have feelings of inadequacy, prompting Paul to write to him, giving him encouragement and direction.

Feeling inadequate is not a problem if it causes us to look to God's truth, as was the admonition Paul gave to Timothy: "Give attention to reading", he said in 4:13, "to exhortation, to doctrine." He said to meditate on them and also reminds him of the gift that is in him, that which is given by God and will enable him to do whatever God has in mind for him. He also tells Timothy to be an example to the believers in word, behavior, love, spirit, faith, and purity. If he did that, his age would be of no consequence- he would be respected by those to whom he was sent. If Timothy were willing to obey God and follow his directions, as given to him by Paul, his inadequacy, due to inexperience, would be of no consideration.

Does a feeling of inadequacy prevent you from doing what God has for you, or in your inadequacy, do you allow HIM to do HIS work?

I Timothy 6                                          November 22

## Fight the Good Fight

Fighting a fight, even for something good, requires the involvement of all of our being. We can't be in a battle while physically being somewhere else, or mentally thinking of other things, or emotionally not being involved, or spiritually not drawing upon the resources that God has given us. In a fight, if we are to win, we need to have all of our being focused and involved.

Paul tells Timothy in I Timothy 6:12 to "fight the good fight of faith, to lay hold on eternal life, to which he was called." In his fight, he is to pursue righteousness, godliness, faith, love, patience, and gentleness, while rejecting unwholesome words, disputes and arguments leading to envy, strife, reviling, evil suspicions, and useless wranglings (verses 3-5). In his fight he is to seek contentment in the Lord and not in that which the world looks to for contentment, mainly material riches, which leads to destruction. Loving money, Paul tells Timothy, is a root of all kinds of evil, causing some to stray from the faith, bringing piercings of sorrow to themselves (verse 10).

Paul writes this to his young protégé, and to us, knowing that it is a battle to stay blameless and not fall into the attitudes, motives, and behaviors of the world. It will require great effort from us.

Do you recognize that you are in a fight to stay centered on the Lord and His commands?

II Timothy 1                                            November 23

## To Share in Christ's Sufferings

In his final letter before his death, Paul writes to his "beloved son", Timothy, receiving encouragement himself as he considers the faith of his disciple.  He then also offers encouragement and important lessons to the young man who, perhaps, was doubting himself.  Paul writes that he was aware of Timothy's tears, and he prayed for him day and night.  He reminds Timothy to "stir up the gift of God," which is in him and not succumb to the fear that plagued him so readily (I Timothy 1:6).   That fear, Paul says, was not from God, Who equipped him with power, love, and a sound mind (verse 7).

Both Timothy and Paul knew what it was to suffer, Paul in literal bonds and Timothy, in bonds of fear and self-doubt as he attempted to lead a church which probably seemed to him beyond his abilities.  Paul calls on Timothy to share with him in the sufferings for the gospel, to share in Christ's sufferings, the One Who saved them (and us) and called them (and us) with a holy calling.

How can we think, after contemplating the sufferings of Jesus for us and the sufferings of these early believers, that we should expect to escape them, or that it would be a good thing for us if we could?  In our valuable and necessary sufferings, we can know, with Paul, that "He is able to keep what I have committed to Him until that day "(verse 12).

Can you say to God that you desire to enter into Christ's sufferings?

II Timothy 2                                                    November 24

## Enduring Hardship as a Soldier

In writing his final letter to Timothy, Paul uses word pictures, in this case that of a good soldier of Jesus Christ. He tells Timothy to be ready to endure hardship much as a soldier does. A soldier goes where he is told, and does what he is told, even to the extent of risking his own life. He does not become entangled with this life, but seeks to please him who enlisted him, focusing only on his mission, giving himself up for it.

Paul reminds Timothy that he himself suffers great trouble for the One Who enlisted him, even to the point of being imprisoned. Not only is he enduring the hardship of Christ but for "the sake of the elect," others who need to hear so that they can come to salvation.

Paul knows that if we died with Him, gave up ourselves, we shall also live with Him (verse 11). Any hardship endured now will be like nothing in the light of the glory of eternity.

Paul not only is delighted in imparting these truths to Timothy but in 2:2 he also instructs Timothy to commit them to faithful men who will be able to teach others. It is not enough to be given truths and use them in our own lives, but we are called upon to multiply, to pass them to others who will be faithful themselves in giving them out to those who will also pass them on to faithful men.

While being diligent to present yourself approved to God, a worker who does not need to be ashamed, do you ever encounter hardship?

If so, how do you deal with it?

II Timothy 3                                        November 25

## Persecutions

"All who desire to live godly in Christ Jesus will suffer persecutions " is one of the last messages Paul sends to the young pastor, Timothy. He does not say MAYBE they will suffer persecutions but that they WILL suffer persecution. Paul writes from experience, having endured much but also having been delivered from them all by the Lord ( II Timothy 3:11& 12). He knows that Timothy will experience much persecution also, since "evil men and imposters will grow worse and worse, deceiving and being deceived" (verse 14). He begins chapter 3 by describing the perilous times to come because men love themselves, they love money, they are unloving and unforgiving, they are without self-control, brutal, despisers of good, and this is only part of his description of men. He tells Timothy to turn away from such people, which in itself is a set-up for persecution. Evil does not like when we refuse to become a part of it, and it will attack.

My nephew, a medical doctor, and his family have been missionaries in Central Asia. Just being allowed to stay there has been a constant difficulty, even though they have accomplished so much good. Many missionaries suffer much just to remain in the countries where God has placed them, and often can share very little of their afflictions. Evil despises good.

Most of us know little of that kind of persecution but are perhaps more familiar with being shunned in our places of work for living a different life or being ostracized by family members who desire us to be like them. Whatever we face regarding persecution, Paul's advice is to "continue in the things which you have learned and been assured of ." Return to the truth of God's Word so you are equipped for any form of persecution.

Meditate on what you have learned and been assured of so you can withstand any form of persecution.

II Timothy 4                                        November 26

## Departing Well

Paul, knowing that his death is near, depicts it as being poured out as a drink offering, knowing he has fought well and finished what God gave him to do. He looks forward to his crown of righteousness. He is dying well because he has lived well, having done what God gave him to do: establishing churches, mentoring followers of God, establishing sound doctrine, writing letters to guide God's people, both in his time and continuing now in this day. Imagine what it would be like for us if we did not have Paul's writings? Yes, he was dying well because he had lived his life not for himself but first for his Lord and secondly for the good of his fellow believers. He was dying well, even in prison, and after enduring hardships and afflictions that we can only imagine.

In this last writing, what is one of the things he wants to impart to Timothy? He tells him to endure afflictions, knowing they will come and knowing the pain of them. We get a glimpse into some of them in his departing words- he is feeling very alone, asking Timothy to come to him quickly since others have forsaken, abandoned or betrayed him; he is suffering physically, asking Timothy to bring him his cloak and to try and be there before winter; he is in need of encouragement, asking for books and parchments. Even in his own needs, with his departure imminent, Paul continues to pour out onto others just as he had done in his entire life as a follower of God.

Most people don't like to think of departing this life, but if we, like Paul, have lived well, we can die well, knowing we have fought the good fight until our last moment and that our joy will be seeing the One for Whom we fought and endured. Consider this.

Titus 1                                              November 27

## The Sacrifice of Mentoring

Timothy was not the only young man blessed enough to be mentored by Paul. Titus was another believer on whom Paul poured out himself. He taught Titus how to bring order to a church, in this case the one in Crete, as he showed him how to establish leaders and resolve problems. Paul prepared Titus well to fulfill the specific tasks he was given, teaching him that problems exist and must be dealt with directly. He then gave Titus all the God-given truths to solve the problems.

Mentoring, equipping and then letting go does not come without a great deal of love, time, energy, patience, and trust expended. Good parents experience all of these as they prepare their children for the rigors of life. It is so much easier and energy efficient to do a task for a young one rather than taking the time, patience, and energy to lovingly teach how to perform the task, but once it is successfully taught, the child can forever more do it on his own and eventually even teach it to another, freeing the parent to move on to something else. I had the privilege just last evening to witness my grandson helping his mother in the cooking of a delightful meal. I saw the patience and extra time it took for her to mentor him in the food preparation, and I also saw the results as I asked, while we were enjoying the meal, what he had learned. I saw the pride of accomplishment in his being.

I have always loved the saying, "Give a man a fish and he eats for a day, teach him to fish and he eats for a lifetime." Paul knew the long-term value of putting in the time and energy to teach his young apprentice well, for his own sake, for the sake of God's people, and for the glory of God. To be a good mentor, like Paul, we need to be willing to give freely and selflessly for the advancement of God's kingdom. We are called to pour out into others.

Talk with God about the value of sacrificing yourself in mentoring others with what God has given you.

Philemon                                                        November 28

## Challenging a Brother

Philemon was a friend and fellow laborer of Paul's, having helped him in starting the church in Colosse. Philemon had a slave, Onesimus, who had run away, found Paul in prison, and came to accept Christ as his Savior. In this very personal letter, Paul is writing to Philemon, asking him to receive his runaway slave back, not only as a slave but as a fellow believer, a brother. Paul is asking a great deal of Philemon, especially when we consider the time in which he lived. The master-slave relationship and the economic issue are considerations making it more difficult for Philemon, but Paul's approach would be impossible to deny.

Paul begins by commending Philemon for the joy he brings to him because of his love and work among the believers, then appeals to him on the basis of that love, presenting Onesimus as his "son," a new believer. He respects Philemon's position as the slave-owner, but then relates to him that his desire is to keep Onesimus with him, but doesn't want to do anything without the voluntary consent of Philemon. He also reminds Philemon that Onesimus' running away resulted in his coming to the Lord, making his relationship as a brother far more valuable and eternal than the slave-master relationship. Paul then encourages Philemon to receive Onesimus, just as he would receive Paul, and even offers to pay to Philemon anything that Onesimus may owe him. He concludes by writing of his confidence in Philemon's obedience in doing the right thing even MORE than the right thing (Church history suggests that he did). What a wonderful account of challenging a brother who had been wronged, to act with forgiveness and grace.

Do you challenge others in the manner that Paul did?

How would you receive the challenge if you were Philemon?

Hebrews 2:9-18 & 4:15                          November 29

## Jesus' Sufferings in Temptations

The unknown author of Hebrews presents Christ as suffering for us, so we would have the opportunity of being like Him. He tasted death for everyone (verse 9), "in bringing many sons to glory, to make the captain of their salvation perfect through sufferings" (verse 10). Because Jesus Himself has suffered, being tempted, He is able to aid those who are tempted.

We recognize His sufferings in His death for us but don't often consider His sufferings in being tempted. He was tempted by Satan for forty days in the wilderness. What did it cost Him in His extreme hunger to refuse to turn stones into bread, as the tempter suggested? He was willing to remain hungry and stay centered on His Father, while not taking sufficiency into His Own hands. What did it cost Him to refuse all the kingdoms of the world for Himself and instead live the life that would offer salvation to all mankind? That choice led to suffering beyond our comprehension. It led to His death. What did it cost Him the night in the garden when He contemplated separation from His Father as He took on all our filth? "Nevertheless, Your will" was His answer to the suffering He knew He would have to take on if He were to make propitiation for our sins.

Because "He has suffered being tempted, He is able to aid those who are tempted." Our temptations, while important and meaningful to God, cannot compare to His. Nevertheless, He is able and willing to aid us in them.

Hebrews 4:15 says, "For we do not have a High Priest who cannot sympathize with our weaknesses but was in all points tempted as we are, yet without sin."

Talk with God about the temptations He suffered through for you.

Let Him aid you as you are tempted.

Hebrews 5:12-14                                         November 30

## Spiritual Immaturity

As a baby grows, what would happen to him if he continued to take in only milk, never progressing to solid food?  He would not grow in a healthy manner, and eventually there would be deficiencies in his diet which would manifest themselves in his being, causing him difficulties.  The author of Hebrews, as he writes to the Jewish believers, confronts them with their need to grow and mature.  By this point, he says, they ought to be teaching others, but instead are still drinking only milk, needing someone to teach them.  They are babies, unskilled in the Word and in the knowledge of Christ.  They cannot take in solid food (Hebrews 5:14), as a mature person can.  Why?  They have not taken the "milk" that has been given them and made use of it, making it their own, so cannot now move on to discern what is good and what is evil.  God cannot give them more until they make use of what he has already given them.

Spiritual immaturity is expected of a new believer, a baby in Christ, but remaining in that state opens the door for unnecessary problems in one's life.  If he cannot discern between good and evil, sometimes he will choose evil.  If he cannot or will not take in the "solid food" God has for him, he will not know how to live.  When I hear, "I'd rather listen to Christian music or watch TV preachers," or "The Bible is too difficult to understand," etc., I know the result will be spiritual immaturity and a life full of unnecessary trouble, trouble that comes from not knowing and living in the truth.

Have you progressed from "milk" to the "solid food" which comes from sitting in the Presence of God with His Word?

Hebrews 7:19-28; 9:12-14, 22 & 10:10            December 01

## Jesus' Offering of Himself

One of the purposes of the Book of Hebrews is to show the weakness of the law- it made nothing perfect (Hebrews 7:19) and to show the need for a better covenant and hope, that being Jesus, the Son. While the Old Testament animal sacrifices were a reminder of sin, their blood could not take it away. "We have been sanctified through the offering of the body of Jesus Christ once for all" (10:10). "With His Own blood He entered the most Holy Place once for all, having obtained eternal redemption" (9:12). It is through the shedding of His blood "who through the eternal Spirit offered Himself without spot to God to cleanse our conscience from dead works to serve the living God." He had to die for our reconciliation to God to occur, for "without shedding of blood there is no remission" (9:22). He offered His body for us.

That being true, how can we expect to escape suffering in our lives? Jesus is our Savior, but He is also our model in how to live. He shows us the purpose of life- not comfort, nor happiness, not avoidance of suffering, but a yielding to the Father so that holiness will ensue through deep relationship with Him. We need to continually remind ourselves what our purpose is- union with the Father through His perfect Son. That purpose is often found through suffering.

Are you daily mindful of your purpose?

Do you accept your suffering as part of that purpose?

Hebrews 11                                                December 02

## God's Hall of Faith

Hebrews 11 is God's "Hall of Faith" because it chronicles people who obeyed God, were faithful and had the victory, while often enduring much in the way of suffering.

Abel offered the sacrifice which God required, even while being the subject of his brother's wrath.  Noah, believing God, took on the ridicule of his society while building a huge boat on dry land and proclaiming the coming catastrophe to an unbelieving people.  Abraham, also obeying God, set out for a place that he did not know, living in an environment totally foreign to him.  He also was called upon by God to offer his long-awaited, beloved son, Isaac, back to God, which he willingly, but sorrowfully, did.  Moses, as a baby, having been protected and hidden by his faithful parents, refused to be called the son of Pharaoh's daughter, choosing instead to cast his lot with God's people, giving up many pleasures while suffering great affliction for his faithful choice, "esteeming the reproach of Christ greater riches than the treasures in Egypt; for he looked to the reward" (Hebrews 11:26).  By faith he led God's people, suffering much at their hand.  Other heroes of the faith "stopped the mouths of lions, quenched the violence of fire, escaped the edge of the sword, out of weakness were made strong, became valiant in battle..." (verses 33 & 34).  Hebrews 11:35 says others were tortured, some endured mockings and scourgings, chains and imprisonment, and stonings, while some were sawn in two or slain by the sword.  They were destitute, afflicted, tormented.  God says the world was not worthy of them.  Yet, they did not receive the promise in their physical life, but triumphed, being assured of what would come.

Can you do more than endure your difficulties and afflictions- can you triumph in them, knowing and holding onto what God has promised, even though you can't see the promises now?

Hebrews 12:1-11                               December 03

## Endure Chastening

Hebrews 12 begins by commending the faithful men in chapter 11 as encouragers to us to "lay aside every weight and the sin which so easily ensnares us" so we can run the race God has set before us as we look unto Jesus, the One Who endured the cross and despised His shame. When we consider Him, we will not grow weary or discouraged.

As we look to Him to run our race, He will need to chasten us, because He loves us and wants the very best for us. Verse 5 tells us to not despise that chastening nor to be discouraged when He rebukes us. When I am sitting under the conviction of the Holy Spirit, at first it is so painful and demoralizing to see myself as I am, but then I quickly realize how privileged I am to have the Creator of the world, the Savior, care so deeply for me that nothing about me escapes Him. He is so invested in me that He wants me to be like Him, to be a partaker of His holiness. As verse 11 says, chastening is not joyful for the present, but painful, but "afterward it yields the peaceful fruit of righteousness to those who have been trained by it."

Talk with God about how you view His chastening. Receive it as a privilege.

James 1:1-20                                           December 04

## Count it all Joy

In the first chapter of his book, James, in his practical and pragmatic way, writes that we should consider it a joy when we fall into trials. What did he say? We should consider it JOY- because we learn patience from testing. We need to be tried so that patience can do its work of making us whole and complete, lacking nothing. When we remain unsure, either of God or ourselves, not having been tested in trials, James says we are "like a wave of the sea, driven and tossed by the wind," "unstable in all our ways." He goes on to say in verse 12 that "Blessed is the man who endures temptation" for he will receive from God the crown of life.

Both trials and temptations have their purpose of refining us, making us complete in the Lord. We don't have to go looking for adversities, but they WILL come, and with them the offer of our lacking nothing when we have negotiated them. Our feelings will tell us things like, "This should not be happening. This is not fair. This is too hard. I can't do this. Why me? Why would God do this to me?" And on it goes, until we THINK correctly. One of the ways to do that is to center on this passage in James. The truth is that we WILL fall into trials and temptations, and as we go through them, we can become complete in the Lord, knowing Him more fully. Therein lies real joy.

When trials come, what is your first reaction?

Is it based on feelings or the truth from God's Word?

James 1:17                                                    December 05

## Psalms 25:8

### God Is good- All the Time

"God is good." I often cringe when people say that because they usually say it just after He has done something that fits into what they think He should do. It meets with their approval. We had this event planned for today, and we had great weather: God is good. We got good medical reports back: God is good. We got enough money to pay off a bill: God is good. What if the weather for the important day was cold and wet, the medical report came back positive, or there isn't enough money to pay the bill? Does that mean on those occasions that God is not good?

There is a much loved and admired man in our church whom I have known for more than thirty years. He was a physical education teacher, is a coach, a loving husband, a devoted dad to four daughters and now a grandfather. He and his wife had difficulty conceiving, and I was one of the people who prayed for them. After the fourth daughter he told me I could stop now, demonstrating his sense of humor. Matt also loved physical activity, particularly rugby, which he continued to play into adulthood. One Saturday in September, over 20 years ago, he was playing in a game, just as he had done on many occasions before. Only this Saturday was different. In a scrum, he suffered an injury, one that would leave him a quadriplegic for the remainder of his life. Matt is well known for saying, "God is good, all the time." A vibrant man in the prime of his life finds himself unable to move anything in his body, other than his head, says, "God is good all the time." Where does that come from? From a deep, secure knowledge of Who God is and what life is really about. It is about God's redemption and our relationship with Him through His Son, Jesus Christ. In adversity, we are given an opportunity like no other time to see Him, really see Him. He means all of our circumstances for good, no matter how we, in our limited understanding, might view them and no matter from what source they come upon us. He is good when we are on a mountaintop, and He is just as good when we are in the depths of despair. He is good, all the time. If you ever meet Matt, he will tell you that, as he sits in his wheelchair, unable to move. Satan meant it for evil, but God meant it for good. And good it is.

Sit with God and let Him help you remember how He used adversity in your life to show you more of Himself.

James 3:1-12 & 1:19                                      December 06

## The Tongue Brings Pain

James, in his quest for actions to back up what we say we believe, likens the tongue to a fire and the devastating results that can come when it is unbridled. He says it "defiles the whole body, and sets on fire the course of nature," calling it "an unruly evil, full of deadly poison." We can use it for good or bad, for blessing or for cursing. He had previously given the admonition in James 1:19 to be swift to hear and slow to speak, again recognizing the power of our words.

He uses two other pictures to show the enormity of what the tongue can do: A bit in a horse's mouth can turn his whole body just as a small rudder can turn a massive ship. "The tongue is a little member and boasts great things".

How different life would be for so many if they learned to control their tongues, if they realized they don't have to say everything they think, and if they brought their thinking into captivity, using principles from God's Word. Are my words edifying, meant for the good of another? Are they consistent with the truths of God's Word? Am I allowing the Holy Spirit to determine what I should be saying? Do I allow Him to convict me when I use my tongue wrongly and then seek His forgiveness as well as the forgiveness of the one I have wronged?

Think about your speech patterns.

Talk with God about your desire to bring your tongue under the power of His Spirit.

James 4:1-3                                                    December 07

## Why We Fight

James very simply and directly answers the question as to where wars and fights come from- from our own desires for pleasure. We lust, and we do not have. Essentially we want what we want when we want it, and when we don't get it, we protest, often resulting in fights.

James goes on to say that we do not have, because we don't ask or because we ask amiss. Maybe we don't ask because we are too ashamed to ask for what we want because it is so far off the mark from what God lays down as His principles. We ask amiss. When we are living in the power of the Holy Spirit, what we desire are His desires- we can't ask amiss. When we are living in our own power, we are going to be focused on ourselves, and we are going to be angry when our desires are not met.

In counseling when I am attempting to see what has gone wrong between two people, that is it- each is angry because he is not getting what he wants. Each is only concerned about himself, discounting God's principles of esteeming the other better than himself, not looking to edify the other, not loving the other as he does himself. If we would think God's principles and act on them, many of the fights and quarrels we have with others would be eliminated. How much energy we would have for other productive things and how much more peaceful and enjoyable life would be.

Think of the last fight you had with someone. Was it because you weren't getting what you wanted?

Talk with God about it.

James 5:13-18                                          December 08

## In Your Suffering, Pray

James says that if anyone is suffering, he should pray. His first thought should be toward God, not toward running to another person. There is a time and place for that but it should come later, as James says, "Is anyone among you sick? Let him call for the elders of the church, and let them pray over him..." If we go to others first, before God, we are bypassing an opportunity, while in our need, to have that intimacy with God that is at the heart of the Christian life. That life is about community for sure, but it has to have as its source, the vital connection with God. Out of that will flow relationship with other believers.

If you are suffering, pray. First, take responsibility and see what God is going to do with that suffering. James also says in verse 13 that if you are cheerful, you should sing psalms. Praise God first for your blessings, then share your joy with others. Where we go first, either with our sorrows or with our joys, tells us on whom or what we depend.

After our private time with God, then it is good and necessary to involve others: "Confess your sins to one another, and pray for one another, that you may be healed" (James 5:16).

When adversity comes knocking unexpectedly, think about where you go first.

Talk with God about His place in your life.

I Peter 1                                                December 09

## Be Holy as He is Holy

Peter, Jesus' disciple who suffered great persecution and opposition, and the same one who denied Jesus three times, now writes to Jewish Christians who themselves are enduring persecution and opposition. Who would be better than Peter to encourage them, he who having failed, and then having grown to a place of maturity through his suffering? He can recognize how "they have been grieved by various trials" (I Peter 1:6) and " have been tested by fire" (verse 7), because he was also. Through these griefs of trials, the genuineness of their faith may come to the surface and be a glory to Christ, a joy to themselves, and will result in a heavenly inheritance.

Despite their sufferings, Peter tells them to focus on being holy in all their conduct, being holy for He is holy (verse 16), remembering that they were redeemed by the blood of Christ. He earned the right to tell them this since he himself matured from a fearful follower of Jesus, who abandoned and denied Him more than once, as he was in the process of emerging into the man who would one day accept crucifixion, but demanded, as tradition suggests, that it be upside down, not seeing himself worthy of dying as his Savior did. He endured mockings, rebukes, imprisonment, arrests, beatings, as he followed Christ. Who better to encourage other believers as they suffer similar experiences? Who better to instruct us, as we go through various trials, to "gird up our minds" and "to be holy as God is holy?"

How far away are you from seeking holiness when you are in the midst of pain?

I Peter 2:13-25                                    December 10

## Suffering Patiently

Peter writes how commendable it is if, because of our relationship to God, we are willing to endure grief and suffer wrongfully at the hands of another, particularly an authority figure. We are to submit to those He has placed or allowed in various positions, not for their sake but for HIS sake. He says in I Peter 2:17 that we are to honor all people. We think this is difficult in the times in which we live, but consider the time in which Peter writes - a time when men were treated in the most barbaric of ways, when there was no thought of justice, when innocent men were crucified.

Peter asks, "What credit is it, when you are beaten for your faults, you take it patiently?" There is no credit in that, but when you do good and suffer for that, God receives and commends that. Peter says we are called to that because our Savior, our example, also suffered for us, He Who deserved none of it, He Who was without sin, He Who did not have to submit, but willingly did without a threat, committing Himself to the Father: "Not My will but Yours." He did it for us that we might live, being healed by His suffering. Whatever our suffering, HE knows and called us to it, and commends us for it when we bear it patiently with our eyes on the One Who bore all for us.

Talk with Jesus about the suffering He endured for you.

Consider how you go about bearing your suffering.

I Peter 3                                              December 11

## Submission to God

Peter makes it clear in I Peter 3 that we are to do what we do because of our relationship to God, then partly because of the impact on other people, not because of what we desire.  For example, women are to submit to their husbands partly so they are a witness for Christ but also so that the husband may be won to Him by their conduct.  When a woman presents herself in this way and is concentrating on inward beauty, that is "very precious in the sight of God."  Her behavior is always about her relationship with her Lord.

Likewise, a husband is to give honor to his wife, consider her an heir together with him, which she is- so that his prayers may not be hindered (verse 7).  Again, his thinking and behavior are partly for the good of his wife but they are more so about his relationship with God.

Peter, in verses 8 and 9, says how we are to interact with other believers: Be of one mind, have compassion for them, be tenderhearted and courteous.  Why?  Because GOD called us to that.  "The eyes of the Lord are on the righteous and His eyes are open to their prayers", Peter says in verse 12.  We are to do what God's Word tells us because of our relationship to HIM- and, by the way, we will bless others in the process, and find peace and fulfillment in our own lives as we are received by Him. We will sometimes pay a price for living differently than others, but verse 7 says, "It is better, if it is the will of God, to suffer for doing good than for doing evil."

Talk with God about making HIM the reason for your behavior.

I Peter 4:12-19                                     December 12

## Do Not Think it Strange

In the midst of a trial I used to long for an ordinary day and think, "This should not be happening." Now I realize that to be in a difficult situation IS ordinary. It IS to be expected. It says so right here in I Peter 4:12, "Do not think it strange concerning the fiery trial, which is to try you, as though some strange thing happened to you." There WILL be fiery trials, and we are "to rejoice to the extent that we are partakers of Christ's sufferings ". We are, after all, co-heirs with Him, so will participate in His sufferings as well as His glory. Peter specifically targets the suffering that comes from being a follower of Christ. When that happens we are to glorify God in it and consider ourselves blessed because His Spirit is resting on us (verse 14).

Aside from being thought foolish or ignorant or being mildly ostracized for our beliefs or manner of life, most of us in our country know little of suffering for the cause of Christ, going through real reproach and persecution as Peter suggests here. Yet, we do face trials on a regular basis, and Peter says they should be expected. "Let those who suffer according to the will of God commit their souls to Him in doing good, as to a faithful Creator" (verse 19). The principle is to expect trials and have the mind of Christ while in them. He will use them to "perfect, establish, strengthen, and settle us" (1 Peter 5:10).

Do you consider it strange when trials come upon you, or do you consider it part of the territory- and an opportunity to join with Christ?

II Peter 2                                                December 13

## Destruction From false Teachers

Peter writes in II Peter about being steadfast and vigilant, and one of the reasons he finds that so necessary is because of false prophets and deceptive heresies among the people. He says in chapter 2, verse 1, that they "will secretly bring in destructive heresies, even denying the Lord who bought them, and bring on themselves swift destruction.´ In verse 12 he says, "They speak evil of the things they do not understand, and will utterly perish in their corruption..." He says they "entice unstable souls," having gone astray themselves and "speak great swelling words of emptiness." That last phrase, "speaking words of emptiness," reminds me of being at the crash site of Flight 93 in Pennsylvania in the days after September 11th, along with other family members and friends of the loved ones who were lost there, those so in need of comfort and hope. What we received from some of the speakers who should have been able to offer real hope, was only "great swelling words of emptiness," as Peter says. I don't blame them- in fact, in one respect, I felt sorrow for them. They could not give what they did not have, and yet there was an anger welling up in me also, for the mourners there needed and expected something of value from these ones who should have had something to offer from those who allowed themselves to be put in that position, but nothing was given. I remember during one of the prayers offered, my daughter and I looking at each other and saying, "WHAT is he talking about?" Emptiness.

I feel that same anger (and sorrow on my better days) when I hear people telling me something they heard from a televangelist, something not based on Scripture, something that makes the hearer feel good, but is not truth. "By covetousness they will exploit you with deceptive words. ... and their destruction does not slumber" (verse 3).

Talk with God about the necessity of being steadfast and vigilant against deception.

I John 1                                           December 14

## The Pain of Not Seeking Forgiveness

John, "the disciple whom Jesus loved," the one whom Jesus chose to care for His mother after His death, writes in I John 1:9 that "If we confess our sins, He is faithful and just to forgive us our sins and to cleanse us from all unrighteousness." If... We carry a great deal of pain when we don't confess and don't receive the forgiveness and cleansing from the only One Who can give it.

God allowed His Son to go to the cross to die for our sins, and Jesus went willingly, suffering beyond our understanding as He hung there alone, separated from the Father as He took on our sins, so that we could be forgiven and be reconciled to the Father. So how do the Father and Son feel when we essentially say, "I can't bring this to Him. It is so grievous that I must carry it myself. I must pay. I cannot and will not forgive myself." If we say those things, we go through life carrying the dirty load, feeling ashamed, and remaining useless in the work of the ministry. What we are saying to God is that His death was not enough for this particular sin. We are also saying that we have a higher standard of holiness than God- He is willing to forgive but we are not. No, it cannot be. When we refuse to give Him our sin and walk away cleansed and free to serve, we hurt Jesus again and suffer much pain ourselves. "If we say that we have not sinned, we make Him a liar, and His Word is not in us."

Are you quick to confess your sin and receive His forgiveness?

As you sit in His Presence, let His Spirit show you where your are in this.

I John 2:18-27                                          December 15

## Denying Jesus

John has a harsh word for one who denies that Jesus is the Christ- a liar (I John 2:22). He who denies the Son, he says, does not have the Father either: "He who acknowledges the Son has the Father also".

John also uses the same word, liar, for a person who says he knows Christ but does not keep His commandments. He says the truth is not in such a person, "But whoever keeps His word, truly the love of God is perfected in him" (verse 5). That is how we know that we are in Him, if we have a desire to keep His commands. There must be a difference in us, a new path, after receiving Jesus. We cannot just say we know Him and continue to live as the world does, with no interest or willingness to follow what He says.

It is a hard thing to observe that many people who claim Him as their Savior make no attempt to consider Him in their daily lives. They want the fire insurance but have denied the homeowners insurance, really knowing Him, and protecting and feeding their relationship with Him.

My observation has been that of all the scenarios in a person's spiritual condition: (1) Unsaved with no knowledge of Him (2) Claiming Him as Savior but never making Him Lord, or (3) Knowing and obeying Him, living fully for Him, that second scenario brings the most pain and discomfort in this life. John says such people are liars.

In which of the three scenarios are you?

Read again I John 2 with Him.

I John 2:28-29 December 16

## Not Being Ashamed

One of the themes John writes about often in his letters is abiding in God. What does that mean? When we come to a knowledge of Who Jesus is and receive Him into our lives as our Savior, His Spirit comes into us and abides. He is there, never to leave. He abides in us, and we need to abide in Him. Doesn't abiding include seeking unbroken communion with Him, being in Him, constantly giving up our right to ourselves, being united in Him? We are His, and He is ours. We allow Him to carry out His will and work through us, and since we are constantly seeking Him, we know what that is. He wants to make us like Himself.

Being in union with Him can only come as we sit in His Presence. It requires the best of our time, concentration, and attention. It is a struggle for most of us to go in and stay in His Presence- we prefer to DO, but we can't DO unless we are abiding in Him. Even though it is a struggle, the more we go there with Him, the more we want to be there. Since we are made for union with Him, we will want to take in His Word and obey it.

If we are not abiding in Him, John says, we will lack confidence at the thought of His coming, and we will be ashamed. We will be ashamed because we have neglected our relationship with Him and do not know Him as we should. We don't look forward to coming face to face with someone whom we have disappointed by our neglect.

Abide in Him.

How are you doing with sitting in Jesus' Presence, with aspiring to know Him to the degree that you are abiding in Him?

I John 3:10-23                                        December 17

## Lack of Love

"Whoever does not practice righteousness is not of God, nor is he who does not love his brother" (verse 10). If we are continually practicing sin or we have no love for other believers, John says we are not of God. He goes on to say in verse 14 that he who does not love his brother abides in death, and in verse 15, that he who hates his brother is a murderer. Later he also calls him a liar.

Jesus, having laid down His life for us, has shown us love, the same kind of love that God expects us to have for one another. It would be a rare occurrence for us to have to lay down our physical life for another, although some have encountered that, but it would be fairly common to be faced with having to give sacrificially of ourselves, our material possessions, our money, our time, our understandings, for another. We will be called to pour out whatever we have on another, and very often it will not be convenient or comfortable. John poses the question: If we have what another believer needs, and we refuse to give it, how does God's love abide in us? (verse 17). We cannot just say we love, but we must manifest it in our behavior. By this working out of our love, we will know that it is God in our lives and not ourselves. If we see no acting out of His love, our own hearts will condemn us. Love is not a feeling but a willful choice to act for the good of another.

As you abide in Him, do you see the pouring out of His love in your life toward others?

I John 4:1-6                                      December 18

## They Do Not Hear

I have heard it said that living without sound is more isolating and difficult than living without sight. I am sure neither is very pleasant. In I John 4, John writes that a test as to whether a person knows God is whether or not he hears the truth when it is presented: "We are of God. He who knows God hears us; he who is not of God does not hear us" (verse 6). The idea of not hearing God's Word is frightful, and yet, that is the case of many people.

Verse 5 says they who are of the world speak of the world, and the world hears them. That is all they can hear, until they come to the truth of Jesus Christ being sent by God in the flesh to make the payment for their sins. Until they receive that, they cannot hear. They can only hear what the world has to offer them. They have not the Spirit of God within them to open their ears, and that will not happen until they confess that Jesus is the Son of God. I John 5; 20 says, "And we know that the Son of God has come and that we may know Him Who is true...".

I often wonder how people can think and believe some of the things they do. Here lies the answer: They can only hear the lies that Satan wants them to hear. They are deaf to the truth because of their refusal of Jesus. What a painful circumstance to be in, and what suffering will result.

When you are talking to someone about God's truth and they cannot hear, ask God to show Jesus to them.

II John                                                December 19

## Do Not Receive Him

In John's short, second letter he uses the word "truth" five times, emphasizing the necessity of holding onto it above all else. He rejoices that some are walking in the truth of the commandment that God has given (verse 4). But then he writes about many deceivers, those who disavow truth, those who do not confess Jesus as having come in the flesh, and those, he says, should not be received into the homes of the believers, nor should the believers even greet them, for if they do, they share in their evil deeds (verse 11). How this flies in the face of the climate we see around us today where the emphasis is so strongly on tolerance and acceptance of anything and everything.

John says he who "does not abide in the doctrine of Christ does not have God. He who abides in the doctrine of Christ has both the Father and the Son" (verse 9). Jesus is the test to be used- if someone does not bring this doctrine, he is a deceiver, according to John, and should not be received into the homes of Jesus' followers, nor be greeted by them. John does not tolerate any deviation from the truth and sees the destruction that comes when that doctrine is not followed. He defines love as walking according to God's commandments. It is a loving thing to give people the truth, even though it may not seem loving, nor is it popular. He is the truth, Jesus Christ, and it is only He Who can give eternal life. There is nothing more loving for us to present to people.

Do you present Jesus as the only way, even though it may set you apart and cause you some pain and discomfort?

III John                                                    December 20

## Not Seeing God

John writes that he has "no greater joy than to hear that his 'children' walk in truth" (verse 4). Then he goes on to name one of them, Demetrius, who he says, has a good testimony, according to others and according to the truth. It is indeed joyful to see our own children or our spiritual children living a good testimony for the Lord. John also commends the followers who are showing love and being faithful to the brethren and to strangers and are being good witnesses for God.

John, however, notes another, Diotrephes, who while in the church, has his own interest in mind- he seeks his own preeminence, wanting to be first. He talks against John and the leadership. He does not receive the brethren and even puts out of the church those who wish to receive them. Diotrephes was doing harm to other believers, bringing discouragement so that John had to write encouragement to Gaius and Demetrius via letter until he could visit and support them in person.

Verse 11 says, "He who does good is of God but he who does evil has not seen God." There it is: how we behave shows whether we have seen God and to what extent. When we are not gazing upon Jesus, we have no hope of seeing God as He is. Diotrephes, we can assume, was a man who did not see God and so was incapable of doing good, ultimately bringing great pain on himself and others.

Are you on a quest to see, through Jesus, Who God is- and be like Him?

Jude                                          December 21

## Condemnation of False Teachers

Jude, the brother of James and the half-brother of Jesus, writes to make believers aware that ungodly, dangerous men had crept into their midst and were denying the Lord Jesus Christ (verse 4). Apparently they had previously been warned, but perhaps had become complacent of the subtle assaults. He reminded them that God, after saving the people out of Egypt, later destroyed the unbelievers. He is not a God to be put to the test. Jude is implying that these false, deceitful men would also be judged, just as other false believers were judged in prior times, including the sexually immoral of Sodom and Gomorrah. He says they will suffer the vengeance of eternal fire.

There will be no thwarting of God's demand for holiness. Sin and rebellion will be crushed, no matter how much we would prefer to center only on God's love and mercy. Denying the Lord Jesus can only bring untold eternal suffering and pain as yet unknown to man. False teachers speak evil of what they do not know and so, corrupt themselves. Jude says in verse 11, "Woe to them!" He goes on to say how they speak of God but have nothing of substance to present. At some point, God will come "to execute judgment on all, to convict all who are ungodly among them of all their ungodly deeds which they have committed in an ungodly way, and of all the harsh things which ungodly sinners have spoken against Him" (verse 15).

In the midst of this, Jude's encouragement to the believers is to build themselves up in their faith, to pray in the Holy Spirit and to keep themselves in the love of God, even while looking out for the good of other believers.

Are you able to discern false teachers?

Revelation 1:1-8                                    December 22

## With Clouds

There are various kinds of clouds, some less ominous than others, but generally we think of clouds as marring the clear, crisp beauty of a perfect, blue sky. Clouds tend to carry with them the idea of trouble or the presence of something negative. In Revelation 1:7 it says, "Jesus is coming with clouds, and every eye will see Him, even they who pierced Him, and all the tribes of the earth will mourn because of Him."

We look forward to His coming, but He is coming "with clouds," which indicate sorrow and mourning. Scripture says all the tribes of the earth "will mourn because of Him." Those who have rejected Him will mourn as in no other time. He comes to bring joy and reunion to many, but to those who do not know Him there will be mourning at the sight of Him.

In the clouds HE will be seen then, as is His desire in the "clouds" we all face today. They give us an opportunity to see HIM. In them His desire is that we take our focus from the clouds and look in His face and know Him in a way that we never have before.

In your clouds do you see Him?

Revelation 2:1-7                                        December 23

## Removal of Their Lampstand

John was given the Revelation of Jesus Christ by God and was told to send it to the seven churches in Asia. Ephesus was the first church to whom the apostle wrote. He began by commending their faithfulness to the Word and of living lives of perseverance, patience, and good works, but then he told them what He had against them. They had left their first love, had turned away from the love of the Lord, causing him to implore them to remember where they used to be in their love for Him, then to repent or to change their thinking and behavior, and then return to their first love. Perhaps adherence to their beliefs had replaced their relationship with the living God, or duty replaced devotion in their lives. However it happened, the result was that Jesus no longer had their hearts, even though their lifestyle was exemplary.

Can that happen in our Christian circles - that we are busy with ministry and programs, maybe even witnessing, but it is not out of a deep, loving devotion to Jesus?   No one could find fault with our lifestyle, but Jesus does not have our heart.

God told the church of Ephesus, through John, that if they didn't repent of their lack of love for Him, He would remove their lampstand. They would suffer the pain of losing their testimony, not be a light any longer. The greater suffering would be, however, that there would be no warmth in their relationship with the Lord.

Does Jesus have your heart? Do you do what you do solely because of your love for Him?

Revelation 2:8                                             December 24

## Do Not Fear Your Suffering

The message Jesus gives to the church at Smyrna is that He knows about their tribulation and poverty but also knows that they are rich, perhaps meaning with the truth of God. He also commends their works and encourages them not to succumb to the sufferings and persecutions of Satan which are about to befall them. Some of them, He says, will be imprisoned and will be tested in that experience. He admonishes the church in Smyrna to "be faithful unto death", and then they will be given the crown of life.

Jesus conveys to the church that He knows them, He knows what they have been through as well as what they will go through in the days ahead. He has compassion for them and also calls them to courage, telling them not to fear any of the things they are about to suffer because in the end they will be rewarded by Him. Suffering is temporary, the crown of life is for a lifetime.

Do you think of suffering as being temporary, while eternity with Jesus is permanent? Talk with God about that.

Revelation 3:1-6 December 25

## Dead Churches

John continues in his prophecy of the various churches, including one that compromises, and another that is corrupt. In chapter 3 of Revelation his prophecy for the dead church in Sardis is that if they are not watchful and "strengthen the dead things which remain, that are ready to die," He will come as a thief, and since they will not know what hour He will come, they will not be found ready. What greater misery could befall us than for Jesus to come and find that we have allowed His things to go by the wayside, to die? To not have Him confess our names before His Father would be the greatest of suffering.

"He who overcomes shall be clothed in white garments, and I will not blot out his name from the Book of Life, but I will confess his name before My Father and before His angels." We were made for HIM, to glorify HIM and enjoy HIM forever. Sin has done its best to take us away from that reality, so we must continually go into His Presence to seek forgiveness and be renewed. Through Jesus we are perfectly fit for God. Nothing must be allowed to take us away from that, or we will be like the dead church of Sardis.

If Jesus came back today would He find you centered on glorifying Him, being IN Him and doing those things He has called you to do?

Revelation 3:14-22                                    December 26

## The Lukewarm Church

"I will vomit you out of My mouth" (Revelation 3:16). That is what Jesus says of the church that is lukewarm, neither hot nor cold, the church of the Laodiceans. They do not even know that they are wretched, miserable, poor, blind, and naked, but instead think they are well off and have no needs. In verse 18 Jesus says He wants them to buy from Him gold that has been refined in the fire, then they will be rich, they will be clothed, and they will see. Once again, here is the idea that to come to the place of being "rich" in Jesus, refining through suffering is a must. In verse 19 Jesus says, "As many as I love, I rebuke and chasten." To the ears of us today that sounds like a contradiction. Can it really be true that Jesus rebukes and chastens us because He loves us? His desire is to give us real wealth, Himself. His desire for us is found in verse 21, that we will overcome and come "to sit with Me on My throne, as I also overcame and sat down with My Father on His throne." He is not looking for our present comfort now but wants us with Him for all of eternity.

"Behold I stand at the door and knock. If anyone hears My voice and opens the door, I will come in to him and dine with him, and he with Me" (Revelation 3:20). He desires to enter our lives and invites us into His, with all that that entails.

Have you been lukewarm or have you allowed Jesus to refine you, to be clothed with Himself, that you may really see?

Revelation 5                                          December 27

## Worthy is the Lamb

In John's vision he sees a scroll with writing inside but no one is able to open it, so he weeps much. But then he sees a Lamb, One Who had been slain, Who takes the scroll, and those who are present sing a new saying:

"You are worthy to take the scroll,

And to open its seals;

For You were slain

And have redeemed us to God by Your blood" (verse 9).

Jesus is worthy because He was slain, because He shed His blood for us. Blood had to be shed, and suffering and pain beyond measure had to take place for our redemption. Jesus was willing. Remember in His agony in the garden, His saying, "Father, not My will but Yours?" He accepted the suffering and now is being worshipped by every creature.

"Worthy is the Lamb Who was slain

To receive power and riches and wisdom,

And strength and honor and glory and blessing".

Contrast what occurred in Jesus' life in the days of and preceding the cross, with this scene in Revelation 5. Jesus went to the depths to be lifted to the heights:

"Blessing and honor and glory and power

Be to Him Who sits on the throne'

And to the Lamb, forever and ever" (Revelation 5:13).

Consider what Jesus suffered for you. Exalt Him.

Revelation 7:9- 17                                        December 28

## Wiping Away Every Tear

John continues in his vision, describing the end of the world events: war, scarcity of basic resources, death, martyrdom of faithful men, earthquakes, darkness, falling of stars, movement of mountains and islands, receding of the sky as a scroll and men of all stations in life, hiding themselves and calling for the mountains to fall on them, putting an end to their fear and horror. John is describing the great day of God's wrath. He asks, "Who is able to stand?" He later writes of fire, thunderings, hail, the sea turning to blood, torment from locusts... He says, "Woe, woe, woe to the inhabitants of the earth."

Amongst all this pain and destruction is an account in Revelation 7 of a multitude crying out in praise to the Lord that salvation belongs to God and to the Lamb (verse 10). They are ones who come out of the tribulation and are washed and made white by the blood of the Lamb. They are before the throne, serving God continually. Revelation 7:15 says, "And He Who sits on the throne will dwell among them". There it is: That deep fellowship which came out of their tribulation. They will not hunger or thirst anymore, they will be shepherded, and God will wipe away every tear from their eyes". It is difficult to sit still when we see God's victory which is to come!

Talk with God About His desire to wipe away every tear from our eyes.

Revelation 18                                          December 29

## Final Destruction

Chapter 18 of Revelation records the final destruction of all that has been anti-God, all those things that look so enticing to men, those things that speak to our sinful nature, but bring sure death.  Up until now Satan's representatives have had free rein, battling anything of God, bringing great suffering to all men, feeding us the lie that we don't need God, that we can be independent from Him and be our own gods.  That is what brings the ultimate pain- that idea that we can manage ourselves, that we don't need Jesus, the Lamb, Who paid for us and is the only way for us to be reconciled to God.  That is from where our innate emptiness and loneliness come, that refusal to be reconciled.  Satan knew that would be the case and loves to foster that in us.  We are made to need deep connection with God through Jesus, and it doesn't matter what else we have, if we miss that, nothing will ever satisfy, and we are then set up for immense suffering.

If we carry this separation from God to the end of time, we see the ultimate destruction in Revelation 18: Desolation of all that men have looked to for any hope of satisfaction.  Chapter 19 records the beast and false prophet being cast alive into the lake of fire (verse 20) and the coming of Jesus, King of Kings and Lord of Lords (verse 16) to reign eternally, just as God had promised throughout His Word.

Contemplate the suffering in the end times of those who would not receive Jesus.  It compares to nothing we know.

Revelation 21                                                    December 30

## No More Sorrow

In the final chapters of Revelation, John tells us about the binding of Satan for one thousand years in the bottomless pit, his release after the appointed time when he once again concentrates on deceiving men, only to eventually join the beast and false prophet in the lake of fire and brimstone where thy will be tormented day and night forever and ever (Revelation 20:1).

John also tells us of the great white throne judgment where men will be judged according to their works (Revelation 20:13). The really distressing news is in verse 15, "And anyone not found written in the Book of Life was cast into the lake of fire."

Now the good news, so good that the word "good" hardly does justice to it: In Revelation 21 John writes about the new heaven and new earth where those who have received the Son will dwell with Him and be His people (verse 3), as a bride dwells with her husband. "And God will wipe away every tear from their eyes; there shall be no more death, nor sorrow, nor crying. There shall be no more pain, for the former things have passed away" (Revelation 21:4).

HE knows about every tear we have shed in our lifetime, and HE will wipe them all away, even the ones we have forgotten, and there will be NO more of them. How could there be when we are with HIM? HE will make all things new. I cannot wait!

"He who overcomes shall inherit all things, and I will be his God and he My son (Revelation 21:7). What a way to end this study of pain and suffering. Thank You, Lord Jesus.

Let Him redeem all your tears now, bringing His good out of them. Rejoice for the day when He will wipe them all away and there will be no more, the day when you will be with Him.

Revelation 22:20-21                                    December 31

## He Comes Quickly

On this last day of the year, we also come to the end of Revelation in our journey through Scripture, in our quest to see what God has presented to us in regard to pain and suffering.  It is a time to look back over the past 365 days and ask, How have I progressed in dealing with my losses?  Do I know Jesus better as a result?  Do I think more like He does in regard to suffering?  Do I look at my pain as opportunities for Him to show Himself in a fuller way to me and others?  Do I seek to pour out on others what He has shown me?  Do I allow Him to redeem my pain for His glory and my good?

On this day we are aware of the passage of time and how we have used it.  In Revelation 22:20 Jesus says, "Surely I come quickly".  How is He going to find us when He does come?  Will He see us having embraced all that has occurred in our lives as from Him, having been willing to carry it for Him?  Will He see us having endeavored to make the most of every opportunity?  Will He say, "Well done My good and faithful servant", not only in the way we have handled suffering but in how we have related to Him and others, always realizing that what happens is always between Him and us, first and foremost?  Have we allowed Him to take our pain and make us into the people He always intended for us to be?  Have we been willing to carry it for His glory?  Have we allowed Him to redeem it?

Thank Him, as you sit with Him, for all He has shown you in this year as you have gone through His Word.  Covenant with Him to continue in it and with Him daily.

# ABOUT THE AUTHOR

Lorraine Brosious earned a Masters of Arts degree in Christian counseling from Liberty university and has been on staff at the First Baptist Church in Peekskill, New York as a Board Certified Christian Counselor for over twenty years, ministering to people in the throes of difficulty and loss. She has had speaking engagements in various venues, covering Christian issues, particularly in regard to pain and loss.

In her personal life she has experienced several painful losses, including the sudden death of her husband in 1984, which left her with four children to rear alone. Again on September 11, 2001, her son-in-law, Todd Beamer, was killed when the terrorist attacks took down flight 93 in the field in Pennsylvania, leaving her daughter without her husband and her three grandchildren without their father.

Walking with counselees through their grief, being ministered to by God in her own, and studying the Word of God and seeing what He says about pain and loss prompted her to write a daily devotional, 365 Days of a Journey through Loss and Pain.

Made in the USA
Middletown, DE
26 January 2017